# Philosophy and Archaeology

This is a volume in

*Studies in Archaeology*

*A complete list of titles in this series appears at the end of this volume.*

# Philosophy
# and Archaeology

## Merrilee H. Salmon

*Departments of
Anthropology,
History and Philosophy of Science,
Philosophy
University of Pittsburgh
Pittsburgh, Pennsylvania*

1982

## ACADEMIC PRESS
*A Subsidiary of Harcourt Brace Jovanovich, Publishers*

New York    London
Paris    San Diego    San Francisco    São Paulo    Sydney    Tokyo    Toronto

CC
72
S24
1982

ACADEMIC PRESS, INC.
111 Fifth Avenue, New York, New York 10003

*United Kingdom Edition published by*
ACADEMIC PRESS, INC. (LONDON) LTD.
24/28 Oval Road, London NW1 7DX

Library of Congress Cataloging in Publication Data

Salmon, Merrilee H.
   Philosophy and archaeology.

   (Studies in archaeology)
   Bibliography: p. 183-193
   Includes index.
   1. Archaeology--Philosophy. 2. Archaeology--
Methodology. I. Title. II. Series.
CC72.S24  1982        930.1'01        82-8828
ISBN 0-12-615650-6                     AACR2

PRINTED IN THE UNITED STATES OF AMERICA

82 83 84 85    9 8 7 6 5 4 3 2 1

# Contents

*Preface*      *ix*

*Acknowledgments*      *xi*

ONE.  Introduction      1

TWO.  Laws in Archaeology

Introduction and Examples      8
Some Features of Laws: Generality and Truth      9
Determinism and Statistical Laws      14
Methodological Determinism      16
Differences between Laws of Physics and Laws of the Biological
    and Behavioral Sciences      18
Are There Any Laws of Archaeology?      19
The Importance of Laws for Archaeology      20
Are There Any Nontrivial Laws of Archaeology?      23
An Attempt to Employ Laws in an Archaeological Explanation      26
Conclusion      29

THREE.  Confirmation in Archaeology

Introduction      31
The Logic of Confirmation      32
The Hypothetico-Deductive Method      34
Relative Confirmation and Absolute Confirmation      36
Inadequacy of the H-D Method as a Model of Confirmation in Archaeology      39
Prior Probabilities      42
An Alternative Pattern for Confirmation      49
Bayes' Method      51
Alternative Hypotheses      55
Conclusion      56

# FOUR.   Analogy and Functional Ascription

Introduction      57
Form and Function        58
Context      59
Analysis and Evaluation of Arguments from Analogy        61
An Attempt to Provide a General Method for Ascribing Functions        65
Criticism of the Attempt        67
Ethnoarchaeology and Analogy        74
Conclusion      82

# FIVE.   Functional Explanation

Introduction and Examples of Functional Explanations        84
Functional Explanations versus Functionalist Theories
    of Anthropology      85
The Consistency of Functional Explanations with Scientists' Understanding
    of Causality      87
Some Connections between Functional Explanations and Systems        90
Models of the Phenomena and Models, or Patterns, of Explanation        93
Difficulties in Fitting Functional Explanations with Some Standard Models
    of Scientific Explanation        97
Some Inadequacies in the Standard Philosophical Models, or Patterns,
    of Scientific Explanation        105
An Attempt to Preserve Causal Features in Functional Explanations        106
An Attempt to Preserve Structure and Causality        108
Conclusion      111

# SIX.   Structure of Archaeological Explanation

Introduction        113
Explaining the Character of a Faunal Assemblage        115
Structure of the Explanation        117
Deductive-Statistical Explanation—Explaining Regularities        120
Explaining the Occurrence of a Pattern        122
Problems with the High Probability Requirement        124
Causal Relevance and Statistical Relevance        131
Probabilistic Causes        134
Common Causes        136
Conclusion      138

# SEVEN.   Theory Building in Archaeology

Introduction        140
The Definitional Approach        141
Operational Definition        143

# Philosophy and Archaeology

This is a volume in

*Studies in Archaeology*

*A complete list of titles in this series appears at the end of this volume.*

# Philosophy
# and Archaeology

## Merrilee H. Salmon

*Departments of
Anthropology,
History and Philosophy of Science,
Philosophy
University of Pittsburgh
Pittsburgh, Pennsylvania*

1982

## ACADEMIC PRESS
*A Subsidiary of Harcourt Brace Jovanovich, Publishers*

New York   London
Paris   San Diego   San Francisco   São Paulo   Sydney   Tokyo   Toronto

CC
72
S24
1982

ACADEMIC PRESS, INC.
111 Fifth Avenue, New York, New York 10003

*United Kingdom Edition published by*
ACADEMIC PRESS, INC. (LONDON) LTD.
24/28 Oval Road, London NW1 7DX

Library of Congress Cataloging in Publication Data

Salmon, Merrilee H.
   Philosophy and archaeology.

   (Studies in archaeology)
   Bibliography: p. 183-193
   Includes index.
   1. Archaeology--Philosophy.   2. Archaeology--
Methodology.   I. Title.   II. Series.
CC72.S24   1982         930.1'01         82-8828
ISBN 0-12-615650-6                       AACR2

PRINTED IN THE UNITED STATES OF AMERICA

82 83 84 85     9 8 7 6 5 4 3 2 1

# Contents

*Preface*    *ix*

*Acknowledgments*    *xi*

ONE.  Introduction    1

TWO.  Laws in Archaeology

Introduction and Examples    8
Some Features of Laws: Generality and Truth    9
Determinism and Statistical Laws    14
Methodological Determinism    16
Differences between Laws of Physics and Laws of the Biological
    and Behavioral Sciences    18
Are There Any Laws of Archaeology?    19
The Importance of Laws for Archaeology    20
Are There Any Nontrivial Laws of Archaeology?    23
An Attempt to Employ Laws in an Archaeological Explanation    26
Conclusion    29

THREE.  Confirmation in Archaeology

Introduction    31
The Logic of Confirmation    32
The Hypothetico-Deductive Method    34
Relative Confirmation and Absolute Confirmation    36
Inadequacy of the H-D Method as a Model of Confirmation in Archaeology    39
Prior Probabilities    42
An Alternative Pattern for Confirmation    49
Bayes' Method    51
Alternative Hypotheses    55
Conclusion    56

FOUR. Analogy and Functional Ascription

Introduction   57
Form and Function   58
Context   59
Analysis and Evaluation of Arguments from Analogy   61
An Attempt to Provide a General Method for Ascribing Functions   65
Criticism of the Attempt   67
Ethnoarchaeology and Analogy   74
Conclusion   82


FIVE. Functional Explanation

Introduction and Examples of Functional Explanations   84
Functional Explanations versus Functionalist Theories
   of Anthropology   85
The Consistency of Functional Explanations with Scientists' Understanding
   of Causality   87
Some Connections between Functional Explanations and Systems   90
Models of the Phenomena and Models, or Patterns, of Explanation   93
Difficulties in Fitting Functional Explanations with Some Standard Models
   of Scientific Explanation   97
Some Inadequacies in the Standard Philosophical Models, or Patterns,
   of Scientific Explanation   105
An Attempt to Preserve Causal Features in Functional Explanations   106
An Attempt to Preserve Structure and Causality   108
Conclusion   111


SIX. Structure of Archaeological Explanation

Introduction   113
Explaining the Character of a Faunal Assemblage   115
Structure of the Explanation   117
Deductive-Statistical Explanation—Explaining Regularities   120
Explaining the Occurrence of a Pattern   122
Problems with the High Probability Requirement   124
Causal Relevance and Statistical Relevance   131
Probabilistic Causes   134
Common Causes   136
Conclusion   138


SEVEN. Theory Building in Archaeology

Introduction   140
The Definitional Approach   141
Operational Definition   143

Systematics        150
Formal Theories        157
Mathematical Modeling        160
Constructing Theories by Borrowing        165
General Assumptions, Common-Sense Hypotheses, Induction,
    and Theories        166
Conclusion        177


Concluding Remarks        179


Bibliography        183


*Author Index*        *195*

*Subject Index*        *199*

# Preface

This book was conceived in the mid-1970s, when I first became aware of the strong interest of the "New Archeologists" in problems central to contemporary philosophy of science. These new archaeologists undertook the task of establishing archaeology as a scientific discipline, and as a step toward this goal, they urged the adoption of standards outlined by philosophers of science for scientific confirmation and explanation. Numerous discussions of these issues have appeared in the archaeological literature, including some written by philosophers, and some of this literature has been strongly polemical in tone.

The heated controversies over archaeology as a science have abated somewhat since the 1970s. In the wake of those debates there have appeared a number of studies in which the authors have attempted to summarize and integrate the changes stimulated by the work of the new archaeologists. Nevertheless, many of the issues raised in the earlier studies remain unresolved. These are the problems that are addressed in this book: the existence of laws of archaeology; the circumstances under which archaeological hypotheses can be considered confirmed or disconfirmed; the role of analogy in archaeological reasoning, especially in ascribing functions to archaeological items; the structure of archaeological explanation; the particular problems associated with functional explanations; and the issues surrounding attempts to construct theories of archaeology. Each of these important problems is covered in a separate chapter of the book. Such problems do not lend themselves to easy answers, nor will their solutions have an appreciable impact on the practical activities of "dirt" archaeologists. Nevertheless, there are very good reasons for trying to deal with them.

Principally, discussion of these issues has become a part of the archaeological literature. Knowledgeable archaeologists are thus supposed to have some acquaintance with these problems and their resolutions. Unfortunately, there has been a tendency to demonstrate the required familiarity by simply citing results of one author or another who has pronounced on these issues; as if, for example, a theoretical account of the nature of scientific laws could be cited and used in further work in just the same way as an empirical study. The situation is further complicated because one can find a "philosopher-authority" to cite in support of almost any position on any topic. Archaeologists should have some access to an extended discussion of the issues as they apply to archaeological cases so that they may avoid prejudicial decisions. This *negative* reason, that is, to clear away confusion and misunderstanding, is important, but there is a *positive* reason as well. Fully as important is the ability to come to a deeper understanding of one's discipline. In considering such problems as the nature of explanation in archaeology, one is forced to relate archaeology to other disciplines—to compare and contrast—and to reflect on more general problems, such as the importance of regularities in our understanding of the world. The intellectual satisfactions of such deepened understanding are worthwhile in themselves, regardless of any useful applications that may result.

Although this book was written primarily for archaeologists, it has something to say to philosophers as well, particularly those who are interested in the philosophy of the behavioral or social sciences. I have attempted to deal with genuine philosophical concerns of archaeologists. Philosophers who work in a vacuum, isolated from the problems that distress practicing scientists, risk forfeiting the chance to say anything meaningful about the nature of scientific knowledge.

No work of this sort can be without bias. However, I have attempted to state my assumptions throughout the work, to recognize that reasonable persons can disagree on these difficult questions, and to make the reader aware of some new ways of approaching these topics. I have tried to state opposing views fairly, and I have given bibliographic references for those who want to pursue these views, as well as other related topics. My hope is that this book will build a bridge between archaeology and philosophy, and strengthen the bonds between philosophy and the other behavioral sciences.

# Acknowledgments

This book was written with the generous assistance of the National Science Foundation (Grant SOC 78-15276) and a sabbatical leave from the University of Arizona. Part of that sabbatical year was spent in Melbourne: at Ormond College there was a congenial and stimulating atmosphere for living and working; in addition, the chairman of the Department of History and Philosophy of Science at the University of Melbourne made available an office and research facilities. The prehistorians at LaTrobe University—N. Oram, D. Frankel, P. Ossa, and R. Vanderwal—extended many courtesies and introduced me to fascinating aspects of archaeology in Australia.

Many of the ideas expressed here took shape in discussions and in correspondence with P. J. Watson. It is a pleasure to acknowledge her kind support.

Throughout my years at Arizona, my colleagues in archaeology— T. P. Culbert, W. Dever, A. Jelinek, W. A. Longacre, W. Rathje, J. J. Reid, M. B. Schiffer, and R. Thompson—were incredibly generous with their time and expertise, unfailing in their patience, and unstinting in their support of my work. Although it is inadequate repayment for all they have given me, this book is gratefully dedicated to them.

Very special thanks go to Mike Schiffer, who has read, discussed, and constructively criticized almost everything I have written on these topics. Peter White kindly read and criticized an early draft of the manuscript. Others who read and made helpful comments on portions of the work are Diane Gifford (Chapter Four), Sandra Mitchell (Chapter Five), and Robert Hamblin (Chapter Seven). For her help in typing the manuscript, and for her cheerful support in other ways, my thanks go to Ann Hickman.

Every teacher learns much from her students: I am grateful to mine and to those of my colleagues at Arizona for their enthusiasm for the subject and their persistent demands for clarity. I particularly want to thank Alison Wylie for her contributions in this respect.

The deepest debt I owe is to my husband, Wesley Salmon, for his intellectual contributions to this manuscript, and for every other sort of support throughout the writing of this work.

# CHAPTER ONE

# Introduction

> The archaeologist's spade
> delves into dwellings
> vacancied long ago,
>
> unearthing evidence
> of life-ways no one
> would dream of leading now,
>
> concerning which he has not much
> to say that he can prove:
> the lucky man!
>
> Knowledge may have its purposes,
> but guessing is always
> more fun than knowing.
>
> (from "Archaeology" by W. H. Auden)

Philosophy and archaeology, some would say, make strange bed-fellows. Traditional problems in archaeology—locating, excavating, and dating sites and their contents, and interpreting material culture—seem remote from the concerns of philosophers. However, there are archae-ologists willing to forego the indulgence of guessing (pace Auden) in order to reconstruct *on a firm evidential basis* past cultural, social, and economic systems. They want to explain, as well as describe, develop-ments in the lives of the people who produced and used the excavated remains. They want to understand how changes occurred, such as from a hunting–gathering to an agricultural subsistence pattern, or the growth and subsequent decline of some of the great population centers. They want to "know" all this, and use the "knowledge" to deepen and extend our understanding of human behavior.

This is an ambitious program, and it quite naturally leads those involved to raise questions about the nature of evidence, the circum-stances under which hypotheses should be accepted or rejected, and the character of scientific explanation—in short, about the difference be-tween *guessing* and *knowing*. Such questions have been a major preoc-cupation of contemporary philosophy of science.

1

Archaeologists' interest in philosophical aspects of their discipline is not new. Familiarity with relevant philosophical work is evident in much of the mid-century literature concerning proper classificatory schemes for American archaeology. (See Willey and Phillips (1958) for discussion of this issue, as well as for many references.) However, I do not intend to present a history of archaeological theorizing here. My starting point is rather the efforts of "New Archeologists," to seek, in works of philosophy of science, fairly specific guidelines for ways to make their discipline more scientific, that is, to ensure that archaeological claims embody knowledge rather than guesswork.

Lewis Binford, one of the founders of the New Archeology, writes that his own involvement with philosophy of science began at a meeting in the 1950s with the renowned cultural anthropologist Leslie White, one of his teachers at Michigan.

> He said, Mr. Binford, do you know the meaning of relevance? Boas is like the *Bible*, you can find anything you want in his writings. He was not a scientist. Scientists make their assumptions explicit and are ready to defend their arguments within an explicit logical framework. Boas was muddle-headed. Better to read clerical literature, at least the priests know why they hold their opinions! "I suggest that you read some philosophy of science." I did (Binford 1972:7–8).

One might protest that White's advice to Binford was surely a *non sequitur*. The study of science itself, not the philosophy of science, would seem to be the way to learn about the scientific method. Nevertheless, Binford did read the philosophers—for example, Hempel, Brodbeck, Popper, and Nagel. Their influence on him is apparent, although only a small proportion of Binford's publications deals specifically with such philosophical issues as the requirements for scientific explanation and the nature of scientific confirmation.

More explicit use of the philosophy of science occurs in *Explanation in Archeology* (Watson *et al.* 1971). In this work, which relies extensively on Hempel (1965, 1966), the authors urge archaeologists to use the hypothetico–deductive model of confirmation and the deductive–nomological model of explanation in designing their research projects, and in presenting the results of their investigations of archaeological sites.

This work, and others in a similar vein, brought forth a vigorous debate on method and theory in the archaeology journals. Two philosophers (Morgan 1973; Levin 1973) were early contributors to the discussion: they specified archaeologists' failure to grasp adequately the Hempelian models, as well as their lack of understanding of the relations between these models and scientific activity. Morgan and Levin did not, however, consider in any detail the problem that motivated archaeologists' to appeal to the Hempelian models in the first place, which was whether scientific archaeology itself was desirable or even possible. Hempel's models had been used to show that many of the so-called explanations offered by archaeologists could better be described as fanciful reconstructions than as scientific explanations, and also to provide some insight into the nature of scientific reasoning. In a reply to Morgan's criticisms, the authors of *Explanation in Archeology* expressed apprehension that such criticism could be misinterpreted and understood as an attack on scientific archaeology (Watson *et al.* 1974).

Philosophers were not the only critics of the proposals of those who insisted on a new, more explicitly scientific archaeology. Archaeologists themselves raised objections against their colleagues. Some, such as Hawkes (1968, 1971), were concerned with the alleged "de-humanization" of archaeology. They perceived the discipline as a humanistic, historical enterprise in which certain scientific practices, especially explanation by subsumption under universal covering laws, not only were inappropriate, but damaging to the dignity of archaeology. These archaeologists claimed that such explanations disregard the importance of human freedom and accomplishments of the individual.

Others, notably Sabloff *et al.* (1973), raised doubts about the possibility of a genuinely scientific archaeology because they believed that the uniqueness of the events that archaeologists study ruled out gaining understanding through experimentation. Because they also doubt that the "the potentially crucial psychological data, such as motivation, desires, goals, and social forces" can be quantified, they question whether any behavioral laws of archaeology can be established. Those who agree with them obviously see no point in trying to develop archaeological explanations that would essentially depend upon such laws. Similar doubts about laws are often put forth by those who deny that any of the so-called "sciences" of human behavior can be genuine, or at least "scientific" in the same sense as physics, chemistry, and other "hard sciences." In their view, archaeology is no less (and no more!) scientific than psychology, sociology, anthropology, or history.

Still others (Tuggle *et al.* 1972), while sympathetic to scientific archaeology, question the archaeological laws required for deductive–nomological explanation. They urge archaeologists to adopt a systems model of explanation, in which, as they see it, no laws are needed. According to their view, which is modeled on Meehan (1968), explanations are "dynamic descriptions" involving interrelated sets of variables that express regular connections among phenomena. To most philosophers, and to many archaeologists, such expressions of regularities seem indistinguishable from the laws involved in scientific explanations as construed by Hempel. These "systems theorists" are reluctant, however, to admit that such connections between variables are the same as laws. They prefer to regard them as "regularities" that may not be independent from any particular space–time reference, and that may lack some of the causal and predictive force of ordinary scientific laws.

Most of the issues raised by Meehan (1968) and Tuggle *et al.* (1972) are unresolved; however, in recent years many articles have appeared that attempt to analyze current trends and point to new directions in archaeology. The relationship between new and traditional archaeology—the question of whether the ideas of the new archaeologists constitute a genuine "revolution" in archaeology—the growing importance for archaeology in such fields as ecology, demography, and economics have been discussed by Trigger (1978), Meltzer (1979), and Schiffer (1978, 1981). While this new work is exciting and interesting, I think that there is still much more to be said about the issues originally posed by the new archaeologists. In the following chapters, I have tried to come to grips with six topics that have received considerable attention by archaeologists, and that also pose a serious challenge to philosophical thought.

The first of these topics, presented in Chapter Two, is a discussion of laws in archaeology, for a proper understanding of the nature of scientific laws leads to a somewhat broader conception of science—and of scientific explanation—than that which is held by those who, like J. Hawkes, draw a sharp boundary between humanistic and scientific disciplines. Then an account of "explanation" can be given, somewhat more appropriate to archaeology than the deductive–nomological model.

The problem of explanation certainly dominates theoretical discussion, not only in archaeology, but also in history, anthropology, and biology. A key issue is the appropriateness of a similar mode of explanation for physical, biological, social, and behavioral sciences. Because archaeology involves elements of all these sciences, the question has particular interest for archaeologists. Much of the debate about explanation centers on the laws that occur in explanations. That laws are involved in any genuine scientific explanation is a principle widely accepted by philosophers, though with some dissent (Dray 1964; Scriven 1962; Nickles 1977). Even among those who accept the requirement, however, the nature of these laws and the exact role they play in explanation have been sources of great disagreement. Because questions about the nature of these laws have perplexed many archaeologists, it is entirely appropriate to begin a study of philosophy and archaeology with an attempt to clarify the notion of scientific laws.

Confirmation in archaeology is the next topic, presented in Chapter Three, as we consider how the laws needed for these explanations might be established, or confirmed. Recent attempts to present the hypothetico–deductive model of confirmation as a normative model to guide archaeologists in designing and executing their research have been somewhat misleading. The hypothetico–deductive method of confirmation is an over-simplified account of scientific reasoning. There are severe limitations for its application, particularly in archaeology. In fact, the hypothetico–deductive method is not the pattern adopted in actual cases of confirmation in archaeology, even by those who endorse it in their theoretical writings. It is quite common to find these archaeologists proposing statistical generalizations as hypotheses worthy of testing. They consider alternative hypotheses and weigh their prior probabilities, that is, any plausibility these hypotheses may have before they are subjected to testing, and they reject any hypotheses whose prior probabilities are so low as to disallow acceptance on the basis of tests that can be performed. They adopt statistical sampling techniques in order to control bias, and they employ sophisticated confirmation theory to assess their results. All of this is sound scientific practice, but it does not fit well with the accounts of confirmation that are often presented in the theoretical parts of the archaeological literature. I believe that a more adequate account of confirmation can be developed along Bayesian lines.

The topic examined in Chapter Four, deals with analogy and functional ascription, another problem that arises in connection with the confirmation of law-like hypotheses and other archaeological statements that go beyond simple reports of observed phenomena. Analogical reasoning has traditionally been used to support most of the claims made by archaeologists about prehistoric peoples. In recent years, however, many archaeologists have questioned the sort of support analogies can provide for hypotheses. There is some tendency to regard analogy as merely a heuristic device, and to insist on the necessity for "deductive" testing in order to establish reliable results. At the same time, with the development of ethnoarchaeology, new emphasis has been placed on various uses of analogy, particularly on its role in ascribing functions to archaeological objects.

This fourth chapter deals with the logical structure of analogical arguments, and with the criteria for assessing their strengths and weaknesses. The uses of analogical reasoning on many levels are discussed, and the central importance of such reasoning for the discipline is reasserted.

Functional explanation is considered in Chapter Five. To ascribe a function to an object is to describe the use or uses to which it was typically put. This is not quite the same thing as offering a functional explanation of the presence of such objects in the material culture of some society. Functional explanations in archaeology most often account for the presence of an item by showing how the accomplishment of some task, or the achievement of some goal by means of that item, contributed to the stability or success of some system.

Functional ascriptions are an integral part of functional explanations, for a correct assignment of the function to an object is required before one can say how the object was used to achieve that function in the system under consideration. However, even when evidence and argument can convince us that a function was correctly assigned, there still remain numerous problems with functional explanations per se. This discussion is important, I believe, because many widely accepted explanations of archaeological phenomena, including many so-called "systems explanations," and evolutionary explanations, are functional. Yet, according to some philosophical models of explanation, functional explanations do not really meet strict scientific standards. According to the deductive–nomological model, for example, they are best regarded as mere explanatory sketches, or partial explanations. Nevertheless, not only in archaeology, but in biology and other social and behavioral sciences, functional explanations are pervasive.

At the very core of the debates between new and old archaeologists—that is, between those who see archaeology as a science and those who regard it as a humanistic discipline—is a question about what constitutes satisfactory explanation. Because both old and new archaeologists have been content, for the most part, to identify scientific explanation with adherence to the deductive–nomological model—which requires universal laws, and rejects functional explanation—they have been forced to disagree about whether explanations in archaeology are, or can be, scientific. I argue in this fifth chapter that functional explanations in archaeology are appropriate and necessary, as well as scientific, and that any philosophical model of scientific explanation which cannot accommodate functional explanation is itself inadequate.

The outlines of some standard models of explanation, including the deductive–nomological model, are presented in this fifth chapter. One model—the statistical–relevance model—which does permit recognition of functional explanations as genuine scientific explanations, is also discussed. This model, like those presented by Hempel, requires laws for explanation of phenomena, and thus, it too is a covering-law model. But the laws may be statistical, and this model also permits explanation of low-probability events. The model also imposes certain relevance conditions upon explanations, which are lacking in other models.

The *structure of archaeological explanation,* is the major focus of Chapter Six. Several explanations in the archaeological literature are examined

with an eye to certain features outlined in various models of explanation proposed by both philosophers and archaeologists. The aim here is not only to measure these explanations against the models, but to test the models themselves, that is, to see whether they have done an adequate job of capturing the beneficial features of respected archaeological explanations. One frequently can recognize that an explanation is adequate, and yet be unable to state all the criteria necessary for correct scientific explanation. The development of an adequate theory of explanation for archaeology will depend on a delicate balance between logical principles, which might be suggested by philosophers of science and the considered judgments of practitioners of archaeology concerning what constitutes good explanation in their discipline.

The final chapter consists of a discussion of a variety of attempts by archaeologists to construct archaeological theories. Other closely related issues, such as problems with definition and classification, are discussed as well.

Many archaeologists are concerned over the impoverished and confused state of archaeological theory. A theory of archaeology that would provide a coherent set of reasonably high-level generalizations relating material culture and human behavior is considered an important desideratum by all those who wish to see archaeology firmly established as a scientific discipline.

There is some disagreement concerning the slow emergence of such a theory. One widespread belief is that much more work needs to be done at low- and mid-range levels before any plausible general theory can be advanced. The idea here is that a high-level theory will, or can, develop naturally after certain groundwork has been laid. Others (e.g., Dunnell 1971:4) insist that the theory, although unstated, is already present, and that this implicit theory guides and informs the lower level work. Dunnell believes that confusion in terminology is the chief deterrent to making this implicit theory explicit, and has tried to remedy that situation.

Other writers feel that the best way for archaeology to acquire a theory is to "hook in" with General Systems Theory. Because archaeology deals with systems of varous sorts, and since a General Systems Theory claims to have a set of general principles applicable to any system, such a move appears attractive to many. Still others (e.g., Read and LeBlanc 1978) believe that archaeological theory can be advanced by the construction of formal theories dealing with restricted topics, such as the relation between population size and the area of habitation. Advantages and disadvantages of the various approaches to theory building are considered in this final chapter.

# CHAPTER TWO

# Laws in Archaeology

## Introduction and Examples

Discussion of the nature of laws and of their theoretical importance for such disciplines as history, anthropology, and archaeology provides a good starting point for a study in the philosophy of archaeology. Questions about the existence of any laws of archaeology, what form such laws would take, how such laws might be established, the role of laws in explanation, and the importance of laws for a theory of archaeology have all figured prominently in recent literature. Disagreement about these questions has helped to shape the discipline, for the answers are inextricably tied to whether or not archaeology should be regarded as a science, and if so, what form of science. In this chapter an attempt will be made to state clearly the problems concerning laws and to make some progress toward their resolution.

Careful observers are aware of many regularities in the world around them: Large bodies of water appear bluer on clear days than on cloudy days; usually children of two blue-eyed parents have blue eyes; in many cities water pressure is low during commercial breaks of televised professional football games; most cut flowers wither when deprived of water.

Homely observations such as these have inspired many people to try to understand why such patterns occur. Such attempts to answer questions about observed regularities often lead to the discovery of related patterns and connections. When the connections are persistent and significant they—or the statements that describe them—are called scientific laws.

Of course, the observations given in the preceding paragraph are not intended to be an account of how most scientific laws are discovered. The point is just to dispel some of the mystery apparently surrounding the notion of a law in the minds of many archaeologists. Nor are the examples intended to provide a definition of scientific laws. Although many topical studies begin with definition of terms, it is possible to postpone definition while still elucidating the concept of a scientific law. Because there are serious difficulties in defining *law*, this approach has much to recommend it.

Every reader is already familiar with some scientific laws, such as

1. In an energy-isolated system the total energy content always remains constant (the first law of thermodynamics).

2. $PV = nRT$ (the ideal gas law, which relates the pressure, volume, and temperature of gases under certain conditions).

3. If a certain gain (a certain amount of goods or money) is added to an initial fortune $f_0$, then the utility of this gain is smaller, the higher $f_0$ (the law of diminishing marginal utility, Carnap 1950: 266).

4. Persons who smoke more than two packs of cigarettes daily are more likely to develop lung cancer than nonsmokers.

5. The greater the distance between groups in time and space, the more unlikely it is that diffusion will take place between them (Sanders and Price 1968:59).

## Some Features of Laws: Generality and Truth

Examination of law statements such as these can reveal some commonly accepted features of laws. One of these features is that laws are formulated in general statements, where *general* is understood in two distinct senses. One sense refers to the form of the statement; the other to the content.

In the first place, law statements are general with respect to their logical structure or form. All logical generalizations state relations between classes or sets of entities. The logical generalizations in which laws are formulated may be further distinguished on the basis of whether these generalizations are *universal* or *statistical*.

The statement, "All kinship relations that are important in a society are expressible in the language of that society," is a universal affirmative generalization: one class is included in another, that is, all the members of the first class are also members of the second. "No pre-ceramic societies are societies which practice copper metallurgy" is a negative universal generalization. This type states there is no overlap in membership between the classes mentioned, in other words, that one class is excluded from the other.

Statistical generalizations, sometimes called probabilistic generalizations, state that a certain proportion of the members of a class is included in or excluded from another class. The proportion may be specified numerically, as in ".51 of live human births are male," or the proportion may be indicated less precisely, as in examples four and five. Universal generalizations may be thought of as limiting cases of statistical generalizations in which the numerical proportion is either 0% or 100%.

It is important to remember that the property of being either a statistical or a universal generalization is a logical property of a statement, that is, a matter of whether or not the statement has a particular logical structure, regardless of its content. However, the precise logical form of a statement may not be immediately apparent from its linguistic or grammatical structure. When logicians talk about "logical form," they mean the form that reveals the logical relationships which are important in that statement, although grammar may conceal rather than reveal such relationships. When a logician says that (affirmative) universal generalizations are statements which have the form "all As are Bs," this is a kind of shorthand for expressing the point that in a universal generalization the subject class (denoted by A) is included in the predicate class (denoted by B). The relation of logical inclusion is of crucial logical importance. The logician does not mean that any statement with the grammatical form "all As are Bs" is a universal generalization. With suitable linguistic manipulation, many statistical generalizations may be expressed in that grammatical form. One method is simply to let the predicate carry the probabilistic features of the statement, for example, "All human babies are such that there is a .51 chance of their being born male."

*All* has several uses in English, and its occurrence in a statement sometimes obscures the fact that a generalization is statistical rather than universal. An example of this occurs in Fritz (1968:86), where Sahlins and Service's law of evolutionary potential is presented in the form: "For all cultural systems and for all evolutionary stages the more specialized and adapted a cultural system in a given evolutionary stage, the less likely it is to evolve to the next stage." Although Fritz reads this as a universal law, the law actually attributes different degrees of probability to certain kinds of changes in a cultural system under various conditions. The law does not exclude the possibility of evolution in any cultural system, no matter how specialized and adapted it might be. The law links the probability of evolutionary change to the degree of adaptation:

The more specialized the system, the less likely it is that evolution to the next stage will occur.

The function of *all* in the statement of Sahlins and Service's law is not that of expressing a universal generalization, but rather that of indicating generality of another sort. This second type of generality is equally important for statements of laws. Law statements must be general in the sense that their application is not restricted to any particular time, place, or individual. The use of *all* in Sahlins and Service's law is to emphasize this lack of dependence on specific times, places, and individuals. *All* should be read in its first occurrence in the law statement as "regardless of time or place" and as "regardless of the particular stage" in its second occurrence. This nondependence on specific individuals is a sort of generality that statistical laws, as well universal laws, must exemplify. This sort of generality is a matter of content rather than logical form.

A statement that is a logical generalization possibly lacks this second type of generality. For example, "All pottery made in the Carter Ranch Pueblo was used by the family group which made it," is a universal generalization, but it lacks the other type of generality because it states a restriction to a particular place in the southwestern part of North America. Such restrictions make the statement an unsuitable candidate for a law statement, even though there is a regularity expressed in the statement. Conversely, a statement may be general in the sense that it is not restricted to particular times, places, or individuals, and still fail to be either a statistical or a universal generalization. An example of such a statement is "Some hunter–gatherers are sedentary." This statement has the form of an existential generalization. Such statements express the overlap of two classes to the extent that they share at least one member. But laws must be expressed in either universal or statistical generalizations. The preceding examples show that logical generality and generality with respect to content are different; and law statements must have both.

Another noncontroversial requirement for law statements is that they must be true. The truth requirement is perhaps obvious when we remember that law statements are simply statements which embody, express, formulate, or describe regularities that are real features of the world. Because this is the case, it should also be obvious that scientific laws, or laws of the natural and social sciences, have some empirical content. This is the feature which distinguishes these laws from laws of pure mathematics, which are also true, but whose truth does not depend on physical or behavioral features of the world. Even highly theoretical laws in physics and other advanced sciences are supposed to be connected, through bridge principles or correspondence rules, with em-

pirical phenomena, though the connections may be tenuous and difficult to trace. In less developed sciences, the laws are usually linked
much more closely with the phenomena, and their empirical content is
easily discernible.

In connection with the truth requirement for law statements, we
should remember that there is an important difference between being
true and being known to be true. Statements can be true, though their
truth may be unrecognized. Of the statements "Man was in North
America 30,000 years ago" and "Man was not in North America 30,000
years ago," exactly one is true, but which one is not known. While
statements can be true without being known to be true, most analyses of
knowledge insist that if something is known then it must be true. At the
same time, this requirement is not a demand for infallibility. When we
are in possession of certain sorts of evidence, we believe that we are
sometimes justified in saying that we *know* some statement which, in the
light of further evidence, proves to be false. When this occurs we usually
modify our claim to have known in the first place—perhaps by saying,
"We thought we knew . . ." or "We once claimed to know. . . ."

Part of what is involved in taking a scientific attitude toward the
world is to recognize that our understanding of it is less than complete,
not only in the sense that there are things we do not know, but also in
the sense that some of the things which we now claim to know may not
be true, and that future knowledge will force revision of our present
claims to knowledge. Against this general background of fallibilism,
application of the term *law* or *law statement* is usually reserved for those
generalizations that are highly confirmed (either directly or by virtue of
belonging to some well-confirmed theory) or at least are undisputed in a
given context. When a would-be law statement is under scrutiny, or
when its truth has not been well established, the term "law-like statement" is appropriate.

Occasionally, new evidence leads to outright rejection of statements
that formerly were believed to be laws. "All mammals bear live young"
was once regarded as a law, but discovery of the platypus put an end to
that. "Savages (i.e., those without the benefits of urban civilization and
advanced technology) are incapable of monumental architecture" was
disproved with the advent of radiocarbon dating (Renfrew 1973). While
such rejection of generalizations can occur, quite often the law statements are modified in ways that allow their retention while accommodating the newly acquired evidence. Newton's laws of motion, formerly viewed as presenting an accurate account of all motion of physical
particles, are now understood as giving a very good approximate account of the motions of particles at speeds that are not close to the speed

of light. Archaeologists no longer accept the unqualified statement that agricultural adaptation is a prerequisite for a sedentary lifeway. However, they are attempting to specify the environmental conditions under which this claim is true.Another example of a restriction on the scope of a generalization occurs when: "All potters in societies where pottery is manufactured only in households are women," is changed to "All potters in societies where the social unit of pottery manufacture is a subset of the social unit of pottery use are women" (Schiffer 1976:23). Notice that although the second formulation is more restricted in generality than the first, the second statement is nonetheless still general in both of the senses required for it to be a law statement. It is a universal generalization, as the first one was, and like the first, it is not restricted to any particular times, places, or individuals. The restriction on the second statement occurs by limiting its application to a *subclass* (domestic potters who manufacture pots only for their own households) of the subject class (domestic potters) in the first generalization. Because the subclass can be specified in a general way without reference to any individuals, there is no loss of generality in this restriction of scope. The point is an important one, for often the problem of finding a true law-like statement that applies to a particular situation is one of restricting the scope of a generalization so that both accuracy and generality can be retained.

One important difference between universal and statistical generalizations concerns the requirements for falsification. Whenever a single genuine exception to a universal generalization occurs, the generalization must be rejected or modified if truth is to be preserved.† Statistical generalizations are not vulnerable to counter examples in quite the same way, but they also are modified or rejected in the light of new evidence. Use of extended samples or new sampling techniques often leads to revision of the numerical values stated in some statistical generalizations. New theoretical information may also cause revision or rejection. For example, although modern evolutionary biologists agree that mutation is the ultimate source of genetic variability, there are strong theoretical reasons for believing that such mutations occur far less frequently than was formerly believed. Other factors, such as selection operating on variability which is already present in the gene pool, are also invoked to account for the appearance of most new characteristics in the population. Thus many biologists would not accept the statistical generalization that most changes at the level of the phenotype are

---

†There are problems in determining just how "genuine" a purported exception is. Apparent counterexamples may be the result of mistaken observations, carelessness, delusions, or a number of other factors.

caused directly by genetic mutation. Many archeologists formerly accepted a (statistical) diffusionist principle of the form: "Most technological innovations in less developed societies come from more advanced societies by a process of cultural diffusion." Now this principle seems false in the light of theoretical advances in dating techniques and in a deeper understanding of the technical capabilities of pre-literate peoples.

Alternatively, the scope of a statistical generalization may be restricted in a way similar to that for universal generalizations. For example, "Most cases of valley fever do not lead to serious complication," may be revised in the light of further evidence to "Most cases of valley fever which are contracted by light-skinned people do not lead to serious complications." The archaeological principle upon which seriation dating is based, "Most aspects of man's culture follow the developmental sequence of initial small beginnings, growth to maximum popularity, and finally, small endings (Deetz 1967:27), might be restricted in scope to apply to societies that are relatively free from such disruptive forces as wars and famines.

## Determinism and Statistical Laws

Almost any well-developed science includes statistical laws and universal laws among its basic principles. An interesting and important question is whether, at the most fundamental level, there are really these two types of laws or whether statistical generalizations merely reflect our ignorance of connections that are actually universal. Many scientists and philosophers of science believe that there are universal laws that govern (determine) every event, though of course we do not now know all these regularities. The view that every event which occurs is subsumable under some universal law is called *determinism*. The denial of this view, which allows universal laws but denies that such laws can provide a complete account of the world, is called *indeterminism*. The question of the truth of determinism is one of the oldest questions about the nature of the universe. It has been a topic of philosophical speculation for centuries. No attempt will be made here to argue either for or against the truth of determinism. This discussion is merely an attempt to establish what is involved in each view. It is not necessary to settle the issue, or even to adopt a tentative position on the problem of determinism in order to proceed with theoretical studies of archaeology, or any other science. However, it is advisable to be aware of the issues involved, so that we can avoid committing ourselves to some position that assumes a particular answer to this unsolved problem.

First, let us look at an example. When a statistical generalization, such as "25% of cases of syphilis which are untreated in the primary or secondary stages advance to the form of tertiary syphilis known as paresis," is offered as an account of our present stage of medical knowledge on this issue, there is no universal generalization that can be advanced, even tentatively, to account for any further differences between the cases of untreated syphilis that result in paresis and those that do not. Failure to treat syphilis in its earlier stages is, so far as we know, the only relevant causal factor in the development of paresis, but only about a quarter of the untreated cases result in this manifestation. At the same time, most people believe that this statistical generalization reflects our ignorance of some crucial causal factor or factors, whose presence accounts for the difference between the two groups of cases. It is possible that with the advance of medical science we may discover this factor ($X$) that will allow us to substitute the universal generalization "All cases of syphilis that are untreated in the primary or secondary stages and have factor $X$, advance to paresis" for the statistical generalization that represents our present knowledge.

In the light of past successes in medical research, this belief is well founded. The history of epidemiology provides many examples of the refinement of crude statistical generalizations and their replacement by universal generalizations when some specific organism or circumstance has been isolated as "the cause" of a particular set of symptoms. The discovery of these hidden causal factors is easily absorbed into current medical theory that is heavily committed to the view that most diseases are caused by the activity of microorganisms. Tentative laws are framed in such a way that they can accommodate the hidden factors, once they are discovered, with no loss of consistency or major revision of the theory.

However, epidemiology may not be the best model for all of science. There are branches of science in which deeper investigation has displaced universal laws with statistical laws. There was a time, from late in the seventeenth century until late in the nineteenth, when universal laws represented the most advanced scientific knowledge of the physical world. Newton's successes created a new standard for science. He had discovered universal regularities where others had failed to discern these connections. With Newtonian physics as a model, it was reasonable to believe that only limits on our knowledge prevented us from discovering the set of universal laws that completely characterize the universe.

In the twentieth century, increased evidence (acquired partly through greatly improved instruments and techniques of measurement) has forced revision of some of Newton's laws, and a whole new physical theory has emerged. One part of the new theory is quantum physics, which is fundamentally statistical. To say that the laws of quantum physics are irreducibly statistical means that there is no bit of extra knowledge, no hidden factor $X$, which could fit into this theory in order to transform it into a theory having only universal laws. In quantum physics, according to the best current theory, we know there is and can be no hidden factor that determines, for example, whether a particular silver atom fired through an inhomogeneous magnetic field in a performance of the Stern–Gerlach experiment will be deflected up or down. The addition of such a factor would render the present theory inconsistent.

Twentieth-century science, unlike nineteenth-century science, does not support the belief that all the most fundamental laws are universal and await only a genius of Newton's caliber to discover them. This is not to say that present physical theories will not be modified or replaced as our knowledge of the world expands. But there is no empirical evidence to support the view that such improved and expanded knowledge will involve the discovery of universal laws. The present theory may be replaced by a better statistical theory. Under these circumstances, a commitment to the view that the universe behaves in ways that can be completely described in universal law statements is based not on scientific evidence, but on a metaphysical view. Furthermore, we cannot use scientific evidence to support the claim that the ultimate truth about the world contains statistical regularities either. For these reasons, we should keep an open mind on the issue of determinism, and not commit ourselves to some position that assumes its truth or falsity.

## Methodological Determinism

Some scientists and philosophers have suggested that although we do not know if determinism is true, it is a sound methodological principle to act as if determinism were true, and to look for universal laws. This view, called *methodological determinism*, receives considerable support because the truth of determinism is psychologically tied to views about the world being orderly, understandable, predictable, and controllable. Moreover, if determinism is not true, its adherents say (that is, even if *some* fundamental laws are statistical), most or many laws may be universal, and it is certainly important to discover these. They claim that only by adopting methodological determinism will we pursue our research far enough to discover which laws are universal and which are statistical.

A number of insidious assumptions are found here. One is that methodological determinism only can lead to truth and never result in error, using the reasoning that if there is no universal law we will not find one, but if we do not assume there is such a law, we may give up too soon and miss it. Such an approach is harmless with respect to avoiding error only if the most fundamental laws are deterministic. If these regularities are actually statistical, and we get an approximation with a deterministic set of laws (where divergence may be due to inaccurate measurement) we will stop too soon if methodological determinism is our guide.

Another assumption seems to be that unless we are methodological determinists, research will halt at the first glimpse of a statistical regularity. This belies much of the work that is currently being done on statistical theories. Those concerned with developing statistical laws are constantly refining methods of handling data in order to get the most reliable and accurate statistical descriptions and projections. They are not motivated in this work by the hope of finding universal laws, but by understanding as much as possible about the phenomena that they are studying.

Methodological determinism seems pointless unless we are committed to the view that the only truly coherent world is one in which determinism is true. But our committment as scientists should be to understand as much about the world as we can, regardless of what kind of world it is. It is difficult to see how methodological determinism will assist this search.

Perhaps the strongest attraction of determinism is the predictability that apparently goes along with it. Deterministic laws do seem more satisfactory in this respect, for given a law and the assurance that a given case falls under that law, prediction of an outcome is possible. But this view loses some of its attractiveness when we take account of the enormous complexity in the world. Even with deterministic laws, the prediction of the outcome of most events would require far more information than is usually either available or usable in order to assess initial conditions accurately and to see which laws were applicable. Thus, the knowledge of deterministic laws does not by itself guarantee accurate predictions.

In some cases, even when we have deterministic laws, our predictions are based on statistics. For example, we may have the knowledge that a particular disease can occur only if an identifiable microorganism is present in the blood. Rather than administer the blood test, however, we might rely on the generalization that 96% of individuals who are subjected to a certain sort of exposure contract the disease, and treat those who had been exposed rather than those who showed evidence of the microorganism. The point is that prediction is, to a large extent, a practical matter, and questions such as ease of application of precautionary measures or severity of possible consequences may outweigh the value of deterministic precision in such contexts. Even if we develop deterministic theories in fields such as biology and the social sciences, statistical laws may be the ones most often used for purposes of prediction, for the deterministic laws may be impossible to apply.

## Differences between Laws of Physics and Laws of the Biological and Behavioral Sciences

The preceding discussion of the importance and widespread use of statistical laws should help to persuade archaeologists that their discipline will not be judged a real science simply on the basis of whether it can establish a set of deterministic laws, and make predictions with deductive certainty. Statistical laws are perfectly respectable, and are of crucial importance to the so-called "hard" sciences as well as to the biological and behavioral sciences. There are important differences between the laws of physics and chemistry, and those of less developed sciences, but it is a serious mistake to believe the line is to be drawn on the basis of whether the laws are universal or statistical.

One of the most lucid discussions of the difference between the laws of physics and chemistry and the laws of other sciences, such as biology and psychology, occurs in Smart (1963:50–63). The laws of physics and chemistry, as Smart observes, are more general than the laws of biology, for they are not limited to occurrences on one particular planet. We have evidence to support the view that the regularities that govern physical and chemical interactions on earth also apply to physical and chemical interactions in distant parts of the universe. We do not even know if there are any forms of life in other parts of the universe, let alone if the regularities of genetics and evolutionary biology would be applicable to such forms. Therefore, if we are to assert these generalizations of biology with any degree of confidence, they must be restricted to a particular region in space and time—although the present planet's biosphere is a rather large region. For this reason, Smart is reluctant to apply the term "law" to these statements, and prefers to call them "empirical generalizations." It is clear that expressions of any regularities in human behavior ("laws of the behavioral sciences") are similarly limited in scope. The only genuine laws in biology, Smart claims, are certain laws of biophysics and biochemistry, but this is to say that the genuine law-like portions of biology are reducible to physics and chemistry, for only these laws are general in the requisite sense.

None of this is intended to raise any doubts about the *scientific* nature of biological studies or about the importance and truth of the generalizations that are used in biology. Smart's point is methodological. Recognition of the limited generality in biological and behavioral sciences has methodological consequences, including certain views about reductionism and the appropriate use of mathematics in sciences that are restricted, such as biology.

Although Smart expresses a preference for the term "empirical generalizations" to refer to the well-confirmed regularities in biology and behavioral sciences, this semantic point is not crucial. The term "law" is widely used, and seems harmless, so long as we recognize that these "laws" are restricted to terrestrial developments, and also that they are not further restricted to any specific individual, time, or place. Biological laws have an appropriate type of generality for the subject matter: the study of life. Furthermore, there are no known counter-instances to these laws elsewhere; if there were known exceptions, this would prevent acceptance of some claims we now regard as laws. In view of astrophysicists' investigations of organic molecules, and our increased understanding of the nature of other planets, such possibilities are less remote than they once seemed.

## Are There any Laws of Archaeology?

If the main points in Smart's discussion of the difference between the laws of physics and the laws of evolutionary biology can be accepted, then a resolution of some important methodological issues in archaeology is possible. One such issue is whether or not there are any laws of archaeology.

Just as some of the laws that form part of biological theory have their foundation in physics and chemistry, so do some of the laws which form part of archaeological theory. The statistical laws governing the decay rate of $^{14}C$ and the rate of obsidian hydration may be considered archaeological laws in the same sense that biochemical laws which govern the chemical behavior of components of cells may be considered biological laws. Furthermore, insofar as these laws are reducible to laws of physics and chemistry, they are laws in the unqualified sense recognized by Smart.

A more interesting question is whether there are any laws of archaeology that are not reducible to laws of physics and chemistry, or at least not reducible in such a straightforward way. Archaeology draws on many other scientific disciplines for the interpretation of material that is found at archaeological sites: geology, climatology, botany, physiology, ethnography, and psychology. Insofar as any laws that fall under these categories are used by archaeologists for their purposes, or are developed by archaeologists, these too may be considered archaeological laws. These shared laws will probably not have the full generality of the laws of physics and chemistry, because they will contain at least implicit reference to our own planet.

The laws that seem to be most properly characterized as "laws of archaeology" are the regularities or empirical generalizations that relate various items of material culture to one another, or connect aspects of material culture with patterns of human behavior. The central problem for archaeology is that of understanding the past through material remains, and *any* laws that are primarily concerned with this problem are at the center of archaeological theory. Even these laws may be shared with another discipline. The principle of *superposition*, allowing archaeologists to infer temporal arrangements of archaeological materials on the basis of their spatial arrangements, is obviously closely related to the geological principle of superposition. Any laws connecting material culture with economic behavior might be claimed as laws of economics as well as laws of archaeology. The boundaries among all the social and behavioral sciences are somewhat blurred, and there is no particular reason why archaeology should be more sharply delineated than any of the others.

## The Importance of Laws for Archaeology

Some archaeologists who would go along with this discussion so far might balk at spending research effort to establish laws of archaeology. They claim that the only generalizations that connect material culture with behavior, and which can be established with any degree of reliability, are going to be useless, or at least not very helpful, in understanding the past. Trigger, for example, sees his own work as aimed at "a better understanding of the past as distinguished from formulating timeless laws about human behavior (1978:xii)," and he complains about the fact that "appalling trivialities have been dignified as laws (1978:7)". Charges of triviality will be addressed in connection with some specific examples taken from recent archaeological literature in a later section.

Some recent discussions of whether laws are important in archaeology have focused on whether or not archaeology is, or even ought to be, a science. The proponents of scientific archaeology insist that their task is not merely to describe and date archaeological sites and their contents, but to explain these findings, in the sense of reconstructing the behaviors of the societies that produced the material culture. On most standard accounts of scientific explanation, laws are required; thus, the concern with laws in archaeology. Opponents of this view (e.g., Hawkes 1971) protest that archaeology is not a nomothetic discipline, but a humanistic one. In the eyes of these writers, the attempt to make archaeology scientific is an attempt to dehumanize it, to strip it of all concern with human achievement and values. In quantifying, tabulating, and formulating generalizations, these critics claim, all the important and interesting features of the subject are lost.

However, the dispute about the importance of laws need not take the form of whether archaeology is a science or a humanistic discipline. It might rather address the issue of what form of science archaeology is, or what type of model for becoming a science archaeology should adopt. This problem is not one for archaeology alone. Many writers interested in theoretical foundations of social and behavioral sciences believe that physics, with its high-level theories, abstract entities, and deductive-nomological explanations, is not the best model. Certainly, the claims offered as laws in human sciences look fairly unimpressive when compared with the laws of physics and chemistry. The laws offered by the social sciences, which are both plausible and very general, seem to be either commonplace truths or, especially in economics, mathematical laws devoid of all empirical content. A standard criticism of good deal of work done in sociology, psychology, and political science is that it consists of vast amounts of empirical data invoked to support tautologies. In the area of cultural anthropology, one of the most articulate critics of adopting the "hard science" model has been Clifford Geertz:

> Believing, with Max Weber, that man is an animal suspended in webs of significance he himself has spun, I take culture to be those webs, and the analysis of it to be therefore not an empirical science in search of law but an interpretive one in search of meaning (Geertz, 1975:5).

Geertz claims that what interests him is not laws, but rather interpretation, explication, and "thick" description. Cultural anthropology is a science, he says, but a different kind of science, "softer" than a physical science. In a somewhat similar fashion, Trigger (1978) does not deny that archaeology is a science, but he implies that it is possible to understand the past without regard to the existence of laws. It is possible that such comments are meant to apply only to the search for deterministic laws. If one were to deny that there were any statistical laws, it would be much more difficult to make a case for the existence of laws of social science. But, as I shall try to show, appeal to laws is just as necessary for adequate interpretation and understanding as for explanation.

Geertz is perfectly correct in saying that it is wrong for cultural anthropologists to try to ignore the particular features of the peoples they study in favor of trying to learn what is common to all cultures. But it does not follow from this that anthropology is not concerned with generalization as well. Consider the following remarks:

> Looking at the ordinary in places where it takes unaccustomed forms brings out not, as has so often been claimed, the arbitrariness of human behavior . . . , but the degree to which its meaning varies according to the pattern of life by which it is informed. *Understanding a people's culture exposes their normalness without reducing their particularity.* . . . It renders them accessible; setting them in the frame of their own banalities, it dissolves their opacity (Geertz 1975:14, emphasis added).

What can it mean to expose the normalness of a people if we do not know what normality is? Some account of what is normal provides the framework for our recognition and understanding of traits in another culture. But to have an account of what is normal is to be in possession of a (statistical) generalization or law of human nature: Humans usually believe, say, or do thus-and-so under such-and-such circumstances. Geertz's arguments support anthropologists' (and archaeologists' and historians') concern with the particular; they do not support indifference to generalizations. At least part of interpretation or understanding is positioning the idea within an intelligible framework or pattern. And intelligible frameworks and patterns are exemplary of the regularities that are expressed in law statements. For this reason, the importance of laws should be recognized regardless of whether archaeology is regarded as one of the humanities or as a soft science.

To say that laws are important in archaeology is not to say that they play exactly the same role in explanations there that they do in physics. The way laws are used to explain why gases expand when they are heated seems much more straightforward and simple than the way laws are used in attempts to explain the widespread extinction of megafauna, the abandonment of pueblos in certain regions of the American Southwest in the fourteenth century A.D., or the absence of fish from the Tasmanian aborigine's diet. It is not that we don't know any laws that might govern these phenomena: (a), We know that extinction can be caused by destruction of habitat; (b), there are regularities linking the destruction of species with certain kinds of predatory behavior; (c) various kinds of stresses, such as prolonged periods of drought or heavy attack from invaders, will cause humans to leave their dwellings; and (d), even the vagaries of the human diet are subject to some regularities. Of course, many of the laws which express these regularities are much rougher and less precise in their formulation than the laws used in explanations in physics. But that is not the only problem.

A more serious difficulty is that we do not know which of the laws is applicable in the situation under consideration; nor, if several are applicable, do we know how to assess their relative importance, or how to calculate the effects of any interaction between operative regularities. Furthermore, it is difficult to sort out the initial conditions that are relevant from those that are not, and in many cases we have very little information of any kind about the initial conditions. These problems are genuine, and I believe they are the legitimate concern of those who, like Trigger and Hawkes, criticize excessive attention to the problem of formulating laws in archaeology. But the solution to these problems is not hastened by claiming that laws are unimportant. Laws are crucial for understanding as well as for explanation, as Geertz himself recognizes (1975:21), but there is more to the job than just discovering the appropriate regularities. Some of these complexities are discussed in Chapter Six. There exists a prevailing need for laws in understanding the past.

## Are There Any Nontrivial Laws of Archaeology?

With respect to Trigger's charges of the triviality of proposed archaeological laws, it is appropriate to examine some of the work (Schiffer 1976) he has criticized. In the opening chapter of *Behavioral Archaeology*, Schiffer (1976) refers to philosophers' discussions of laws (Nagel 1961; Hempel 1966; Salmon *et al.* 1971) and says that his own work will maintain this philosophical perspective on laws. However, he then goes on to characterize a law as "an atemporal, aspatial statement relating two or more operationally defined variables" (1976:4), and he concludes that because many archaeological statements fit this characterization, it is appropriate to call these statements "laws." Schiffer calls his account a "working definition," and clearly he does not intend to give a precise characterization of the concept. Indeed, the philosophical literature that he cites points out just how difficult it is to provide such a definition. Unfortunately, this working definition has inadequacies which lead Schiffer to present examples that could not be genuine scientific laws, and that could cause serious misunderstanding about the nature of laws of archaeology.

The chief difficulty with the working definition is its failure to require empirical content. Although in his general remarks about laws Schiffer recognizes this requirement, his working definition fails to capture it. Two or more operationally defined variables may be related to one another by *definition*. If this is the case, then the statement of their relationship is some kind of law, but it is not an empirical law—one expressing a substantive truth.

Many familiar examples of these definitional relationships occur in dimensional anaylsis, such as the formula ($d = r \times t$) relating distance $d$ to rate of travel $r$ (velocity) and elapsed time $t$ . Even though both distance and time may be operationally defined, this statement of their relationship is not an empirical law; the relationship is a matter of definition and mathematics. Put another way, velocity is not something independent of distance and time, but rather is defined in terms of a mathematical relationship between the two: $r = d/t$. In light of this, another way of expressing the relationship $d = r \times t$ is $d = (d/t) \times t$, and this makes its tautological character obvious. Note that to characterize a relationship as depending on mathematics and definitions is not to deny its importance. It is just that relationships of this type should not be confused with those having empirical content. Different means are used for establishing the two sorts of laws. In the empirical case, laws must be confirmed in some sense by the empirical evidence, but no empirical data could serve to establish or to undermine the claim that $d = r \times t$. Such laws are either stated as an explicit convention, or are deductively derived from other conventions using only logic and mathematics. In scientific explanations, the two types of laws play very different roles. Only an empirical law can play a substantive role in explaining empirical phenomena.

In contrast to the formulas of dimensional analysis, consider the relationship expressed in the ideal gas law, a genuine empirical law: $PV = nRT$. Pressure ($P$), volume ($V$), and temperature ($T$) are all capable of operational definition, *and* none is defined in terms of the other. ($R$ is a constant, and $n$ refers to the number of moles of gas.) This law is restricted in its application to certain sorts of gases under moderate pressure and temperature, but these restrictions do not detract from its empirical content. Pressure, volume, and temperature of gases are connected in a lawlike way, and the discovery of this relationship represented a genuine advance in our knowledge of what the world is like. Logically, things could have been otherwise.

If we look at the set of quantitative transforms that Schiffer (1976:58–65) presents as explicit examples of archaeological laws, we can see that each of these is a formula that is much more like the distance formula than like the ideal gas law. These laws have no empirical content, and so cannot be scientific laws, in the sense in which we have been using that term. Consider, for example, the "basic equation" that relates the total number of discarded elements of a given type ($T_D$) to the average number of elements of that type normally in use in a system (*S*), during a given time (*t*), and the average uselife of that type of element (*L*). The equation is: $T_D = St/L$ (1976:60). Several background conditions are stipulated: no instances of the element type are traded in or out, and there are no state-to-state (S–S) transformations of the element type within the system, other than discard. The latter stipulation is designed to ensure that when an element's uselife is over, it is discarded rather than recycled, curated, or modified for secondary use. Schiffer also states that, during the period of use in the community, both *L* and *S* are constants, but this stipulation seems unnecessary, because both these quantities are averages.

The dimensional character of this formula becomes more apparent when the expression $T_D$ is written as a product of rate of discard ($F_D$) and time, for then the equation can be written $F_D t = St/L$ (1976:60), and when *t* is cancelled on each side the equation becomes $F_D = S/L$, which says that under the given stipulations the rate of discard is equal to the average number of elements in use divided by the average uselife of an element. But under the stipulation that discard is what happens to an element in a system when its uselife is over, the rate of discard is *definitionally* connected to the number of elements in the system and the uselife of the elements in just the same manner that the rate of travel is connected to the distance covered and the time elapsed in travel. Similar analyses can be performed on the 28 other equations in his chapter to show their nonempirical character. In light of this, we must reject Schiffer's claim that these are examples of *laws of archaeology*, according to his own criterion of laws as "certain relational statements having empirical content (1976:4)."

With respect to these formulas, it is also interesting to note that none of them succeeds in relating material culture, taken in a strict sense, to human behavior. The variables which do refer to material culture are already "contaminated" by behavioral notions. For example, *S* refers to the number of elements *normally in use* and *L* to average *uselife* of a type of element. In this context, Schiffer's own comment on the value of the equation $F_D = S/L$ is instructive: "This is a useful relationship because *S* often can be reliably estimated archaeologically and *L* frequently can be obtained from experimental or ethnoarchaeological studies (1976:61)." This comment reveals that the genuine archaeological laws, made as explicit and precise as possible, are those that enable archaeologists to estimate *S* and to obtain *L*. These are the laws that enable the archaeologist to relate material culture, that which is uncovered and observed at the site, with human behavior.

Before examining attempts to use the quantitative transformations in archaeological explanations, it is important to say why these quantitative transformations are *not* trivial, although they lack empirical content. Dimensional analyses organize and make explicit relationships that might have been blurred, confused, or only implicit. Variables most amenable to observation may not be the most useful variables for purposes of comparison and contrast. For instance, if we want to formulate generalizations based on sites that were occupied for very different time spans, then using rates at which various processes occurred will make comparisons easier than using total output figures.

In setting up equations, certain stipulations about background conditions are made in order to ensure the correctness of the equation. Seeing whether or not these background conditions are applicable in particular cases is an important empirical exercise. Mere recognition of the importance of various dimensions is crucial to the development of a science. The formulas presented in *Behavioral Archaeology* call attention to the variables that are most relevant for understanding the past. They also make explicit the fact that some quantities that are important for archaeological understanding cannot be discerned by counting material elements, but must be inferred. For example, the total number of elements *discarded* by a past system is not the same as the total number of elements *recovered* by the archaeologist in most cases (Schiffer 1976:65). Such observations serve to stimulate research that tries to answer questions about the best methods of inferring such values. Precisely formulated problems about important issues can result from such work, and the gain in clarity is valuable. The mere absence of empirical content does not make formulas in dimensional analysis trivial; on such grounds, all of mathematics would be judged trivial. It is entirely appropriate for any science to employ mathematics for purposes of organization and clarification, though of course it would be a mistake to regard these mathematical principles as "laws" of the science or as having the explanatory force of empirical laws. With respect to this last point, it is useful to look at Schiffer's attempt to explain changes in the flow rate of chalcedony at the Joint Site (1976:158–178).

## An Attempt to Employ Laws in an Archaeological Explanation

To explain these changes, Schiffer suggests using the equation which relates frequency of discard ($F_D$) to the ratio of the average quantity of an element type ($k$) in a given social unit, times the number of such units ($c$), times the frequency of use of that type ($F_U$), to the average number of uses per element ($b$): $F_D = kcF_U/b$. This equation makes explicit that any change in $F_D$, which here represents the frequency of discard of chalcedony implements, is associated with a change in at least one of the other variables. In this particular situation, the number of social units is fixed, so any change must be associated with $k$, $F_U$, or $b$. Schiffer next asks what could *cause* change in these variables, and suggests four possible answers:

    1. The efficiency of the use of chalcedony tools decreased (suggesting a cause for a decrease in $b$).
    2. Chalcedony tools were in more widespread use among households ($k$ increases).
    3. The range of tasks involving chalcedony tools increased (possibly causing an increase in $k$ or $F_U$, or a decrease in $b$).
    4. Chalcedony tools were used for the same tasks, but the *rate* of task performance increased ($F_U$ increases, but no cause for the increase is suggested until later) (Schiffer 1976:173; remarks added in parentheses).

All of these hypotheses are testable. After testing and analyzing the results carefully, the first three hypotheses are tentatively rejected. The fourth hypothesis is discussed not just in terms of the stated rate increase, but in terms of what *caused* this increase. The sole causal factor suggested is that there was an increase in hunting by groups of males (1976:175).

The quantitative transform does not play the usual role of a law (i.e., a "covering law") in explaining the change in flow rate of chalcedony. The covering laws which are employed in explanations must have empirical content if they are to provide the appropriate links between initial conditions and the phenomena to be explained. This quantitative transform lacks any empirical content. An example using the formula concerning distance, velocity, and time may make the point more clear.

Suppose we want an explanation for an apparent increase in velocity during a particular auto race. We notice that whereas in other years it was possible to read the names painted on the sides of cars as they passed, this year everything is a blur. Others remark on the same phenomenon, so we are convinced that it is not merely a problem with vision. Having satisfied ourselves that there is a change in velocity, we set about to explain it.

The distance formula, transposed to the form $r = d/t$ assures us that the change in velocity is associated with an increase in distance or a decrease in elapsed time. Suppose that we know that the distance is fixed, that it is the same as in previous years. The course has not been redesigned, nor has the number of laps been increased. So the change in velocity must be associated with the change in $t$. Of course, it is obvious that there is no explanatory value in just pointing out that the race was completed in a shorter time than in previous years; we want to know *why t* decreased. At this point, we entertain hypotheses about increases in engine sizes, improvments in body designs, and better track conditions.

Suppose that after testing these hypotheses, we ascertain that the engine capacities have been increased by a specific number of cubic centimeters and that the bodies have been redesigned in a specified way. Have we now explained the increase in velocity? Not quite, although at this point we are at the same stage in constructing an explanation that Schiffer was when he found confirmation of the hypothesis that there was an increase in hunting by groups of males.† The statements about increased engine size and streamlined body design, like the statement about the increase in hunting, are statements of initial conditions. Such statements are essential parts of explantations, but if we adopt the view that explanations involve *laws* (as does Schiffer, 1976:17), then the statements of initial conditions are not in themselves explanations.

What sort of covering laws are required to provide the appropriate link between the initial conditions and the event to be explained? In the case of the auto race, it is not even tempting to consider the formula of dimensional analysis, $r = d/t$ as a covering law. Its lack of empirical content is obvious, and the covering laws we seek are those that connect increased cubic capacity of engines with greater power and correspondingly greater speed; or those relating streamlined body design to reduced air drag and the resulting increase in velocity.

The lack of empirical content in the archaeological formula of dimensional analysis is not so obvious; however, this transform is just as unsuited to be a covering law in an explanation. The kind of law required here is one that could link hunting activities to chalcedony use, for example, "Whenever there is an increase in hunting by males, there will be a corresponding increase in chalcedony use." Such a law might be rather difficult to formulate in precise quantitative terms, but without some such law there is no reason to connect the (confirmed) increased utilization of chalcedony on the Joint Site with the (confirmed) increase in hunting by groups of males.

Schiffer never actually says that this quantitative transform plays the role of a covering law in his tentative explanation of changes in chal-

---

†This hypothesis has found only *tentative* confirmation, but this point is irrelevant to the discussion of the *structure* of explanation which is being conducted here. For our purposes, we can assume that the hunting hypothesis has been confirmed.

cedony flow rate. He only uses the transform to generate multiple working hypotheses, that is, to suggest which related variables might have taken on different values. This is certainly an appropriate use for the quantitative transforms. However, because he does emphasize the importance of laws for explanation, and because he offers no other laws here, one could easily infer from the context of the discussion that the transforms could be used as covering laws. This is neither correct, nor is it consistent with Schiffer's own stated theoretical views about the nature of laws and their role in explanation.

Although these quantitative transforms lack any empirical content, most of the other statements that Schiffer suggest as laws or tentative laws are not deficient in this respect—"Pottery paste and fired-on design elements are preserved under most soil conditions;" and "If the social unit of pottery manufacture is the same as, or a subset of, the unit of use, and women make the pottery, then there will be matrilineal transmission of style (Schiffer 1976:24)." Furthermore, in the final chapter of Schiffer's book, when he talks about how to establish laws of archaeology, the ties to empirical reality are made evident by his insistence on the sort of empirical research needed to establish laws. Even though some of the observed regularities that are mentioned seem rough or obvious, they are not trivial. Recognition of such regularities is often the starting point for developing interesting, useful, and powerful theories.

## Conclusion

At this point, it may be useful to summarize the discussion of archaeological laws. Some essential features of law statements have been given: Any statement of a scientific law must be an empirically true universal or statistical generalization that does not make explicit or implicit reference to any individual time, place, or thing. For laws of the biological, behavioral, and social sciences, an implicit or explicit reference to our own planet is a permissible exception to the last requirement.

To avoid the difficulties in trying to distinguish statements that express genuine regularities from those that are merely coincidental, a definition of "law statement" was not attempted. Specifying criteria that could enable us to say why, for example, "No signal can travel faster than light" is a law, whereas "No gold spheres weigh more than 100,000 kilograms" is not a law, even though both are true and general in the appropriate senses, is the chief obstacle to providing such a definition. Although the issue is not crucial to an understanding of laws in archaeology, if the reader wishes to pursue it, an appreciation for the difficulty of this problem can be gained by examining several sources (Reichenbach 1976, especially Foreword by W. C. Salmon; Nagel 1961; Hempel 1966).

It was argued that any laws that relate archaeological objects to one another, or state relations between material culture and human behavior, deserve the name "archaeological law." Laws shared with other sciences, and employed by archaeologists in their attempts to understand the past, are also archaeological laws.

The importance of statistical laws was defended, and their fundamental status in contemporary physics was noted in this chapter. Some questions about the suitability of physics as a model for social sciences were raised. Finally, the importance of laws for archaeology was argued, and some charges about the trivial character of proposed laws of archaeology were rejected.

If one can accept the case made here for the existence and importance of archaeological laws, the question naturally follows of how such laws can be established. This problem, part of the larger issue of establishing as true any statements that go beyond what is immediately observed, is discussed in the next chapter.

# CHAPTER THREE

# Confirmation in Archaeology

## Introduction

Archaeology began with the recognition that certain oddly shaped bits of stone and metal resulted from the activities of people who once inhabited the areas where these remains were found. Intense curiosity about the lives of these vanished people was coupled with the realization that any *knowledge* that could be gained about them would be founded, for the most part, on such remains of their material culture. Thus, the problem of confirmation, which deals with the relation between claims to *know* something and the evidence for such claims, was recognized by the first archaeologists in the context of trying to decide the parameters for claims about the producers of these artifacts.

Most early claims to knowledge of the lives of prehistoric people were based on analogies between buildings, weapons, tools, and household utensils used in contemporary societies and items found in excavations. There are drawbacks to analogical reasoning, however: Many items have no known analogues, and a single item may be analogous in different respects to several distinct things that do not have overlapping functions. Such problems raise questions about the nature of inference from analogies, and provide motivation for a precise characterization of its possibilities and limitations.

Recognition of the limits of analogical reasoning also prompts a search for other methods of confirming statements about archaeologically-known societies. To initiate our discussion it will be useful to state the problem of confirmation in general way: What sorts of observations or experimental results constitute evidence for or against a given hypothesis?

The term *hypothesis* is used throughout this discussion to refer to any statement subjected to evidential testing. Hypotheses may be of various logical types: generalizations, which may be universal, statistical or existential; particular statements; or mixed statements. Some examples of these different types of interest to archaeologists might be

1. All hunters and gatherers are patrilocal (universal generalization).

2. "The initial Lapita colonizers of West Polynesia were agriculturalists who transferred with themselves a horticultural complex that included crop plants, with attendant technology and agronomic lore (Kirch 1978:116)" (particular statement).

3. "Today nomads usually bury their dead in a simple grave in the nearest convenient spot (Hole 1978:155)" (statistical generalization restricted to a particular time).

4. "Some ring-built and coil-built pottery is indistinguishable from single lump wheel-thrown pottery (Coles 1973:148)" (existential generalization).

5. "As the use intensity of an activity area increases the size threshold of tolerable primary refuse will decrease (Schiffer 1976:189)" (statistical generalization).

A brief look at examples like these makes it clear that archaeologists are interested in confirming both statements that are law-like and non-law-like generalizations. Concern with confirmation is not confined to those trying to establish laws of archaeology.

Although frequently reference is made to the support that *observations* or *experimental results* could lend to an hypothesis, in this discussion we consider confirmation as a relation between the hypothesis *statement* and the *statements* that express the observations or results of experiments. See Hempel (1965:22) for arguments showing that this involves no loss of crucial features. Thus, when we refer to data that support or undermine a particular hypothesis, these data are in the form of *sentences* describing the observations or experimental results.

## The Logic of Confirmation

Once confirmation is construed as a relation between statements, it is quite natural to turn to logic, for the fundamental relation of logic—the consequence relation—is concerned with the circumstances under which the truth of some statements guarantees the truth of others. Furthermore, logic provides guidelines that enable us to reject some statements on the basis of others. Statements that stand in certain relations to one another are logically incompatible that is, the truth of one precludes the truth of the other. For example, "All hunters and gatherers are patrilocal" is incompatible with "Group A, who are hunters and gatherers, are not patrilocal." If the second statement is true, then the generalization must be false.

Insight gained through deductive methods is insufficient, however, for most of the interesting archaeological hypotheses are not connected by deductive relations of logical consequence or incompatibility to statements whose truth is known. Deductive reasoning *is* important in archaeology, as it must be in any science that employs statistics. Nevertheless, in spite of the support given by mathematics and deductive reasoning, the problem of confirming statements about the past on the basis of contemporary archaeological evidence is basically a problem in inductive logic.

Inductive logic is concerned with the support some statements can provide for others when the statements neither deductively entail nor contradict one another. Inductive logic tries to analyze and appraise arguments in which the premises lend some support, but not conclusive support, to the conclusions. Good inductive arguments can be distinguished from their deductive counterparts by three key factors:

1. The *validity* of deductive arguments is a formal matter depending only on the structure, that is, the logical relations between the terms or statements. This is why we can say, for example, that *any* argument of the form "All As are Bs; all Bs are Cs; therefore, all As are Cs," is correct, regardless of the classes which A, B, and C designate. Inductive arguments are somewhat dependent on structure for their correctness, but content and background information are also important.

2. Inductive arguments, unlike deductive arguments, are "ampliative" (Salmon, 1967:8). This means that the conclusion of an inductive argument contains more information than its premises. In a deductive argument, the conclusion can only recombine or repeat those elements already in the premises.

3. Deductive arguments, unlike inductive arguments are "truth preserving." This point is related to the preceding one, for if the conclusion of a deductive argument can contain only what is implicit in the premises, and if the premises are true, then the conclusion also will be true. In contrast, because "new" information can occur in the conclusion of an inductive argument, it may be false even though the premises are true and do lend support to the conclusion.

Inductive logic allows for degrees of support, so we may speak of a hypothesis being "weakly confirmed" or "strongly confirmed." The question now becomes: What sorts of inductive arguments can be used to support archaeological hypotheses, and how can the strength of such arguments be assessed? We shall now consider several types of inductive arguments that have been advocated or employed by archaeologists.

## The Hypothetico–Deductive Method

One kind of argument, favored by many New Archaeologists, and often presented in texts on scientific methodology, is the hypothetico–deductive form of argument—or, as it is often called, the H–D method of confirmation. According to the standard accounts, the method works as follows: (a) Formulate the hypothesis, $H$; (b) deduce (hence, the "deductive" part of the name) some prediction, $P$, which is amenable to observation; and then perform the observation to see whether the stated prediction is true or false. If the prediction is true, the hypothesis is confirmed; if not, it is disconfirmed. The following schemata represent the structure of the two cases:

1. $H$ deductively implies $P$    2. $H$ deductively implies $P$
   $P$                              not $P$
   $H$ is confirmed.                $H$ is disconfirmed.

To illustrate confirmation, consider the following attempt to support the hypothesis: "A prolonged drought in years prior to the abandonment of Grasshopper Pueblo caused its abandonment." One deductive implication of the hypothesis is the statement "There was a prolonged drought at Grasshopper in the years prior to abandonment." While this period of drought is not directly observable, its indicators, such as tree ring data, are so reliable that the presence of drought may be counted as an observable prediction; and in fact, the indicators show that the drought occurred. It is quite obvious, however, that only limited support is given to the causal hypothesis, for though we may confidently assert the existence of the drought, what is at issue is whether or not the drought *caused* abandonment. It could not have caused abandonment if it did not occur, but its occurrence may have been only incidentally, and not causally, related to abandonment. Thus the claim that abandonment *was caused by* drought is not strongly supported by the evidence that there was a drought.

To disconfirm the hypothesis, "Tribal warfare in Amazonia is caused by protein deficiencies in the diets of the warring tribes and intense competition for locally scarce protein resources," the implication "Protein is scarce in the diets of the Yanomamö (a highly warlike Amazon tribe)" was investigated and judged false on the basis of a 13-month observation period in the field (Chagnon and Hames 1979).

Consideration of these two examples brings out the need for additional complexities that were not presented in the extremely simple version of the H–D method presented above. However, it will also be shown that even with refinements, this method does not present an adequate account of confirmation for most situations in archaeology.

In the first place, we might notice the disparity between the confirmation example, in which the true prediction lends only *some* support to the hypothesis, and the example of disconfirmation, where the false prediction would seem to require the outright rejection of the hypothesis by the rules of deductive logic. This disparity, and the recognition that the form of the disconfirmation argument is a valid deductive form, has led Popper (1963) and his followers to deny that the scientific method involves confirmation, and to admit only the deductive method of falsification. This "deductivism" of Popperians is somewhat moderated by their admission of the related notion of "corroboration." An hypothesis is said to be corroborated when it has survived serious attempts at falsification. However, they insist that corroboration is not confirmation.

Tringham (1978) claims to follow Popper's method in testing an hypothesis concerning the cause of damage patterns on the edge of a flaked stone tool. She and her colleagues "tried to test the tools on as many materials as possible that would have been available and modified by flint edges. . . . By proving that certain materials were not the agents of a specific kind of damage, we can confirm (*sic*) our hypothesis with a greater degree of certainty (Tringham 1978:180)." Actually, although she was engaged in trying to reject hypotheses, Tringham was not really following Popper's method of subjecting a single hypothesis to severe testing to see if it could survive attempts at falsification. Rather, she was testing a variety of *alternative* hypotheses to see whether or not they could account for the observed pattern of wear on flint edges. When these hypotheses failed to yield the expected result, they were rejected. This concern with alternative hypotheses is very important and will be discussed later. In the case of Tringham's work, we find an example of an archaeologist following a sound methodology in practice while misdescribing it and linking it to a controversial philosophical position on methodology.

Closer examination of the process of disconfirming an hypothesis also shows that claims about the deductive nature of falsification are themselves mistaken. Although the premises of the second schema deductively yield the conclusion that *H* is false, this oversimplifies the actual structure of the hypothesis testing situation, because it is hardly ever possible to deduce an observable prediction from *H* alone. Auxiliary hypotheses ($A_1 \ldots A_n$) regarding, at the very least, certain claims about initial conditions of observation and testing, such as the working condition of equipment, accuracy of measurements, reliability of observers, and normality of background conditions, are required to make the deduction succeed. Often other auxiliary hypotheses of a more substantive nature are so intertwined with the original hypothesis that they cannot be separated in a testing situation. So, a more accurate representation of the form of a disconfirming argument is:

3. *H* and $A_1$, and . . ., and $A_n$ together deductively imply *P*.
   Not *P*.
   Therefore, either *H* is false or at least one *A* is false.

Though we may have good reason to believe that the auxiliary hypotheses are true, we are left with good, but not conclusive, reason for believing that *H* is false. The falsity of observational predictions thus offers inductive rather than deductive support for the falsity of the hypothesis that is tested.

Of course, auxiliary hypotheses are just as important in confirmation as in disconfirming arguments, and the schema representing confirmation should also be modified to account for this. Auxiliary hypotheses concerning the accuracy of interpretation of tree rings from the Grasshopper area play a crucial role in claiming that drought caused abandonment of Grasshopper Pueblo, for the long drought is inferred from these. Tree ring analysis provides reliable information about climate, but mistakes can be made through lack of expertise, a sample of trees from "non-typical" locations, and human error.

## Relative Confirmation and Absolute Confirmation

It is important to notice that there are two separate senses of "confirmation" and "disconfirmation," that is, a relative sense and an absolute sense (Hempel 1965:40). An experiment or observation may confirm (disconfirm) an hypothesis in the relative sense by increasing (decreasing) the probability that the hypothesis is true. However, confirmation (disconfirmation) in this sense does not guarantee confirmation in the absolute sense, for an hypothesis would be considered confirmed (disconfirmed) absolutely only if the evidential support for (against) it was overwhelming. This point is easily seen when one recognizes that there exists both confirming and disconfirming evidence for many important hypotheses. For example, the hypothesis that prolonged drought caused the abandonment of Grasshopper, although confirmed by some observations, is disconfirmed by evidence for other prolonged droughts, which were not followed by abandonment, during the century and a half of Grasshopper's occupation.

Awareness of the two senses of confirmation leads quite naturally to the question of how much or what kinds of relative confirmation are necessary in order for an hypothesis to be confirmed in the absolute sense. Although no definitive answer can be given to this question, some guidelines can be offered.

## The Impact of Disconfirming Evidence

An hypothesis cannot be considered confirmed in the absolute sense if there is significant disconfirming evidence, regardless of how strong the confirming instances. For example, even though many archaeologists have accepted mid-continental migration routes for early man in North America, this hypothesis cannot be considered confirmed in the absolute sense in view of the sorts of disconfirming evidence raised by Fladmark (1979). The known distribution of early archaeological sites, as he points out, does not agree with what would be expected from such a population spread (1979:57).

## The Importance of Sampling Variety

In the absence of disconfirming evidence, the more relevant variety in confirming instances, the more strongly confirmed is the hypothesis. This condition is imposed to prevent bias, and is a requirement adopted by archaeologists, for example, in their attempts to establish hypotheses concerning the relations between habitation area and population size. Naroll (1962) investigated only 18 societies in different parts of the world to support his estimates of habitation space per person, but other archaeologists have criticized the lack of variety in his instances, and have tried to broaden the data base in testing his hypothesis (Hassan:1978).

This requirement for variety is important even when one is testing generalizations that are less sweeping than Naroll's. For example, if one is interested in testing hypotheses about the amount of protein in the diet of an Amazonian tribe, it is important not to conduct tests only during the rainy season when fishing is hopeless. Extended studies, lasting for a year or more, such as that of Jones and Meehan among the Australian group of Anbara hunter–gatherers (Meehan 1977), provide better variety in confirming instances. These can take into account broad seasonal and annual fluctuations in the relative amounts of protein and carbohydrates available to hunter–gatherers.

The variety discussed here must be *relevant* variety. One could achieve some sort of variety, for example, by returning to the Amazon year after year to observe the diets of the group being studied. But if these studies were done only during the rainy season of each year, proper or relevant variety would be absent. This is why accounts of confirmation in archaeology that link the strength of confirmation to the *number* of confirming instances (LeBlanc 1973:202) are somewhat misleading. It is true that the number of confirming instances may simply be too small to provide relevant variety. This may have been the case for Naroll's (1962) study. It is quite natural in such a situation to consider improving the strength of confirmation by seeking more instances. But it should be remembered that the real goal is an increase in relevant variety, and that greater numbers are just one means to that goal. Moreover, merely increasing the number of instances does not guarantee variety that is fully appropriate.

Determination of relevance depends on the matter under consideration. One cannot say, in general, which features are relevant to archaeological studies. Seasonal availability of certain foods is a highly relevant factor that controls the diets of hunter–gatherers. If one's studies of protein intake ignore this fact, then proper variety is absent. In order to achieve relevant variety in observable predictions, one must consider the domain of applicability of an hypothesis. In one hypothesis just mentioned, the domain of applicability is the diets of Amazonian tribes. In the case of Naroll's hypothesis, the domain of applicability is all groups with permanent residence quarters.

After the domain of applicability is identified, it should be divided into partitions such that it would be plausible to suppose that the hypothesis would be more likely to hold in one partition than in another. Such partitioning is not a matter for logic, but requires some, often considerable, understanding of the subject matter under consideration. In order to partition the domain of the diet of Amazonian tribes, one needs to know the subsistence strategies of the tribes and to be familiar with the variability of resources with respect to space and time. In order to partition the groups of people with permanent residence quarters, one needs to know about such things as how climate affects the requirement for covered living space. This type of information is acquired through training in a discipline and through fieldwork.

After the domain of applicability has been partitioned, tests in the form of experiments or observations are devised for seeing whether the hypothesis holds in the various partitions. Although logic can be used to check whether predictions follow deductively from the hypothesis, logic does not provide any help with devising or discovering these predictions. Substantive knowledge of the situation as well as ingenuity is required to formulate nontrivial predictions.

## The Issue of Significance in the Value of Evidence

In the absence of disconfirming evidence, the more significant the confirming instances, the more strongly confirmed is the hypothesis. Significance, like relevant variety, cannot be characterized within the framework of the H–D method, for the method cannot distinguish between implications that are trivial and those that are important. Significance is a matter of substance, not form, and a knowledge of the subject matter is required to separate the significant from the insignificant. Archaeologists recognize that some confirming evidence strongly supports an hypothesis whereas other implications are utterly trivial. Archaeologists interested in supporting the hypothesis that the extinction of megafauna in Austrialia was caused by intensive hunting by humans count as confirming evidence the indications that man coexisted with these animals for perhaps 10,000 years (Goede *et al.* 1978). The hypothesis that man hunted these animals to extinction implies that there was coexistence at one time. However, this evidence is regarded as much less significant than evidence of kill sites or butchering sites for these animals would be. In fact, the *long period* of coexistence is regarded by some archaeologists as evidence that the extinction of the animals was not caused by overhunting.

The issue of significance has practical importance, for most hypotheses that archaeologists are interested in testing imply an infinite number of observable predictions. The archaeologist can not afford to waste time and money testing only trivial implications that will not do much for confirming or disconfirming an hypothesis. But no guidance at all on which ones to test can be given by the H–D method.

# Inadequacy of the H–D Method as a Model of Confirmation in Archaeology

A feature that makes the H–D method difficult for archaeologists to use is its requirement that observational predictions follow *deductively* from the hypothesis (along with an auxiliary hypotheses) that is being tested. This makes the method fundamentally inappropriate for testing probabilistic or statistical hypotheses, because it is not possible to deduce statements concerning the composition of any individual sample from a statistical statement. This does not mean that there are no statistical deductions. But all that one can deduce from a statistical hypothesis is a probability distribution for all possible relative frequencies in some sample. If one adds an assumption (or auxiliary hypothesis) of random sampling, then it is still possible only to deduce another probability statement (e.g., "There is a probability of .95 that the observed frequency in a sample of size $n$ is within two standard deviations of the value mentioned in the hypothesis."), and *any* observed frequency of some property in a given sample is compatible with this statement.

Many of the hypotheses that archaeologists are interested in testing, such as most of those previously mentioned, are statistical. And statistical deductions like the aforementioned do play a role in classical statistical hypothesis testing. But these methods involve a significant departure from the simplicity of the hypothetico–deductive method. Although the importance of statistical sampling methods and testing is becoming widely recognized among archaeologists (Thomas 1976; Binford 1977), not explicitly recognized is that these methods do not fit under the rubric of the H–D method of confirmation. As a result, the inadequacy of the H–D method for archaeology tends to be overlooked, and some archaeologists have stated positions in their theoretical works that are not reflected in, or are incompatible with, their substantive work (Binford 1972, 1977).

Aside from the problem with statistical hypotheses, many of the hypotheses that concern archaeologists are statements about the *behavior* of the people who produced the archaeological materials. Yet, there is only a probabilistic chain which connects production of artifacts, their use (and possible reuse), the deposition of these materials, and the discovery of the materials by archaeologists. In view of this probabilistic chain, all predictions that certain items will be found—predictions based on hypotheses that such items were actually produced, used, and deposited by a society—are nondeductive.

Actually, in spite of all the talk about "deductive methods," the major lesson that most archaeologists have gleaned from exposure to the H–D method is not that of the importance of *deducing* observable predictions from hypotheses. Many archaeologists believe that of major importance is the framing of explicit hypotheses, and the devising of observational or experimental tests for predictions based on the hypotheses. They are satisfied with predictions that are inductively drawn from hypotheses, predictions that are very probably true if the hypothesis is true. Insistence on structuring one's field work in this way is what distinguishes the so-called New Archaeologists from some of their predecessors. Many early investigators were not very interested in the connections between the treasures they unearthed and the behavior of those who produced the treasures; others had only vague ideas about what kind of knowledge archaeological excavation could help to establish. Among new archaeologists, insistence on hypothesis formulation and testing is particularly strong, and is regarded as a hallmark (in the same class as the concern for laws) of scientific archaeology.

The emphasis on testing, which demands controlled observations and/or experimentation, is a reaction to what in the past may have been an excessive reliance on imaginative reconstruction, appeals to authority, hearsay, and written records of dubious authenticity or semimythical character. It is a serious mistake, however, to equate the admitted importance of hypothesis formulation and testing with the acceptance of the H–D method, and the rejection of other forms of inductive reasoning.

An additional difficulty with the H–D method is its failure to deal with the problem of choosing among alternative hypotheses that could account for the same observable predictions. Rejection of alternate hypotheses because they failed to yield a predicted result was discussed in connection with Tringham's work The related issue that I wish to discuss here is the consideration of several hypotheses when each could be invoked to account for some observed outcome. The importance of alternative hypotheses in archaeological reasoning is demonstrated in the studies aimed at trying to understand population of the American continent (Dumond 1980). Irving and Harrington (1973), for example, claim that man was in Beringia approximately 27,000 years ago. This hypothesis is invoked to account for the discovery of worked mammoth bones which yielded radiocarbon dates of about 27,000 B.P. Auxiliary hypotheses employed by Irving and Harrington assume that (a) the bone has been correctly identified as bearing the traces of human modification and (b) that such bone becomes too brittle to work after a brief period under normal conditions.

But archaeologists are aware of two other hypotheses that, in conjunction with the same auxiliary hypotheses, could yield the same observation. These alternatives are: (a) radiocarbon dating of the bones is incorrect—the bones are really only 10,000–12,000 years old; and (b) the bones are roughly 27,000 years old, but they were preserved in a frozen state until about 10,000 years ago (a time when man's presence in Beringia is well documented) at which time they became exposed, were found, and worked in their thawed state.

In the light of problems with radiocarbon dating of the collagen fraction of these bones (Dumond 1980:985), and ethnographic support for the working of bones of thawed prehistoric mammals, many archaeologists would prefer to accept one of these alternatives rather than the early occupation hypothesis. Under the H–D method of confirmation, this preference for one hypothesis rather than another is quite inexplicable. The method simply does not handle disputes about the relative merits of competing hypotheses.

## Prior Probabilities

In view of the difficulties encountered with the H–D method, it is time to consider an alternative method. In order to understand the account of hypothesis confirmation that will be presented, the concept of "prior probability" must be introduced. The prior probability of an hypothesis is simply the degree of plausibility that it has prior to the testing situation being considered. We would, for example, assign a probability of approximately .5 to the hypothesis "Mrs. Philips, who is pregnant, is carrying a male child," prior to observing the results of testing by the amniocentesis procedure. Prior probabilities may be expressed numerically, as any real number between 0 and 1, or nonnumerically (high, middling, low, etc.). While these probabilities are assigned prior to a particular test, they are not assigned in a completely arbitrary manner. In assigning the probability of .5 to the claim that a human fetus is male, background information about the relative number of male and female births was employed. Such background information might come from statistical studies, or from other tests that an hypothesis has undergone prior to the primary test in question.

Sometimes, however, an hypothesis has no record of previous testing, so other methods must be used to assess its plausibility. It will be shown that these prior probabilities play an important role in judging the degree to which an hypothesis has been confirmed by a particular test, and that they also help to determine which hypotheses undergo testing. W. Salmon (1968) discusses a number of criteria that can be used to assign prior probabilities. These criteria will be illustrated here with archaeological examples.

In the first place, the prior probability of an hypothesis depends on the logical relations it has with hypotheses that are themselves well confirmed. These logical relations provide a set of formal criteria for determining upper or lower limits on prior probabilities. If an hypothesis is incompatible with some well-confirmed hypothesis, or if it would be very unlikely if some well-confirmed hypothesis were true, then the hypothesis in question is assigned a low prior probability. For example, before some very recent studies, the hypothesis that the diet of Amazonian forest dwellers is deficient in protein was considered well confirmed by many cultural anthropologists (Chagnon and Hames 1979). Because of this, a relatively low *prior* probability would have been assigned to the hypothesis, "The protein intake of the Yanomamö is more than adequate," for it contradicts the accepted hypothesis. Also, the high probability value of a well-confirmed hypothesis is transferred to the prior probability of any hypothesis that it entails. Thus, the prior (before digging) probability that an Anasazi peublo will contain coil-built pottery is very high, because "All Anasazi pueblos contain coil-built pottery" is well confirmed.

This assignment of high or low prior probabilities (sometimes called "priors") on the basis of known probabilities of already accepted hypotheses might sound ultraconservative, but it is a requirement imposed by deductive logic or mathematical consistency. For, prior to a given test and under the assumption of the same background evidence throughout, if a hypothesis ($H_1$) has some probability value $n$, and if $H_1$ entails a second hypothesis ($H_2$), then by the rules of the probability calculus, the probability of $H_2$ can be no smaller than $n$. Similarly, if $H_2$ is incompatible with $H_1$, then the probability of $H_2$ can be no larger than 1-$n$. Assigning prior probabilities in accord with the requirements of mathematical consistency does not make one a reactionary. What would be culpable conservatism would be the failure to recognize that we might be wrong about the accepted hypotheses, or the refusal to test *any* hypothesis whose prior probability was low.

In actual practice, these formal criteria for assigning priors are seldom applicable in archaeology, for most of the hypotheses one is interested in testing do not stand in the deductive relations of incompatibility or entailment to another confirmed hypothesis. Usually the relations between new and old hypotheses are probabilistic. For example, the well-confirmed hypothesis that most Anasazi pueblo sites contain painted pottery provides only probabilistic support for the hypothesis that a dig at a particular Anasazi site will uncover painted pots. In a case like this, there are some formal constraints on the assignment of prior probabilities to hypotheses concerning what a dig will uncover; however, the priors depend not only on the probability of the well-confirmed hypothesis, but on others as well (e.g., Have pot hunters been active in that area?) and these probabilities may not be known with any confidence. In what follows, let $P(H)$ be short for "the probability of an hypothesis $H$"; let $H_1$ represent the hypothesis that most Anasazi pueblo sites contain painted pottery, and $H_2$ represent the hypothesis that a particular dig at an Anasazi site will uncover painted pots. Then, to calculate the *minimum prior probability* of $H_2$,

$$P(H_2) = P(H_1) \times P(H_2, \text{ given } H_1)$$
$$+ P(\text{not } H_1) \times P(H_2, \text{ given not } H_1).$$

$P(H_1)$ represents the probability of the well-confirmed hypothesis. Let us suppose that is fairly high, say .8. $P(H_2, \text{given } H_1)$ represents the likelihood that the dig will uncover some painted pottery *if* it is true that most Anasazi sites contain painted pottery. It would be reasonable to assign a fairly high value here also, say .7. $P(\text{not } H_1)$, the probability that $H_1$ is false, is equal to $1 - P(H_1)$, or .2. The final probability in the formula above, the probability that painted pottery will be found on the site if it is *not* true that most sites contain such pottery, is not dependent on any of the already assigned values. It would probably be reasonable to say that such an event is fairly unlikely, so we could assign a low value of .2, for purposes of illustrating how the formula works. Then using the formula to calculate the minimum prior probability of $H_2$, we have

$$P(H_2) = .8 \times .7 + .2 \times .2, \text{ which is equal to } .60.$$

This information can be presented in rather simple tabular form:

TABLE 3.1

PRIOR PROBABILITY OF DISCOVERING PAINTED POTS

|  | $H_2$<br>A dig at this<br>Anasazi site<br>will yield painted pots | Not $H_2$<br>A dig at this<br>Anasazi site<br>will not yield painted pots |
|---|---|---|
| $H_1$: .8<br>Most Anasazi pueblo sites<br>contain painted pottery | $.8 \times .7 = .56$ | $.8 \times .3 = .24$ |
| Not $H_1$: .2<br>Most Anasazi sites do not<br>contain painted pottery | $.2 \times .2 = .04$ | $.2 \times .8 = .16$ |
| Total | .60 | .40 |

It is fairly obvious that in many situations in archaeology one would not have very accurate assessments of the values required to utilize the formula, so this formal method of calculation would not often be useful. However, an important logical point is illustrated. When an hypothesis has strong inductive support from a well-confirmed hypothesis, its prior probability can be much lower than that of the well-confirmed hypothesis. In the example in Table 3.1, the respective probabilities are .6 and .8. This is different from the case where the well-confirmed hypothesis deductively entails an hypothesis, for in such cases the prior of the entailed hypothesis can be no lower than that of the well-confirmed one.

Even though the formal methods for calculating probabilities may not be applicable in many cases, the inductive relations that hold between hypotheses are extremely important. Inductive support takes various forms; it can be simple or complex, and it can affect plausibility in apparent and subtle ways. The hypothesis, "Most Anasazi sites contain painted pottery," combined with the information that some particular site is an Anasazi site, yields by a common type of inductive argument called "statistical syllogism," the conclusion that this site contains painted pottery. The inductive argument supporting the conclusion that painted pottery will be found at a dig on that site is less straightforward. It depends not only on the pottery's being there, but also on such factors as the archaeologists' competence, whether pot hunters have disturbed the site, and the money and time available to conduct excavations. All of these factors should be taken into consideration when assigning a prior probability to "Painted pottery will be found at this site," regardless of whether or not any formal method for calculating priors can be used. These inductive relations between hypotheses are classified by Salmon (1968) as "material criteria" for assigning prior probabilities, and he regards these as much more important than the formal criteria.

Analogical relations between hypotheses provide another extremely important set of material criteria for assigning priors. At the beginning of this chapter, reference was made to limitations on the use of arguments from analogy for interpretation of archaeological remains. Some new archaeologists have claimed that only *testing* can refute or tend to confirm hypotheses, but that analogies "should be documented and used as a basis for offering a postulate as to the relationship between archaeological forms and their behavioral context in the past (Binford 1972:33)." Binford makes it clear that he sees the proper role of analogy as that of *suggesting* hypotheses about functions of archaeological features when items of similar form are known ethnographically. Analogical arguments of this type are important, and they will be discussed in some detail in the next chapter. Here, our concern is with analogies that are employed to assess the plausibility of a hypothesis. It is not difficult to find examples in archaeology of a new hypothesis being proposed and then judged plausible or implausible on the basis of comparisons with other successful hypotheses considering such parameters as the nature of causal processes invoked and the degree of simplicity involved.

One such example uses the criterion of analogy to assign a low prior probability to a hypothesis before testing it or presenting any other evidence against it. In criticizing Haffer's hypothesis (1969, 1974) that the distribution and diversity of birdlife in Amazonia was caused by drastic ecological change during the Pleistocene, Whitten says, "The archaeologist is immediately struck by the similarity of this idea to Childe's oasis theory of domestication. Both utilize a model of extreme ecological change as a *deus ex machina* to explain changes that otherwise seem inexplicable (1979:238)."

The hypothesis that Whitten criticizes is analogous to Childe's oasis theory with respect to a causal force: extreme ecological change. The kinds of causal processes that are endorsed by hypotheses are factors *relevant* to their plausibility. New hypotheses that appeal to well-known and widely understood physical processes, (i.e., soil and wind erosion), to account for modification of archaeological sites are analogous to hypotheses that have proved successful. On the basis of such relevant analogies, these hypotheses would be assigned high prior probabilities, and would be deemed worthy of testing. Any hypothesis that appealed to a dubious causal process, such as mental telepathy or the activities of visitors from outer space, would likely be assigned a lower prior and considered unworthy of testing on the basis of its relevant analogy to unsuccessful hypotheses. Whether or not "extreme ecological change" is acceptable as a causal force depends, in part, on whether one is willing to make certain theoretical assumptions about the possibility of eventually giving a more precise and detailed explanation of the causal processes subsumed under the broad heading of "extreme ecological change."

Another example of the use of analogy to assess prior probability of a causal hypothesis also highlights the role of theoretical background in determining if an hypothesis is analogous to other successful or unsuccessful hypotheses. After testing and rejecting a number of hypotheses, Jones (1978) offered a causal hypothesis for why the Tasmanians stopped eating fish. He claimed that they did this as a result of a deliberate cultural choice that had nothing to do with such things as the availability of fish, the preservation of an ecological balance, or the absence of appropriate technology. His hypothesis is analogous (with respect to causal features) to hypotheses that are regarded as highly successful by some anthropologists (notably the Structuralists), but as unsuccessful by Cultural Materialists and others.

Depending on the theoretical stance taken, one would be inclined to assign differing prior probabilities on the basis of this analogy. Apparently, disagreement with Jones about the prior probability of the taboo hypothesis has led Vanderwal (1978) and others to formulate further alternative hypotheses. Of course, the availability of suitable alternatives is itself an important factor in assigning prior probabilities to hypotheses. The apparent lack of such alternatives figured largely in Jones's acceptance of the cultural taboo hypothesis. The presence or absence of alternative hypotheses is a *pragmatic* consideration in the assignment of prior probabilities, and it will be discussed later, along with other pragmatic criteria.

Serious disputes arise among archaeologists about the plausibility (or the degree of prior probability) of many hypotheses, and these disagreements are frequently based on the types of causal processes that hypotheses countenance. Diffusion appeals to certain kinds of causal processes; whereas, evolutionary theories appeal to other types. Although some authors argue that both sorts of causal hypotheses are important (Trigger 1978:228), others who are strongly identified with one theoretical position will assign a very low prior to any hypothesis which invokes the "wrong" sort of process. The practical effect of this is that rival hypotheses are often not tested, on the grounds that "It is so unlikely that it is true that it is not worth testing."

In drawing analogies between hypotheses, other factors besides causal ones are relevant. One of these factors is simplicity. While simplicity is itself a notion too complex to define easily, there is a general recognition that successful scientific hypotheses share this feature. Many of the most successful hypotheses, such as those offered by Newton and Einstein, have managed to account for masses of highly complex data while retaining stunning simplicity. On the basis of this relevant similarity to successful hypotheses, it is reasonable to assign a higher prior probability to a simpler hypothesis than to a complex one that accounts for the same data.

Archaeologists often use the simplicity criterion to assign prior probabilities. Meggars, for example, finds the plausibility of her refugia model for interpreting cultural diversity in South America enhanced because "It brings order out of chaos, and reveals unsuspected patterns of similarity in different categories of cultural phenomena" (1979:263). Both features that she mentions are features that contribute to the simplicity of her hypothesis.

While recognizing the importance of simplicity, one has to be on guard against oversimplification. The degree of simplicity involved in successful hypotheses is different for various disciplines. The sort of mathematical simplicity and elegance attainable in physics, for example, is not a feature of the best hypotheses in the social sciences. The type of simplicity appropriate for a particular discipline is an empirical matter that cannot be legislated a priori. Theories that involve ecological determinism have been criticized by anthropologists as being overly simple, for example, because there is strong evidence that humans in similar ecological settings engage in highly distinct behaviors. Such evidence indicates that there are factors other than ecological ones involved in human behavior, and hypotheses that neglect this complexity are too simple.

In addition to the formal and material criteria that can be used to assign prior probabilities, pragmatic criteria also play a role, though a less important one than that of the material criteria, which deal with the content of the hypotheses rather than just their "external" relations with other hypotheses.

Probably the most important pragmatic consideration for an archaeologist who is trying to assign a prior probability to an hypothesis is the status of the hypothesis with respect to available alternatives. Jones' hypothesis that the Tasmanians stopped eating fish because of a cultural taboo is more plausible in view of the failure of hypotheses that claimed a lack of fish-capturing technology and other hypotheses that claimed environmental restraints. When an hypothesis appears to be the only one available to account for the evidence, it is assigned a higher prior probability than when there are a number of available alternatives. Irving and Harrington's (1973) hypothesis about man's early occupation of Beringia has a lower prior than it would if there we no plausible competitors. Archaeologists are aware of the need to consider alternative hypotheses, and they frequently criticize one another for failure to take alternatives into account when proposing that certain hypotheses should be tested (Dumond 1977:332ff).

Another pragmatic criterion to be used in assigning prior probabilities is the *source* of the hypothesis. Put quite bluntly, this means that an hypothesis that is proposed by an established archaeologist has a greater prior probability than one proposed by one who lacks any expertise in the area. This appeal to authority will cause many readers to shudder, but it is not so reactionary as it appears. First of all, it is important to remember that we are talking about *priors* and not about acceptance of hypotheses. This does not exclude outsiders, newcomers, students, or assistant professors from proposing successful hypotheses. Obviously they do. Further, it is not assumed that the established authorities are never wrong. But, *in the area in which one is an expert*, one's hypotheses are apt to be correct more often than conflicting hypotheses proposed in that area by nonexperts. Expertise is not a function of academic position, but depends on such factors as talent, training, and experience. Archaeologists are perfectly justified, on the basis of this pragmatic criterion, in assigning very low priors to archaeological hypotheses proposed by nonexperts like van Daniken. This principle must be used rather carefully in a discipline like archaeology, however, for there are many controversial areas where "experts" disagree. If there is disagreement among experts, the criterion cannot be used to assign the hypothesis of one a higher prior than that of another. There are also many areas in archaeology that are so unexplored that they lack any experts. In such cases, consideration of the source of an hypothesis may be much less important in assigning priors.

In practice, the source of an hypotheses is often a strong factor in determining if it will be pursued. Archaeologists are somewhat reluctant to offer official endorsement of an hypothesis just because it is suggested by an archaeologist who is "a visionary person with uncanny insight (Emil Haury's description of Dr. Frank H. Cushing, quoted in Martin and Plog 1973)." However, few would deny that this consideration is extremely influential in deciding which hypotheses to test in the field, so its importance in assessing plausibility seems incontrovertible.

This discussion of prior probabilities has been designed to show that archaeologists actually consider prior probabilities, although they do not use that terminology, in deciding which hypotheses to test. In many recent accounts of "scientific archaeology" there has been a great deal of emphasis on the importance of testing hypotheses, but too little has been said about how selections among available alternative hypotheses are made. The methods for doing this are not arbitrary, and lend themselves to exposure and justification by criteria discoverable in the substantive works of archaeologists.

## An Alternative Pattern for Confirmation

In addition to help in guiding the choice of hypotheses for testing, priors are important in helping to decide which hypothesis, among competing hypotheses that have the same observational predictions, should be considered confirmed by a true prediction. An account follows of confirmation that makes explicit the role of priors, which are ignored in the H–D account of confirmation.

1. The hypothesis has a non-negligible prior probability.
2. If the hypothesis is true, then the observational prediction is very probably true. (If the hypothesis deductively implies the prediction, then this probability is 1.)
3. The observational prediction is true.
4. No other hypothesis is strongly confirmed by the truth of this observational prediction; that is, other hypotheses for which the same observational prediction is a confirming instance have lower prior probabilities.
5. Therefore, the hypothesis is confirmed (M. Salmon 1976:379, adapted from W. Salmon 1973:114).

The first point requires that hypotheses selected for testing be plausible. As we have seen there are several different criteria for assessing plausibility, or assigning a prior probability. This requirement may be interpreted broadly enough to allow testing of an hypothesis that is judged plausible by any of the criteria. All that is formally demanded by this requirement is that the prior probability be greater than zero. So, for example, some hypothesis that might be assigned a very low prior on the basis of its incompatibility with a well-confirmed hypothesis might nevertheless be plausible through analogy with other successful hypotheses, or when one considers that it was proposed by someone who is an extraordinarily clever and fertile investigator.

The second point in this analysis of confirmation is similar to the first step in the H–D method, but differs from it in allowing probabilistic implication from hypotheses to predictions. Discussion of previous examples has shown that probabilistic connections are more common than deductive connections for observable predictions in archaeology. A wide variety of statistical sampling and testing procedures are used in archaeology. Close analysis of these methods is not appropriate here, and is covered elsewhere in the literature (e.g. Mueller 1975; Thomas 1976). But in any account of the logic of confirmation in archaeology, the importance of testable predictions which are inductively rather than deductively linked to hypotheses must be acknowledged.

As in the H–D method, an obvious requirement for confirmation is that predictions based upon the hypotheses must be true if the hypotheses are to be confirmed, and this is covered in the third point. If a prediction is false it cannot contribute to confirmation, but tends to support rejections of an hypothesis.

It is in the fourth point in this account of confirmation that explicit use is made of priors to determine which of alternative hypotheses is considered confirmed by the evidence. Returning to the hypothesis of man's early occupation of Beringia, the alternative hypothesis that says radiocarbon dates are off by 15,000 years or more has a very low prior probability. Thus, we do not regard it as confirmed by the prediction that the worked bone tools show dates of 27,000 B.P., even though this prediction follows from the hypothesis (along with appropriate auxiliary hypotheses). Some archaeologists regard the discovery of bone tools as support for another hypothesis because the other has a greater prior probability. Suppose that the prior probability of a mistake of this magnitude occurring in the radiocarbon dates is about one in two hundred. And suppose that the chance of man's being in Beringia 27,000 years ago is roughly one in a hundred. Many archaeologists would disagree with these priors, but all that is needed is that the second be higher than that of the mistake in radiocarbon dating. Then, if the confirming instance, that is, the true observational prediction, raises the likelihood of each of the two alternatives by an equal amount, the result is that the early occupation of man is better confirmed than the hypothesis of inaccurate dating. Actually many archaeologists, while preferring the early occupation hypothesis to the poor dating hypothesis, would select the third alternative as the one which the evidence confirms. This is because there is ethnographic support for mammoth bone being frozen for thousands of years and then being thawed and worked just as if it were fresh bone. Related incidents have occurred in recent times in Siberia, and provide some basis for giving a higher prior probability to this hypothesis than that of early occupation, because so few data are available to assign a high prior to man's presence in Beringia before 10,000–12,000 years ago.

It should be remembered that the confirmation referred to here is *relative* confirmation. This means that the hypothesis with the greatest prior probability stands more strongly confirmed than its competitors after the truth of the prediction is observed, but the posterior probability (after testing) may not be high enough for it to be considered confirmed in the absolute sense. Until one hypothesis is confirmed absolutely, it is advisable to seek further observational predictions that could support one of the competing hypotheses.

## Bayes' Method

Readers familiar with statistics and probability theory will recognize this account of confirmation as being modeled on Bayes' method of determining an unknown probability when certain other probabilties are known. Bayes' formula is a theorem of the probability calculus, and its mathematical correctness is unquestioned. Its *interpretation* as a description of the method of scientific confirmation, however, is controversial. Most of the disagreement about its use for this purpose centers on the *sources* of the prior probabilities that are required to use Bayes' formula. Many convinced Bayesians are quite willing to let the opinion of the investigator (the "subjective degree of belief") determine the prior probabilities, on the understanding that continued use of the method to account for new evidence will result eventually in "swamping" or discounting the importance of the arbitrarily selected priors.

Such arbitrariness seems quite unnecessary, however. It appears that any hypothesis that an archaeologist would wish to test would be subject to some of the criteria previously mentioned for determining priors. The assignments might be rough, but they need not be completely without rational foundation. Examples used in discussing ways of assessing the plausibility of hypotheses were chosen with the intention of showing that working archaeologists actually use these criteria. In most archaeological situations, the probability values would not be expressed in precise numerical terms, but rather as qualitative estimates (high, very low, etc.). There is nothing wrong with this, and for this reason the method of confirmation has been presented in such a way that precise values are not necessary for its employment. The mathematical version of Bayes' method is not difficult to understand, however, and it may be instructive to present a quantitative example to make certain logical features of confirmation more plain. The example is based on the work of Turner (1978), although he applies a chi square test for significance and does not use Bayes' Theorem in his discussion. The following example utilizes part of Turner's work.

The hypothesis $(H_1)$ is that there was intensive maize agriculture during the Valdivian Phase in Ecuador. This is argued by Zavallos and others (1977). Auxiliary hypotheses are also used by Turner in formulating an observable prediction. These hypotheses, evidence for which is cited by Turner, are:

1. Dental caries are most frequent and severe in agricultural groups, less so in gathering–collecting–hunting peoples, least severe among hunters.

2. Maize, as it is usually prepared for eating, has strong cariogenic potential in most environments.

3. Stewart's (1931) dental pathology review, which indicates 15.5% of all teeth have one or more carious lesion, provides a good measure for incidence of dental caries among prehistoric Central American Indians whose diet was agriculturally based.

Turner examined crania from a Valdivian Period C cemetery. The prediction was that from a sample of 76 teeth recovered from six individuals judged to be of ages susceptible to caries, approximately 12 teeth should have had at least one carious lesion. However, upon examination it was observed that there was not a single tooth with caries. This constitutes the evidence $(E)$.

For simplicity, let us lump together various alternative hypotheses about subsistence strategy (e.g., hunter strategy, gatherer–collectors, and mixed strategies) into the single alternative hypothesis $(H_2)$, which says that the diet was not agriculturally based. Let us also assume the reliability of all the auxiliary hypotheses for the purpose of testing the main hypothesis $(H_1)$.

On the basis of the arguments of Zavallos and his co-authors (1977), let us assign a reasonably high prior to $H_1$; $P(H_1) = .7$. Because either $H_1$ or $H_2$ must be true, $P(H_2) = 1 - P(H_1)$, or .3. Using Stewart's figures of an expected average of 12 bad teeth in a sample of 76 to determine the likelihood of discovering no caries when $H_1$ is true, we get $P(E$, given $H_1) = .001$. Because our auxiliary hypotheses assure us that the incidence of caries is much lower when the diet is not agriculturally based, let us assign the likelihood of .01 to discovering no caries if $H_2$ is correct. The form of Bayes' theorem that is applicable is:

$$P(H_1, \text{ given } E) = \frac{P(H_1) \times P(E, \text{ given } H_1)}{P(H_1) \times P(E, \text{ given } H_1) + P(H_2) \times P(E, \text{ given } H_2)}$$

Using the assigned values we have $P(H_1$, given $E)$—that is, the posterior probability of the hypothesis, given the truth of the evidence—is equal to

$$\frac{.7 \times .001}{.7 \times .001 + .3 \times .01} = \frac{.0007}{.0037} = .19$$

Thus, the posterior probability that the diet was agriculturally based during the Valdivian period has been reduced dramatically by this test, from .7 to .19, and the probability of $H_2$ has been correspondingly enhanced.

In this particular example, the original hypothesis was *disconfirmed* by the evidence, but the same formula is used for cases wherein the evidence supports the hypothesis. Whether the hypothesis is confirmed or disconfirmed depends on whether its posterior probability is greater than or less than its prior probability; the method of calculation is the same in both cases.

The quantitative presentation of Bayes' theorem presumes nonzero prior probabilities for any hypothesis. If an hypothesis has a zero prior probability, then the numerator of the fraction becomes zero, and the posterior probability cannot take any value except zero.

The role of alternative hypotheses is made explicit in the formal version of Bayes' theorem. In order to know what support some bit of evidence lends to an hypothesis, we need to know how probable the evidence would be *if* the hypothesis were false, that is, if some alternative hypothesis were true. The denominator of Bayes' theorem represents the probability, called the "total probability" that the evidence will occur, regardless of what hypothesis is true. In our example, only two alternative hypotheses were considered, but we could have considered each alternate hypothesis about subsistence strategy, and represented its prior probability and the degree of support it gave to the evidence in the denominator of Bayes' theorem.

The theorem also helps us to understand why some tests are more valuable for confirming or refuting hypotheses than others. This can be translated into qualitative terms even when exact quantitative values are not available. Turner's evidence is particularly damaging to the hypothesis he is testing, for his results are unlikely if the hypothesis is true. As already mentioned, cases in which a particular prediction follows deductively from the hypothesis (and auxiliaries) are rare. So, in the other cases, it is reasonable to ask *how likely* such an example would be if the hypothesis were true, and how likely it would be if the hypothesis were false, or if another hypothesis were true. Bayes' theorem helps us to see how these probabilities, called "likelihoods" raise or lower posterior probabilities by varying amounts. If an outcome which is very likely occurs, it does not affect the posterior probability so much as an outcome that would be very surprising if the hypothesis were true.

W. Salmon (1967:120) argues that Popper's insistence on subjecting hypotheses to rigorous attempts at falsification and regarding those that survive as corroborated can be understood and accommodated in this Bayesian structure. If tests and experiments are chosen such that their likelihood is very low, given the falsity of the hypothesis that is being tested, then the posterior probability of the hypothesis is greatly enhanced if those tests have positive results. Suppose, for example, that Turner wished to test the hypothesis $(H_2)$ that coastal Ecuadorians in the Valdivian Phase practiced a non-agricultural subsistence stratgey. The likelihood of finding no decayed teeth in a sample of 76 from appropriate crania is very low indeed (.001) if this hypothesis is false, that is, if the Valdivians were agriculturalists.

$$P(H_2, \text{ given } E) = \frac{P(H_2) \times P(E, \text{ given } H_2)}{\begin{array}{c} P(H_2) \times P(E, \text{ given } H_2) \\ + P(\text{not } H_2) \times \mathbf{P(E, \text{ given not } H_2)} \end{array}}$$

When the probability is very small that the evidence will occur if the hypothesis is false (represented by the likelihood set in bold), then the second half of the denominator tends to be small, which has the effect of making the denominator not much greater than the numerator, and this, in turn, results in $P(H_2, \text{ given } E)$ taking a larger value. Using the same priors and other values from the earlier example taken from Turner to try to confirm the non-agricultural hypothesis $(H_2)$, and using the above formula, we have

$$P(H_2, \text{ given } E) = \frac{.3 \times .01}{13 \times .01 + .7 \times .001} = \frac{.003}{.003 + .0007} = .81$$

The hypothesis with a low prior probability (.3) has been strongly confirmed by this test, and its posterior probability is quite high (.81).

This introduction of Bayes' theorem should not be interpreted as advice to archaeologist to assign numerical probabilities in all cases and to conduct the calculations according to the formula. The intention is just that of exhibiting the logical structure of a method of confirmation that seems more appropriate to archaeology than the H–D method. In Bayesian confirmation, at least three independent probabilities are required to understand how a given test affects the confirmation of an hypothesis: (a) the prior probability of the hypothesis, (b) the likelihood of the test outcome if the hypothesis is true, and (c) the likelihood if the hypothesis is false. The H–D method takes account of only one of these probabilities, the likelihood of the test outcome if the hypothesis is true, and that only in the special case where the truth of the hypothesis deductively entails the truth of the test prediction (Salmon 1973). The H–D account is a gross oversimplification of actual scientific practice; for this reason, it is not helpful to an archaeologist who is interested in structuring research in a careful way. Fortunately, the methods of confirmation that are actually used in archaeology do not fit this simple pattern.

## Alternative Hypotheses

The problem of *discovering* alternative hypotheses, in spite of its importance, has not been discussed here because it is a matter of substance rather than of the logic of confirmation. Using solely deductive logic, one can only formulate the alternative hypothesis that is the denial of the original hypothesis. Although such a move serves to promote awareness that there are positive alternatives, it does not provide information about the content of the alternatives. For this task, there is no substitute for knowledge of archaeology and related fields, plus imagination and experience.

With respect to causal hypotheses, awareness of some causal fallacies can offer very general help in framing alternatives. Causal hypotheses are usually prompted by evidence that certain sorts of phenomena are correlated. But such correlations may be spurious, hence one alternative hypothesis simply suggests such a coincidence. If the correlation does reflect a genuine causal connection, an alternative hypothesis may suggest an additional underlying causal factor to account for the correlation. Such hypotheses recognize that several symptoms of the same underlying causal mechanism will themselves be correlated in a way that mimics direct causal connection. Dumond (1977:335) praises Deetz (1965) for his recognition of the possibility of an accidental correlation between changes in social organization and changes in ceramic patterning, and also for considering that some as yet unrecognized factor may account for both sorts of change.

Alternative hypotheses that revise the causal ordering of directly causally related phenomena may be devised in some cases. One would not suggest that changes in ceramic patterning *caused* changes in social organization, but in many complex situations it is not easy to sort out what is cause and what is effect. When there is archaeological evidence of prolonged occupation of an area by one group, then a brief period of shared occupation with an ethnically diverse group, followed by the absence of the first group, this may be interpreted as the invasion of the newcomers causing abandonment or it may be said that the influx of a new group was caused, or partially caused, by decisions of the former inhabitants to leave the area. Causal order can be particularly troublesome when there are multiple interacting causes, and it is especially important to be aware of alternative hypotheses in these situations.

Beyond this admonition to look for alternative hypotheses, and warnings not to commit such causal fallacies as confusing cause and effect, ignoring a common cause, or mistaking accidental connections for genuine causal connections, philosophers can offer little advice about alternatives. The formulation of successful hypotheses requires substantive knowledge of archaeology.

## Conclusion

Strong claims for the hypothetico–deductive method of confirmation have been made in recent works by new archaeologists. Although the explicit formulation of hypotheses as well as the testing of these hypotheses by observation and experiment are important to scientific archaeology, emphasis on "deductive methods" is misplaced. An alternative account of confirmation, along Bayesian lines, was presented. This account recognizes the importance of plausibility arguments for assigning probabilities prior to testing. This approach to confirmation also provides a framework for distinguishing between tests that significantly alter the status of an hypothesis and those that make little difference. Popperian claims about the importance of falsification can be accomodated within this pattern of confirmation, and it has the distinct advantage of recognizing the role of alternative hypotheses.

The problem of the limits of analogy as a method of obtaining knowledge of the lives of archaeologically known peoples was introduced to motivate the discussion of confirmation, but was not given much attention in this chapter. A more careful analysis of analogy and its importance for archaeology will be presented in the following chapter.

# CHAPTER FOUR

# Analogy and Functional Ascription

## Introduction

Analogical reasoning, as the name suggests, is reasoning based on analogies, or similarities. Observed similarity in some aspects of things provides grounds for claiming further similarities. In Chapter 3, analogical arguments for the *success* of certain hypotheses were presented. The premises of these arguments involved claims that the new hypotheses were similar to other successful hypotheses with respect to such relevant features as simplicity or the types of causal processes that were employed in these hypotheses.

There are many different uses of analogical reasoning in archaeology. One of the most common uses is to infer similar *functions* for archaeologically found items from the observed similarities between these items and others whose functions are known. Because the function of an item is intimately connected with the *behavior* of those who use the item, inferences about functions are at the very heart of behavioral archaeology.

This central role of functional ascription demands a careful look at the arguments that are used to establish such claims. Toward this end, there follows a discussion of the structure of analogical arguments, criteria for evaluating them, and their relations to the Bayesian arguments for confirmation that were presented in the previous chapter. Other ways of supporting functional ascriptions will also be considered, for it is an interesting question: Are analogies required either for the discovery of such functions or for justifying their ascription to archaeological objects?

Finally, the role of analogical arguments in ethnoarchaeology will be considered, for some of the most sophisticated examples of analogical reasoning occur in these studies. Analogical arguments are used here primarily to assign prior probabilities to hypotheses.

## Form and Function

Knowledge of the *function* of an item of material culture can provide access to behavioral and social aspects of the lives of prehistoric peoples. However, the reliable ascription of functions to items found in archaeological sites can be a serious problem. There is obviously no opportunity to question the makers of these artifacts about their purposes in designing them, nor is there any direct observation of how these items functioned in the society that produced and used them. We can only infer such functions; archaeologists are sometimes concerned about the reliability of these inferences.

How do we know, for example, that the function of the so-called "smoke hole" was to let smoke escape from a dwelling? Perhaps the designers of the house intended the hole for some other purpose, and the hole actually had this unknown function. Experiments with fire in the dwelling might convince us that smoke *could* escape from the hole, and there may be evidence that smoke *did* escape from the hole. But such evidence is not as convincing as it might be, for we can distinguish between the function(s) of an item and other "accidental" uses for it, or ends it may be employed to accomplish. For example, it is not the function of an ice pick to inflict serious wounds, although ice picks have been used as efficient instruments for this task.

To support assertions of function, archaeologists have long made use of analogical inferences from items of similar form, found in ethnographic situations where the functions of the ethnographic items are well known. When a piece of stone at an archaeological site is identified as a mano or a metate, an analogical inference of this type provides the basis for such identification. Many items found in archaeological contexts are so similar to those used in ethnographic contexts that functions are attributed without hesitation. As examples of items that are associated with food procurement and that have ethnographic counterparts, Flannery (1968:69) cites implements such as projectiles, fiber shredders, and collecting tongs, and facilities such as baskets, carrying bags, and storage pits. These functional ascriptions are based on inferences that seem to proceed from similar form to similar function in a very straightforward way.

At the same time, archaeologists are aware that restrictions must be imposed upon the analogical reasoning that infers similar functions from similar forms.† Obviously many items that are alike in form have different functions, even in our own society. A painter's spatula and a pastry cook's scraper look very much alike. A crude principle that would permit the inference from similar form to similar function in all cases would be unacceptable for this reason.

Although archaeologists are not often guilty of attributing a function to some item *merely* on the basis of similar form, the additional considerations that support the inference from form to function frequently remain implicit, and thus can cause confusion.

Some of these implicit principles are fairly easy to expose, and they would be regarded as noncontroversial. "The more severe the limitation on the form of an object that the suspected function imposes, the more reliable is the ascription of that function," is an example of one such principle. Its adoption is reflected in the comparative ease with which we assign functions to many utilitarian objects, and the difficulty we encounter when we try to discern the exact role of items that we believe had some ceremonial function. For some objects, such as grinding stones, there are very few forms that are compatible with reasonably efficient performance of the function. For the objects used in ceremonies or in religious rites, there are far fewer restrictions as to the forms of the objects. Because function determines form most frequently in the design of tools implements, containers, and other objects whose use involves very direct interaction with the physical environment, inferences that go "backwards" from form to function are frequently legitimate in cases where such interaction is apparent.

A more general way of putting the principle just discussed is to say, "Similar function may be inferred from similar form in cases where form is relevant to function." Relevance is the most important consideration in assessing the success of an analogical argument; thus, an effort will be made to explain relevance in this context, and to demonstrate its role in analogies.

## Context

Even in the case of utilitarian objects with a restricted range of possible forms, different functions are possible, as demonstrated by the example of the similar spatula and scraper. In view of this, the inference of similar function from similar form must be further restricted. The con-

---

†Note that "form" in this discussion often refers to the material composition of an object as well as its physical conformation.

text of association in which an item is found imposes another type of restriction.

Context of association, as every archaeologist knows, is a great help in ascribing functions. In the example from Flannery cited earlier, the implements and facilities were found in close association with food remains. This context, in addition to similarities of form, supports his ascription of functions to these objects. In a recent study, Curren (1977) uses context to bolster his interpretation of "relatively flat, variously shaped, ground, and polished slate, limestone, greenstone, hematite, or steatite (artifacts), many times with one or two holes drilled through their breadth (1977:97)" as tools for shaping pots. These artifacts resemble in size and shape the wooden tools, called "ribs," of contemporary potters. Curren points out that these objects, usually labeled "stone gorgets," are found in a wide variety of sites that also contain pottery, but that they have not turned up in any preceramic sites. In at least one case, they have been discovered in a context that may have been a potter's workshop. Whenever an archaeologist attempts to establish the function of some object whose use or purpose is unclear or in dispute, such contextual arguments play an important role. In criticizing Curren's work, for example, Starna (1979) accuses him of neglecting studies that show large numbers of stone gorgets were found at preceramic sites. He also complains of Curren's failure to take note of another context in which the gorgets occur—in many burials.

No archaeologist needs to be convinced of the importance of context for supporting functional ascriptions. However, it is not entirely clear just why context is so important or how contextual considerations are related to analogies between forms. Perhaps the simplest answer to the question of the role of context is that there is a presumption that items found together in an archaeological context were also associated in the society that produced or used them. This inference from association in archaeological context to association in "systemic" context, to use Schiffer's (1976) terminology, is subject to some limitation, like the analogical inference from form to function. Items are reused, carried away, and dumped—all processes affecting association. Intrusions and disturbances by humans or animals, as well as various other natural processes, such as movements of water courses, may associate items that were never in the same systemic context. For this reason, archaeologists must use caution in interpreting their findings. Fortunately, the presence or absence of disturbances can often be recognized, and archaeologists have made great strides in detecting these modifications of archaeological materials (Gifford 1978).

Association alone can never fully reveal an artifact's significance, because association, even in a systemic context, cannot tell us the *role* of various items unless we comprehend the complex within which the items existed. For example, finding sharp, slender objects together with flat clay objects would not suggest the function of either if we had no concept of drawing or writing. Context is important, as Deetz (1967:79) recognizes, because it suggests the unifying complex or activity, such as pottery making, butchering, theatrical performance, or religious rite. Once the complex or activity is recognized, we can draw on analogies with more familiar examples of the same activity to assign functions to various items that form parts of the complex. The arguments involve more complicated reasoning than the "similar form implies similar function" type of argument.

## Analysis and Evaluation of Arguments from Analogy

Before discussing the more complicated analogies, it will be helpful to expose the basic forms of analogical reasoning. The strategy in an analogical argument is to infer on the basis of observed similarities among types of objects that one of the types shares some further, unobserved similarity as well. The logical structure of such arguments may be represented in the following way:

Premise 1. Features $F_1, \ldots F_n$ have been observed in objects of type $O_1$.
Premise 2. Features $F_1, \ldots F_{n-1}$ have been observed in objects of type $O_2$.
Conclusion. Objects of type $O_2$ also have feature $F_n$.

The features $F_1, \ldots F_{n-1}$, which are mentioned in the premises of the argument, are the observed points of analogy. Further *similarity* with respect to $F_n$ is inferred, for while $F_n$ has been observed in type $O_1$, it has not been observed in type $O_2$. Consider the following archaeological example of this type of reasoning, based on Coles (1973:148).

Premise 1. Characteristic ridges and a coil-building techinque that leaves these ridges after smoothing and firing have been observed in pots made by modern potters.
Premise 2. Characteristic ridges (similar to those mentioned in the first premise) have been observed in prehistoric pots.
Conclusion. Prehistoric pots containing the characteristic ridges were made using the coil-building techinque.

A slightly different version of the form of analogical argument occurs when the conclusion refers to a particular instance, rather than making a general claim about some type of object.

Premise 1.   Items $O_1, \ldots O_{n-1}$ are all similar to $O_n$ with respect to features $F_1, \ldots F_{n-1}$.
Premise 2.   Items $O_1, \ldots O_{n-1}$ all have feature $F_n$.
Conclusion.  Item $O_n$ also has $F_n$.

Thus, when an awl-like instrument made from a sharpened deer metapodial is found at a Formative site and has a wear pattern identical to tools used by contemporary Oaxacan farmers for opening cornhusks and removing kernels from cobs, archaeologists assign the same function of the modern tools to the prehistoric instrument (Flannery and Winter 1976:37).

Depending on premises used, therefore, analogical arguments can be employed to establish either generalizations, as in the example from Coles (1973:148), or nongeneral claims, such as: "This stone is a mano." The success of either type of analogical argument, though, depends on more than formal criteria.

Because arguments from analogy are inductive arguments, their premises may provide varying degrees of support for their conclusions. Some analogical arguments are weak; others are quite strong. The crucial factor in evaluating such arguments is the *relevance* of the similar features mentioned in the premises, to the inferred features mentioned in the conclusion. The just-cited inference to the function of the sharpened deer metapodial, for example, is particularly strong because the material from which tools are made, their type of edge, and their pattern of wear are all relevant to the ways in which tools are used. Similarities in wear pattern are especially relevant because there is a *causal* relation between the tasks for which a tool is used and its pattern of wear. Causally relevant factors are extremely important in strengthening analogies.

Relevance can be defined for present purposes in the following way: One feature or property is relevant to another if its presence either increases or decreases the probability of the other's presence. This definition of relevance does not, of course, provide a method for determining if one feature is relevant to another. This must be settled through observation and/or experimentation. Through means such as these, archaeologists have established (a) the relevance of certain types of debitage to techniques of stone tool production; (b) the relevance of porosity in pottery to the use of organic tempering materials; and (c) the relevance of observed variation in soil color and structure to practices of agriculture, irrigation, and burial of the dead.

Other criteria besides relevance are sometimes mentioned in connection with the appraisal of analogical arguments:

1. The greater (fewer) the number of analogous features mentioned in the premises, the stronger (weaker) the argument.
2. The more dissimilar the entities mentioned in the premises, the stronger the argument.

These criteria can be shown to be secondary to relevance, however. With respect to the *number* of points of analogy, obviously the only analogies that are meaningful are those that are relevant, because any two items are similar with respect to an indefinite number of irrelevant features. Houses and horses are similar to one another, for example, in the following respects: they are referred to (in English) by words that differ in only one letter, they are expensive, their maintenance requires a fair amount of work, they come in various colors, their owners often regret having acquired them, etc.

The second criterion recognizes the importance of variety in the objects mentioned in the premises. The dissimilarity (or "disanalogy") is a lack of similarity in *inessential* or *irrelevant* features, and it must be considered along with the demand for similarity or positive analogy in relevant respects. If certain physical features and activities (e.g., "smudge pits" and hide-smoking) are associated in a variety of complexes (e.g., Southeastern Indian tribes, Plains Indians, and Great Lakes Indians, Binford 1972:42–44), the inference that the physical feature and the activity are associated in general is strengthened. The point is that when certain features are associated in disanalogous circumstances, it would seem that their association is nonaccidental—that the presence of some features of the set is *relevant* to the presence of the others.

Context of association is often helpful in suggesting experiments that may be employed to demonstrate the relevance of form to function. In trying to decide whether or not stone gorgets could have had the same function as potters' ribs, Curren presented some of the stones to a potter without suggesting any use for them. The potter used them to construct a coiled pot. Although this type of experiment may show that an instrument can perform some task efficiently, it cannot prove that performing the task was the *function* of the object, as shown in our earlier example of the ice pick used as a murder weapon. The force of these imitative experiments, which attempt to use some object in the way it is believed to have been used in the past, is greatly increased, however, when the wear pattern resulting from such use matches the wear pattern on the archaeological object.

Some special difficulties in assigning ritual functions to objects have already been mentioned. In assigning a burial–ritual function to some type of object found chiefly in graves, the analogical argument that is used may not depend on any similarity in form between the archaeological object and objects found in other burials. The analogy is more complicated. In many different cultures, burials are conducted with some ceremony, and various items are placed with the body of the deceased— items that play a ritual role. In archaeologically discovered burials, the evidence of careful handling often includes uniform orientation of graves, deliberate positioning of bodies in the graves, and the placement of various objects with the bodies. Under such circumstances, it is reasonable to infer by analogy that the archaeologically known burials were also conducted with some degree of ritual, and further that the objects included in the graves played some role in this ritual. Recognition of the archaeological context as a deliberate burial makes clear what type of observed similarities are *relevant* for purposes of assigning functions. When a particular type of item is found only, or chiefly, associated with burials, then we have good reason to suppose that it played a role in the burial ritual even though it may not be similar in "form" to any known ritual items.

Flannery (1976:333) suggests that when an item is found mainly with "elite" households, its ritual function may be to communicate the elite status of the inhabitants of the household. In assigning this function to an object, analogy may be used to designate comparatively substantial dwellings in an archaeological context as elite houses.

Also, by analogy, archaeologists expect such houses to contain some sort of "status symbols." If a dwelling, unlike more humble neighboring houses, contains large pieces of copper, for example, these may be assigned the function of indicating status. This attribution of function is not based on similarities of form with such contemporary status symbols as Picasso prints and Cuisinarts. The relevant points of similarity for status symbols are not points of form, but of costliness, rarity, and difficulty in acquisition. It is in these respects that the archaeological objects and the contemporary objects are similar. The context of "elite household" enables us to recognize which features are relevant in drawing the functional inference.

Sometimes archaeologists are faced with the problem of assigning functions to objects (a) when contextual information is unhelpful, and (b) when there is no ethnographically known item of similar form. Can functions be ascribed to these objects with any degree of reliability?

Historical sources often supply descriptive information or pictures which archaeologists employ in the same way that they use ethnographic studies.

Mesoamerican archaeologists follow this tactic when they use journals of missionaries to assign the function of bloodletting to the stingray spines found in many of their sites (Flannery 1976:343). Flannery futher suggests that a ritual, status-information function was performed by the various materials composing these artifacts. Besides natural stingray spines, there are "cheap" imitations made of mammal bones, and "fine" replicas carved from jade.

McBryde (1979:6) acknowledges the value of such documents and oral histories for assigning functions to materials found at excavations, but she cautions archaeologists who use these resources of the necessity for a command of historians' techniques for dealing with such evidence. Skills in locating and identifying relevant sources, and the development of an adequate critical understanding of such sources are imperative. McBryde identifies the serious mistake of treating travel diaries, reports of administrators, and other documents or oral histories with the same presumed authority as the reports of a trained ethnographer. These materials are produced for different purposes and with different biases, and the archaeologist must consider this when trying to interpret them.

Of course there are many rich sources of historical materials compiled by anthropologists, such as the reports, bulletins, and collections of the Bureau of American Ethnology. These accounts can probably be used for purposes of ascribing functions—as Binford uses them to suggest the function of hide-smoking for the archaeologically known "smudge pits" (1972:42–44)—with less caution than historical sources by nonanthropologists.

## An Attempt to Provide a General Method for Ascribing Functions

Sometimes archaeologists seek functions of artifacts when there are neither historical nor ethnographic analogs to assist them. The difficulties involved in such an enterprise are obvious. Deetz, for example, says "when context, analogy, and imitation fail, little more can be done to clarify their function in the past (1967:79)." However, a philosopher named Michael Levin (1976) has tried to develop a philosophical analysis of functional ascriptions into a general solution to the problem of assigning functions to archaeological objects.

Levin's proposal is worth discussion, and may be especially interesting to archaeologists who are convinced that many analogical arguments are rather weak, for Levin does not mention or use any explicit appeals to ethnographic or historical analogs. Furthermore, Levin claims to provide a method for ascribing functions in the most difficult, context-free case, the one where the object is found in "splendid isolation (1976:228)."

Philosophers have long sought to present an analysis of "function" that could solve the problem of distinguishing between the *function* or *functions* of an object, and other, merely accidental, uses of the same object. L. Wright (1973, 1976) has developed such an analysis. Wright takes the ascription of functions to human artifacts as the clearest cases of functional ascription. His main point is that the function(s) of an object, unlike other accidental uses it may have, plays some causal role in the object's existence or its being where it is. Wright's formulation of the principle is

The function of X is Z iff (if and only if):

1. Z is a consequence (result) of X's being there, and
2. X is there because it does (results in) Z (Wright 1976:81).

Returning to the ice pick example, one can say that the function of ice picks is to chop ice, for (a) the chopping of ice is a result of utilization of an ice pick, and also (b) ice picks were designed (are there) for this function. Inflicting serious wounds on people is *not* the function of ice picks; although they may be used in this way, the aforementioned second condition is not satisfied. Ice picks were not created for this purpose, nor is their being successful murder instruments relevant to their continued existence.

Levin asks what, besides the information that an object would be an efficient means to achieve some goal or accomplish some task, would be required in order to justify the claim that achieving that goal or accomplishing that task is the function, F, of an object, O. He argues that it must be reasonable to suppose that people who possessed the object had some interest in achieving that goal or accomplishing that task. Finally, following Wright, he argues that the object had to come into being because someone who wanted to achieve that goal or accomplish that task determined that the object would be suitable for the job. When there is compliance with the following three criteria:

1. O is convenient for F,
2. F is commonly desired, and
3. O came into existence because somebody who wanted F figured out that O is a good way to get F;

we may then ascribe the function F to the object O (Levin 1976:230).

Levin hopes to accomplish three separate tasks with this analysis of function. The first task is definitional. The three criteria are intended as a set of necessary and sufficient conditions for correctly using the expression "*F* is the function of *O*." If one understands that these are the conditions governing the use of the expression, then one can be said to know the *meaning* of the expression. It is in this sense that Levin uses the criteria to provide a definition of "function."

Secondly, the three criteria are intended as instruments of *discovery*. For example, if one wants to discover the function of some artifact, one can begin by asking: "What is its convenient use?"

Finally, the criteria are intended as statements that can *justify* the ascription of a function, when their truth can be established. In this role, they are supposed to be guides to the forms of evidence that would be relevant. For example, if an archaeologist wants to jusify the claim that the function of smudge pits was hide-smoking, then this can be done, in part, by demonstrating the truth of "Smudge pits are convenient for hide-smoking."

In what follows, it will be shown that Levin's analysis is not adequate to this rather formidable tripartite role of definitional criteria, instruments of discovery, and principles of evidence for functional ascriptions (also see M. Salmon 1981).

## Criticism of the Attempt

Whether *O* is convenient for *F*, or "conduces usually well to *F* (Levin 1976:228)," can sometimes be established by experiment, and may be a relevant factor in discovering a function or justifying a functional ascription. However, it is not a necessary condition for such ascription, and should not be considered part of the meaning of "*F* is the function of *O*." Functions performed very inconveniently may be attributed correctly to poorly designed objects. For example on a rather common type of sponge mop, there is an attachment whose function is to squeeze excess water from the sponge without wetting the hands of the user. This attachment often results in the unwanted splashing and spraying of water, and may fail to remove all the excess water from the sponge, but it is still correct to ascribe to it the aforementioned function. The attachment performs the task it was designed to do, but in an inconvenient, and inefficient way. The squeezer may be replaced in a newer line of mops by an attachment that has the same intended function, but features more efficient design.

The convenience of *O* for *F* should count as some evidence that *F* is the function of *O*, because objects that perform a task efficiently are favored for performing that task. However, as Levin recognizes, some limit must be placed on this principle when it is used as evidence of function. Objects may be convenient for things that their users never recognized, or would not have wanted if they had recognized them. This is why, in an example mentioned earlier, Curren (1977) was hesitant about attributing the function of smoothing pottery to stone gorgets, even though experiments show that they do the job unusually well. There is some uncertainty regarding whether or not this use for the stones was recognized. At this point, many archaeologists turn for help to context of association, but Levin proposes a different sort of supplementary principle: "F is commonly desired." The advantage he claims for this principle is that a general knowledge of human nature, of the ordinary desires of rational agents, would enable archaeologists to determine if F was commonly desired.

There are difficulties both with the principle itself, and with Levin's suggestion about the type of knowledge needed to determine what is desired. An object may have a certain function, even though that function may not be "commonly desired," and may in fact not be desired by anybody. An inventor may devise an instrument for peeling a certain vegetable, even though the vegetable is better, from the standpoints of both taste and nutrition, when it is eaten with the peel. The instrument will not be a success, but it does not seem correct to deny that it is a peeler. There are inventions that have failed because no one wants what the instrument was designed to do. Instruments of biological warfare have some functions which certainly are not "commonly desired"; one hopes they are desired by no one. There is always the danger that an object uncovered by an archaeologist will be one that performed its function poorly (an extremely crude and unsuccesful instrument for keeping a calendar), or was an efficient instrument for doing something no one wanted (a Tasmanian stone knife for fish scaling). It may be possible to assign functions to these objects through appeals to ethnographic analogies, context of association, and oral or written tradition, when these are available. Archaeologists' dependence on such factors is evidenced by their reluctance to assign functions to isolated objects. But none of these factors is embodied in the criteria mentioned by Levin.

My objections to Levin are not based upon the inappropriateness of his appeals to beliefs and desires per se. Some archaeologists may be uneasy about trying, on the basis of the material evidence available to them, to make any judgments about human intentional behavior (i.e., beliefs, desires, etc.) because such judgments pose difficulties. But difficult as it is, archaeologists must somehow come to grips with this problem, for the distinction upon which their discipline is based—that between *artifact* and nonartifactual material—involves recognition of intentional behavior of intelligent, purposive agents, the makers of artifacts. To ignore all considerations of intentional behavior would be to neglect important evidence in the study of material remains. At the same time, because the chief focus of archaeologists' study is the material residue of past societies, important limitations on the use of phychological factors are imposed.

In R. V. S. Wright's treatment of flint from Koonalda Cave, a delicate balance between intentional and material considerations is beautifully demonstrated (1971:48–58). Wright acknowledges that "piece of flint" is a term with merely petrological and not archaeological connotations (1971:48). His reason for believing that some of the pieces of flint in Koonalda Cave are artifacts is the presence and disposition of positive and negative conchoidal fractures on these rocks. It is widely agreed that such bulbs of percussion and flake scars could only be the results of pressures that strike with a particular force at a point of impact. The application of these external forces by any agency other than man's activity is so unlikely that flint pieces bearing such marks are classified as artifacts.

Flint may also fracture as a result of internal pressures, and the pieces may resemble in general size and shape the flakes and flaked pieces produced by external forces. Such internal fractures may leave amorphous fractured surfaces or ripple marks, but they do not leave the bulbs and scars typical of conchoidal fractures. Although amorphous fractured surfaces and ripples *may* be the result of external striking, they cannot be taken to be reliable indicators, because they may also be produced by other means. On this basis, Wright groups the pieces of flint into three categories:

1. Flakes—with bulb and striking platform
2. Flaked pieces—nonflakes which bear a flake scar (negative bulb)
3. Residue—pieces that show neither positive nor negative bulbs

As Wright indicates, his three categories are based on descriptive features. The presence or absence of a bulb is a physical criterion on which it is fairly easy to get intersubjective agreement among observers. The intentional question (artifact or nonartifact?) has been replaced by a question about the nature of the material (bulb absent or present?). The reformulated question cannot be used to sort the pieces of flint into just two categories of artifacts and nonartifacts, for there may be some artifacts in the residue category. But archaeologists can be reasonably confident about the artifactual nature of the material in all cases where there is a positive or negative bulb. Although Wright's categories cannot be used to determine if an arbitrary piece of flint is an artifact, they can be used to give an unambiguous answer to the question of whether or not there was a stone tool industry at Koonalda Cave. To an archaeologist, this is clearly the more interesting question.

In judging that pieces of flint are artifacts, it has been recognized that hominids deliberately produced these objects, but no further appeal to specific intentions has been made. Neither has there been any appeal to "what is commonly desired." Other important questions can be raised about the nature of the material identified as artifactual and the site that contains it. For what was the site used? Were implements being manufactured there? If so, what were they, and what can they tell us about the lives of those who used them?

In trying to answer some of these questions, Wright distinguishes terms of description, such as "piece of flint" and "flake," from terms of interpretation. The interpretive terms he mentions, such as "implement," "core," and "chopper," are all terms that ascribe some function to the artifact. In answering the questions about functional ascription, Wright appeals primarily to the material evidence and analogy. He believes that the site contains very few finished implements. With only two exceptions, the artifacts do not show enough trimming to enable him to classify them as implements of any type. The point is that no analogy on the basis of similar form can be drawn here. He also mentions the lack of similarity of these artifacts to European artifacts that are representative of various tool types (1971:51). Because of the relatively small number of small flakes, which would result if there had been extensive trimming at the site (again by analogy with other sites), Wright does not believe that implements were made at the site and then carried elsewhere (1971:52). Other physical evidence indicates that *lumps* of flint rather than flakes were being formed at the site (1971:56). On the basis of evidence such as this, plus the uncomfortable nature of the cave, Wright concludes that the site was used as a quarry rather than for day-to-day activities. The reference to the uncomfortable nature of the cave involves an oblique appeal to a common desire of humans not to spend most of their time in cramped, dark, wet places.

This brief summary does not do justice to Wright's careful analysis of flint at Koonalda. But it does show the concern of archaeologists with purposive activity of humans, and how archaeological material may be used to provide reliable answers to these questions.

It would seem that Levin's principle, "*F* is commonly desired," although it is sometimes used, is too general to be a help in ascribing functions in most cases. The principle should be restricted, at least, to the desires of the society that produced or used the objects. But when the clause is restricted in this way, a general knowledge of human nature is no longer sufficient for determining what was desired. As many archaeologists are aware, to rely on a general knowledge of human nature, rather than on detailed ethnographic studies, is to build an ethnocentric bias into ascriptions of functions.

The following story demonstrates the dangers of ethnocentrism. When some traders first presented small hand mirrors to a group of American Indians, they were very excited about the new objects and were eager to acquire as many as possible. The traders assumed that the mirrors were wanted for the sort of self-study that amused Europeans. In fact, the Indians immediately recognized the value of mirrors for rapidly transmitting signals over long distances, and this military function belonged to mirrors in their society. If the mirrors had been found in an archaeological context, a general knowledge of human nature would not have been very useful for assigning the correct function to them.

Drawing on his ethnographic study of the Kalinga, Longacre (1981) describes the Kalinga pottery classification that is based on the various functions of pots. Among others, he identifies water jars (Immosso), very large pots for vegetable and meat cooking (Challay), and large-sized rice cooking pots (Lallangan Ittoyom). There is also a pot called "Im-immosso," which is a small version of the water jar. The function of this pot is to allow young girls to learn to carry water jars balanced on their heads. Although this function is certainly compatible with the criteria suggested by Levin, it is very unlikely that the criteria would provide any help in discovering that function, because so many other possible functions are also compatible with the criteria. Examples such as this are particularly telling, for they show the difficulty of ascribing functions in the most straightforward case of utilitarian artifacts. For ceremonial objects, the criteria seem nearly worthless.

The discussion so far shows that neither "*O* is convenient for *F*" nor "*F* is commonly desired" is necessary for ascribing a function to an object, and thus cannot be considered part of what it means to state that an object has a particular function. It has also been shown that these two criteria are not particularly helpful in *discovering* the function of archaeological objects. The most we can say for the criteria is that if we can show that *O* is convenient for *F* and *F* is commonly desired—and this may be very difficult—then we have *some* justification for attributing the function *F* to *O*.

The crucial question then is whether or not the addition of the third criterion ("*O* came into existence because somebody who wanted *F* figured out that *O* is a good way to get *F* (Levin)") results in a set sufficient for the discovery of functions of archaeological objects. This criterion does seem closely related to the meaning of "*F* is the function of *O*" in the sense of being a sufficient condition for ascribing functions. That is, if we could establish that a given object was specifically created to do a certain job, then it would seem unreasonable to deny that doing that job was its function. However, this principle cannot, without modification, serve as a necessary condition for attributing functions. Consider the smooth river stones that were (and are) used by Pueblo Indians for polishing pottery. Although these stones are selected for this purpose, and are passed on from mother to daughter, they certainly do not come into existence because someone determined that they would be good for polishing. L. Wright's (1976:81) formulation of the function principle is sufficiently broad to avoid this difficulty: the object *is there* because it does (results in) the function. His use of "is there" is deliberately vague to accommodate a number of different types of situations, such as this one wherein natural objects are specifically selected to do a particular job.

Regardless of the value of this criterion in helping us to understand assigning a function to an object, the criterion is relevant to *discovering* the function of an artifact only when archaeologists are in a position to establish the requisite causal history of the object. This means that they must be able to show that its usefulness for a particular function was part of the cause either of its coming into existence, or of being in a certain location (in the cases of natural objects employed in the same way as artifacts). For example, to return to the stone gorgets described by Curren (1977); if it were possible to show that these implements were designed expressly for the purpose of smoothing pottery, then we could with complete confidence assign the same function to them as we do to the wooden ribs of contemporary potters.

The appropriate causal history can be established, Levin claims, by appeal to a premise that is always tacitly used by archaeologists when they are willing to attribute functions to material objects. This premise, which he calls the "alertness principle," is "If *O* would be convenient for *F*, *A* (the agent) wants *F*, and *A* is sufficiently familiar with the material *M* of which *O* would be made to know that *O* would be convenient for *F*, then *A* will notice that a thing convenient for *F* can be made out of *M*, and *A* will indeed make an *O* out of *M* for *F* (1976:232)." This peculiar postulate suffers from overwhelming defects: it fails to establish a causal history, it is highly implausible, and it seems to be contradicted by historical examples. Why Levin attributes its tacit use to archaeologists is a mystery.

The alertness principle cannot enlighten us about causes, in spite of

Levin's claims for it. Although the consequent clause, which asserts that an agent intentionally designed an object for the ascribed function, would provide the requisite causal account of the item's origin it can do this only when the antecedent clauses have been established. The first two antecedent clauses have already been discussed. Although experiments can show in many cases that an object would have been convenient for the function, we have seen that a general knowledge of human nature is not sufficient for demonstrating that an agent would have wanted that function. Special knowledge about goals and desires of particular societies and the individuals in these societies is required. Arguments from analogy, based on ethnographic studies, are crucial for this information.

With respect to the third antecedent, Levin claims that "knowledge of the site" can supply presumptive evidence that can show that the agent was sufficiently familiar with the material of which the object is made to know that the object would have been convenient for the ascribed function (1976:231). Sites can vary from those as complete as Pompeii or as impressive and mysterious as Stonehenge, to those as undramatic and uninformative as a few ochre stains on soil or scattered bits of chipped stone in a field. Some sites provide abundant information through context of association, whereas others provide almost none. Only when an object occurs in a site yielding little or no context of association can we say it was found in the "splendid isolation" with which Levin claims to deal, but then knowledge of the sites does not provide the requisite evidence regarding the agent's knowledge or intentions.

*If* we can succeed in showing that an object was designed or selected for a specific function or functions, that is, if we can establish the appropriate causal history of the object, then we are *justified* in making a functional ascription. But the alertness principle cannot be used to *discover* that causal history, for its application requires more than knowledge derived from experiments, a general knowledge of human nature, and a knowledge of the site. Because of this, the criteria that Levin proposes do not provide a general method for enabling archaeologists to discover the functions of archaeological objects.

Aside from difficulties in applying the alertness principle, there is an implausible ring to the principle itself. To accept its truth is to accept the view that each human invention was only a more or less predictable and routine result of rational responses to available materials and the current stage of technological development. To take an important counterexample, consider the stirrup. Stirrups are convenient for allowing a warrior to engage in armed combat from horseback without losing either his weapon or his seat. No doubt this function was considered desirable from the time that armies had cavalry troops. Greeks and Romans were familiar with material of which stirrups can be made. But stirrups were not invented in Europe at a time when all these conditions were fulfill-ed. They reached Europe, probably by a process of diffusion, only in the early eighth century (L. White 1962).

A further objection to the alertness principle is that even when some device has been invented, people are not always "alert" enough to recognize its possibilities. Wheels were not used for work in the New World, although archaeological evidence shows they were used on toys (Heine-Geldern 1976 :289). Hero of Alexandria (around 250 A.D.) is cred-ited with invention of the steam engine (Turnbull 1956:110), but no one thought of using it for work prior to relatively recent modern times. As White (1962:28) says, "The historical record is replete with inventions which have remained dormant in a society (here a footnote refers to his discussion of the mechanical crank, 1962:110–115) until at last—usually for reasons which remain mysterious—they 'awaken' and become active elements in the shaping of a culture to which they are not entirely novel."

Levin does not provide any evidence to support his claim that ar-chaeologists always tacitly accept the alertness principle when attribut-ing functions. There is no reason to burden archaeologists with this untrue and unhelpful tacit premise.

It would seem that in his dependence on the alertness principle, Levin has failed to give an adequate account of the logic of functional ascription. He has ignored the realms of evidence, namely ethnographic analogues and careful analysis of contexts, that archaeologists must em-ploy in ascribing functions to archaeological objects.

## Ethnoarchaeology and Analogy

No discussion of analogical reasoning in archaeology can ignore important current work by ethnoarchaeologists. Some of their studies have been mentioned in passing, in connection with various examples cited in this chapter. A closer look at the enterprise is in order because in ethnoarchaeological studies, analogical reasoning has reached a "new level of systematic sophistication (Schwartz 1978)." Schwartz defines the task of the ethnoarchaeologist, and also acknowledges the importance of analogical reasoning in the history of archaeology:

> The ethnoarchaeologist is an anthropologist conducting ethnographic research for an archaeological purpose, linking material remains to human behavior from which they have resulted. From the inception of archaeology, its practitioners have drawn conclusions about prehistoric material by making comparisons or

analogues to ethnographically derived observations of living people (Schwartz 1978:vii).

Although Schwartz's praise for the new sophistication of analogical reasoning occurs in the foreword to a collection of essays edited by Richard A. Gould (1978), Gould's own position in the matter is less sympathetic to analogy. His own final essay is entitled "Beyond Analogy in Ethnoarchaeology," and he makes his view known again in *Living Archaeology* (1980, see especially 29–35, "Analogy's Last Hurrah"). Whether ethnoarchaeology involves sophisticated appeals to analogy or goes "beyond analogy" is, I believe, a mere terminological debate. If one understands argument by analogy as simply attributing similar functions on the basis of similar forms, ethnoarchaeology certainly goes beyond that. But if analogical reasoning is understood in the manner that has been developed in this chapter, ethnoarchaeologists are involved in some sophisticated analogies.

Examples of this sophistication can be found in the sensitivity of contemporary ethnoarchaeologists to information which can be gleaned from a large variety of human "residues." This term refers not only to artifacts, but also to any deliberate or accidental alterations of the environment resulting from the actions of humans. Their studies also take account of some previously unappreciated features of "context," such as the spatial relations between residues, which can yield information about social relationships in many cases.

All archaeologists study residues of human behavior. Ethnoarchaeologists are interested in a much broader class of residues than artifacts, and they also examine contemporary behavior with an interest in the residues that might be produced by it. They look at the natural processes that might affect deposits of residue over time. Their methods include observation and participation in contemporary societies. They also perform experiments with the goal of producing residues similar to those found in archaeological sites. Analogy is used to infer similar residue-producing behavior in the past from similar residues and observed residue-producing behavior in the present.

Although archaeologists have become aware of many rich possibilities of analogical reasoning, they do not concur in their views about what such arguments are capable of establishing. Longacre (1978) raises the question of whether analogies can yield strong generalizations, or whether their use is confined to that of suggesting hypotheses for further testing and yielding counterexamples to previously accepted generalizations.

For example, Gould sees the purpose of ethnographic studies as that of providing the archaeologist with "alternative modes of behavior that would have been difficult to arrive at by logic alone (1978:254)." As he says, "What we aspire to in archaeology is an idea of the past, and *that idea is based upon a selection of behaviors that can most economically account for the facts* (1978:256, emphasis added)."

Such an account of the value of analogies presents them in an unnecessarily weak light. According to Gould's claim, analogies merely *suggest* hypotheses, whereas the arguments whose conclusions relate behavior to residues are judged primarily on the basis of their economy in handling data. This means that although Gould acknowledges the role of analogies in the discovery of hypotheses, he does not recognize their importance in justifying these hypotheses. For justification he regards a "principle of economy" as paramount.

It is not quite clear just what this principle is, however, because "economy" is ambiguous. "Economy" is sometimes used interchangeably with "simplicity" to refer to a characteristic of hypotheses, explanations, or theories. This view of economy was discussed in the last chapter in connection with its importance as a pragmatic criterion for assessing the prior probabilities of scientific hypotheses. A reasonable way of formulating this principle of economy for judging hypotheses can be expressed as follows: "All other things being equal, the hypothesis that most economically accounts for the data is most apt to be true." Such a formulation, however, reveals the secondary importance of economy, and does not give it the fundamental status that Gould apparently accords to it. Economy is important in scientific reasoning, but most scientists regard it as far less important than other characteristics of hypotheses, such as whether or not the hypothesized behavior is *relevant* to the observed residues.

Because of the ambiguity in "economy," it is unclear whether or not the principle described in the preceding paragraph is the one Gould endorses as fundamental. From his discussion, it is more likely that he is urging a different principle, one that might be expressed in the following way:

> Human beings who have particular goals (such as the production of a type of artifact) usually choose the most efficient way to achieve these goals. Thus, in trying to discern the type of behavior that produced certain residues, we are justified in claiming that the behavior that can be demonstrated to be most efficient for producing the desired result is probably the sort of behavior that actually occurred.

The first principle of economy, which claims that simplicity and truth are conjoined quite frequently in hypotheses, is widely accepted, and not regarded as controversial. This second principle is quite different from the first, however, for it is based upon a factual claim that humans behave in a certain way. Whether humans are efficient in the way claimed is an interesting and important question. Gould cites no evidence for its truth. It may have some plausibility, but there are countless examples of humans' behaving in very inefficient ways, so the claim needs careful restriction or "hedging" at the very least (e.g. Dickson 1980:708). The alleged efficiency of humans poses a fascinating problem for behavioral scientists. Some version of the claim may be true, but it is certainly controversial, and so should not be regarded as a foundation of archaeological reasoning.

Thus, we seem to have two distinct principles of economy. The first principle is widely accepted, but rather weak. The second principle is powerful, but rather implausible. It is a serious mistake to suppose that there is just one principle of economy, which is both powerful and plausible.

If one can establish, by stating suitable qualifications and specifying limiting circumstances, that the most efficient behavior is the most likely, then what is shown is the *relevance* of efficiency to choice of behavior in certain situations. Given this relevance, one can still ask about the importance of efficiency with respect to other relevant factors. For example, with respect to certain types of artifacts, symmetry of the finished product or other aesthetic criteria, or preservation of some rare and valuable material, might take precedence over economy of behavior. Balancing various relevant factors is a delicate task, and one for which there are no set rules.

In Gould's own example—Crabtree's experiment on replicating Folsom points (Crabtree 1966)—it is not at all clear that economy is especially important in the selection of one technique rather than others. Of eleven techniques that attempted to produce the points, only two were successful. Nine techniques were rejected, not because they offered a less economical way of accounting for the data, but because they could not account for it at all. Of the remaining two techniques, one was selected because "it was more reliable in producing the desired results (Gould 1978:257)." The favored technique of direct pressure with clamp thus has greater relevance to production of the desired points than the indirect percussion technique, but this does not guarantee that direct pressure is more economical than indirect percussion. The method that produces the desired results with greater frequency (the more reliable method) would also be the more economical *only if* expenditures of time and energy, including such factors as investment in skill acquisition, plus costs of materials were not much smaller for the less reliable method. Reliability and economy are not always coextensive.

Binford, like Gould, stresses the importance of analogy in suggesting hypotheses about the function of archaeological objects. He says that the proper role of arguments from analogy in archaeology is to enable the archaeologist to formulate "a postulate as to the function of the archaeological features (1972:37)." In contrast to Gould's reliance on *economy* to determine the acceptability of these hypotheses, however, Binford insists on the hypothetico–deductive method of confirmation: "The only method for determining the truth value of a proposition, and hence refuting it, is to devise deductively reasoned hypotheses regarding expected relationships between phenomena in question and other classes of archaeological remains (1972:53)."

Binford's use of analogy goes beyond the mere suggestion of hypotheses though, for he recognizes that arguments from analogy offer inductive support for their conclusions, and that the degree of support is variable and dependent on such factors as the number of analogies and whether or not the points of analogy that are cited in the premises are "important" (i.e., relevant). Although he does not say it this way, it is clear from his remarks that Binford uses analogical arguments to establish *prior probabilities*. Using the standard criteria for evaluating arguments from analogy, Binford claims that "The function of smudge pits was hide smoking" has a greater probability than "The function of smudge pits was pottery smudging (Binford 1972:55)." In summarizing his comments on the alternative hypothesis of pottery smudging, which was offered by Munsen, Binford again emphasizes the importance of testing, claiming that this is the only way to *refute* a hypothesis. But he admits the importance of analogy in helping to "make decisions as to how to invest research time in hypothesis testing (1972:57)." This is an important and widely accepted use of prior probabilities.

One cannot quarrel with this legitimate use of arguments from analogy, but Binford seems to underestimate their role in the *justification* of archaeological hypotheses. First of all, this happens because he does not give adequate credit to the role of priors in the confirmation of hypotheses. The priors are important not only in deciding which hypotheses to test, but also in deciding the relative status of alternative hypotheses after testing. (See Chapter Three.) Because, for example, the pottery smudging hypothesis starts out with a significantly lower prior probability, any test that tends to confirm it might nevertheless fail to raise its relative confirmation by a sufficient degree to guarantee that it was more acceptable than the hide-smoking hypothesis.

Secondly, although this may occur only in rather uninteresting cases in archaeology, sometimes analogical arguments can provide such strong support for their conclusions that further testing would be otiose. The archaeologically discovered awl-like tools, made from sharpened deer metapodials, which are analogous in virtually every relevant respect—including patterns of wear—to the tools used by contemporary Oaxacan farmers (Flannery and Winter 1976:37) are assigned the same function on the basis of these analogies. It is difficult to see how this functional ascription could be strengthened by any further test.

In the third place, cases may arise wherein direct testing of an hypothesis is infeasible. Yet, if the hypothesis rested on an analogical argument, one might look for indirect support by strengthening the analogy. Such indirect support might involve tests, but the tests would not be direct tests of the hypothesis. They would be designed to show such things as the *relevance* of form to function or of environment to a particular form of behavior in a given case. The logical point is that analogical arguments are not *intrinsically* weaker than any other inductive arguments. The sort of conclusion that can be established by any inductive argument depends not only on its form but on its content. Hypotheses with weak priors that can be subjected only to insignificant testing are not going to become well-confirmed just because the H–D method, or Bayesian model of confirmation is applied. In the absence of other possibilities, it would be foolish to disregard or dismiss attempts to strengthen analogies as ways to establish archaeological claims. Ascher's (1961) work on analogy should be seen within this framework.

Archaeologists sometimes worry about the dependence of analogical arguments on an unwarranted commitment to "uniformitarianism." Gould voices the sentiments of many when he says, "The less the archaeologist must depend on uniformitarianism assumptions to infer past human behavior the more valid his explanations will be (1978:2)." Although this is perfectly true, it seems to pose no special problem, because the fewer assumptions of *any sort* on which one must depend, the better the explanations will be. Moreover, "uniformitarianism" is a term that covers many different kinds of principles, some questionable, but some quite innocuous as well.

Simpson (1970) presents a detailed historical account of uniformitarianism wherein he analyzes many of the principles that have been assumed under this label. Of particular interest to archaeologists, I believe, are two senses of "uniformitarianism" that are especially important in today's scientific—particularly geological—literature. The first, called "methodological uniformitarianism" by S. Gould (1965), and "actualism" by Hooykaas (1956), has to do with what Simpson calls *immanent* or inherent properties of the universe (1970:59). This principle states that there are invariable natural laws governing the fundamental properties of matter and energy. These are the laws of physics and chemistry referred to earlier in Chapter Two and considered by Smart

(1963) to be the only genuine candidates for the label "law of nature." These laws govern such regularities as physical and chemical interactions, characteristic spectra, and boiling and melting points of various substances. Archaeologists frequently appeal to such uniformities. The invariance of the half-life of $^{14}$C is crucial to all radiocarbon dating. If cast copper is found in an archaeological site, it is by appeal to a constant melting point of copper that archaeologists infer those who produced the copper had the technological skill to construct furnaces capable of reaching 1083° C. Such appeals seem perfectly legitimate.

The second type of uniformitarianism, called "substantive uniformitarianism" by Steven Gould (1965) has to "do with the *configurations* that have arisen and continue to arise, in historical sequence and in accordance with those immanent properties (Simpson 1970:60)." The geological principle that the types of processes which alter the earth's crust, and the intensity with which these occur, have been the same through the earth's history is uniformitarian in this sense. The assumption that the atmospheric concentration of $^{14}$C has remained constant through time is a substantive uniformitarian claim that formed part of the basis for radiocarbon dating, and that is now known to be false. However, another substantive uniformitarian claim, regarding the production of growth rings in some types of trees, provided a basis for rejecting the absence of variation in $^{14}$C levels. The causal processes that give rise to tree rings are much better understood than those that control the proportion of $^{14}$C to ordinary carbon in the atmosphere, and this is why tree ring results were accepted as corrections of dating by presence of $^{14}$C when the two methods disagreed. What was involved was not a rejection of the principle that causes operating in the present are similar to those operating in the past, and thus capable of giving us information about the past, but rather a deeper and more secure understanding of one sort of causal process and a weak and speculative account of another.

A sound understanding of the causal processes involved in producing edge wear on stone tools forms the basis for archaeologists' assignments of tool functions. The most important factors in determining the edge wear of a tool are the sorts of pressure applied to the tool by the agent and the resistance offered to the tool by the material that is worked. This is why it is safe to infer tool functions from edge wear when it can be observed or demonstrated by experiment that certain ways of applying pressure, such as chopping or scraping, produce characteristic wear patterns. Such inferences depend on rather "safe" uniformities, such as laws of mechanics and physiology. Acknowledging this does not minimize the difficulty of interpreting tool function in many cases, for the problems that concern archaeologists—such as whether edge wear was caused by pressures applied by hominids or by some other natural processs—do not always yield an unambiguous answer. Furthermore, some patterns of edge wear do not correspond to any currently understood process of pressure or resistance. One form of substantive uniformitarianism holds that the causal process that can presently be observed are *sufficient* for knowledge of causal processes in the past (Simpson 1970:58). Such a principle seems unlikely to be acceptable in a science that must deal with behavior of extinct hominids as well as a rapidly evolving *Homo sapiens*, at least without substantial modification and qualification. Archaeologists may simply never know how some apparent tools were used, either because they have no idea of the processes involved or because some knowledge of initial conditions under which such tools were manufactured and used is simply unattainable. But in many cases of assigning functions of chopping, scraping, and other ordinary activities, no questionable uniformitarian assumptions are involved. What is required is an understanding of the relevant laws of nature and how these laws work in a particular well-understood range of applications.

The situation in which archaeologists ascribe functions on the basis of edge wear, however difficult this may be, is probably the easiest one with respect to knowledge of the causal processes and evidence for operation of the same processes in the past. Cases in which the relevant factors are both so few and so well known are relatively rare. Consider, for example, archaeologists' attempts to assess prehistoric population sizes. Some of the factors recognized as relevant are the size and numbers of rooms or houses in an area, the amounts of trash, and the number of burials. Other relevant factors include such things as whether dwellings in an area were occupied on a year-round basis or whether they were seasonal camps. Upper limits on population sizes may be controlled by an area's biomass. It is extremely difficult to take account of all the relevant factors, and to know how to assess their relative importance in such situations. Some writers have tried to support claims that one admittedly relevant factor "screens off," or renders unimportant the other factors. Naroll's attempts to link population size with floor area in a direct way represents such an attempt (1962).

One way to look at studies such as Naroll's and their implications for interpreting archaeological materials is to ask if "uniformity" between ethnographically known primitive societies and archaeologically known societies exists with respect to the connections between population size and floor area. This seems to be an inadequate way of formulating the problem, because it distracts from the chief issue, that is, the exact nature of the relevant connection between floor area and population size. It makes sense to ask questions about uniformity when one is dealing with causal processes that are well known—the question is merely whether or not these same processes were operating in the distant past. But when the processes themselves are obscure or poorly understood or unknown, it is not profitable to concern ourselves with whether or not they operated in the past. If we can observe the association of certain artifacts with particular types of behavior and social organization in contemporary settings, and if we also observe the archaeological remains of similar artifacts, the appropriate question is not "Can we assume that there was a uniform connection between the various items which extends into the past?", but rather "Is the connection genuine or coincidental, and what kind of connection is it?" It is unfortunate that much of the discussion of uniformitarian assumptions in the recent literature tends to obscure the real problem, namely that of determining the relevance of one type of phenomena or process to others, when there is some evidence for their correlation. It is the issue of relevance that determines the success or failure of analogical arguments, not the legitimacy of some uniformitarian assumption in most cases.

## Conclusion

This discussion of analogical arguments and their uses in archaeology, particularly their importance in the ascription of functions, has focused on the importance of relevance for assessing analogical arguments. Archaeologists' traditional concern with context, and their more recent interest in experimental archaeology, are often directed to demonstrating the relevance of one type of feature to another, and have been very helpful in showing the relevance of material remains to behavior and social organization.

An attempt to provide a general method for ascribing functions to archaeological objects was presented. This method, which does not invoke either analogy or context, was shown to be inadequate.

In view of the nature of analogical arguments, and the type of support that they can provide for their conclusions, it seems that there is no obstacle to their use for all three purposes mentioned by Longacre: (a) to yield strong generalizations, (b) to suggest hypotheses, and (c) to yield counterexamples to previously accepted generalizations. What sort of conclusion an inductive argument yields depends not only on its form, but also on the strength of the premises; it seems that in archaeology, given the nature of the data available, the most common and valuable use of analogy is that of establishing prior probabilities of hypotheses.

These priors are used not only to determine which hypotheses are to be tested, but also the relative degree of confirmation after testing. Current work in ethnoarchaeology exemplifies this use of analogy in a striking manner.

One traditional objection to functional explanation has involved questioning the reliability of the functional ascriptions on which such explanations are based. In this chapter, an attempt has been made to show that such ascriptions can be well founded. We are still left with the question of what role such ascriptions play in functional *explanations*. It is to this problem, as well as other objections to functional explanations, that we direct our attention in the next chapter.

# CHAPTER FIVE

# Functional Explanation

## Introduction and Examples of Functional Explanations

A natural way of explaining the presence of many items in the archaeological record involves stating the function of an item or practice. One reads, for example, that stone implements found at a site were used for chopping, and that choppers were required for food processing. Archaeologists explain the barbs chipped on a projectile point by remarking that barbs helped ensure the point's lodging in its target; they explain the choice of prehistoric site locations in terms of the probability that these sites afforded protection from possible enemies; they claim that a corn and bean diet emerged in central America because it provided a complete source of protein; they suggest that certain social practices existed among prehistoric peoples because they served to redistribute wealth; they hypothesize that prehistoric populations ate some plant resources only after the plants had gone to seed and were ready to die to maintain a stable food supply. In some of these cases, the function mentioned is simply the job that an artifact was designed for; in other cases, "function" refers to some deliberately chosen goal of human behavior. In other instances, we say that a practice or activity of people fulfills some function even though this particular result was not a matter of conscious intention. Furthermore, in many evolutionary functional explanations, there is no appeal to conscious design on the part of people, but rather to the mechanisms of adaptation and natural selection. Examples of such explanatory claims abound in any work on archaeology that does more than merely describe the contents of sites.

In spite of widespread use of such claims, and of their intuitive explanatory appeal, objections have been raised against them on many grounds. In the preceding chapter, some questions about the reliability of the functional ascriptions upon which functional explanation depends were discussed. In this chapter, attention will be given to the explanations themselves. Because functional explanations seem to play such a central role in archaeology, any serious objections to them should be considered and—if possible—laid to rest. Even during the era of Functionalism as the dominant general theory of anthropology, an-

84

thropologists were aware of the limitations of this type of explanation. Anthropologists' objections to functional explanation have been concerned primarily with the apparent inability of this type of explanation to account for change and development. Functional explanations seem only to explain the *status quo*. Philosophers, in contrast, have focused on certain logical inadequacies in the form of functional explanation. As Functionalist theories of anthropology have become less dominant, many anthropologists have shown little interest in defending functional explanation as a legitimate form of scientific explanation. In this respect, they differ from many biologists, who see the legitimization of functional explanation as an important point in securing the foundations of their discipline. In what follows, I will try to answer the main objections to functional explanation and to show that any attractive model of explanation in archaeology must account for functional explanations.

## Functional Explanations versus Functionalist Theories of Anthropology

Objections are often raised against functional explanations because of their alleged inability to account for change, their antihistorical character, and their reinforcement of political conservatism. Such objections fail to distinguish between functional explanations per se, and particular functionalist theories of society that have been offered by some anthropologists, notably Malinowski and Radcliffe-Brown. Functionalist theories go beyond the mere employment of explanations that refer to roles and purposes. They require viewing societies as organic units, and demand either that *every* feature of a society be explained with reference to its contribution to the maintenance of the whole or that *every* cultural feature be explained in terms of its role in satisfying some basic need. (See Harris [1968:Chapter 19] for a critical discussion of functionalism in anthropological theories.) One important use of functional explanations *in these theories* is to account for the stability of social arrangements, thus supporting the charges raised above.

Radcliffe-Brown, for example, suggests that *any* social custom can be explained by considering its role in maintaining a smoothly working society, just as the presence of hemoglobin in the blood is accountable by its function in transporting oxygen from the lungs to various parts of the body; "Every custom and belief of a primitive society plays some part in the general life of the organism (1967:229)." Often cited is Radcliffe-Brown's explanation of the role of joking as a means of stabilizing family ties through preventing conflict between a man and his wife's relatives (1952:Chapter Four).

These innovative studies of social structure opened exciting new avenues to anthropologists, and the methods Radcliffe-Brown outlined so carefully, including a heavy emphasis on functional explanation, were adopted by his enthusiastic disciples in Great Britain, Australia, and the United States.

Notwithstanding his important contributions to anthropology, Radcliffe-Brown's negative views about the feasibility of gaining accurate knowledge of the past had some deleterious effects on the development of anthropological archaeology. Mulvaney summarizes these effects in a poignant paragraph:

> Radcliffe-Brown (who held the Sydney University Chair of Anthropology from 1926–1931) laid the foundations for the study of social structure, a landmark in anthropological history. Yet he propounded doctrines which negated the past as a possible subject for scientific study. In a slashing review of one of Davidson's major papers, Radcliffe-Brown laid down in 1930 that anthropology "will make little progress until we abandon these attempts at conjectural reconstructions of a past about which we can obtain no direct knowledge in favour of a systematic study of the culture as it exists in the present." Thirty years later, his former department appointed its first lecturer in prehistory (1975:121).

Small wonder that archaeologists have grave reservations about the value of Functionalism or anything associated with it! However, to regard all functional explanations as good only for the purposes of supporting Functionalist theories of anthropology is to take much too narrow a view, and one that is not in accord with ordinary scientific understanding of the range of these explanations.

First, one may consistently employ functional explanations for some features but not for others. We can admit the value of functional explanation without adopting the view that *every* feature of a society functions to maintain the social structure.

Second, functional explanations are compatible with changes in structure, and thus the charges of antihistoricalism and conservatism fail. Functional explanations are employed in evolutionary biology to explain changes in types of organisms over time as well as to explain stabilities, such as the maintenance of constant body temperature in individuals. The biologist Mayr, who strongly endorses many types of functional explanation says, "it is legitimate to ask with respect to any biological structure, function, or process: Why is it there? What was its selective advantage when it was acquired? (1978:52)." The functional explanations that Mayr envisions as the correct answers to these legitimate questions involve the *history* of the structure, function, or process, not merely its present contribution to some whole. These evolutionary functional explanations are different from those used by Radcliffe-Brown, but they are no less "functional."

Requests for functional explanation occur occasionally even in physics, that paragon of "hard science": "For a long time physicists have been perplexed as to the reason for the muon's existence. It is so like the electron that its role in nature would seem to be obscure. What purpose does it serve? (Davies 1979:149)."

Functional explanations are as important to the archaeologist as to the evolutionary biologist, and they are used not only to explain evolution but also to explain why prehistoric peoples settled at particular sites, why certain items occur in these sites, why tools or facilities have a particular form, or why certain processes (such as the abandonment of a pueblo) occurred. However, many archaeologists would hesitate to call these explanations "functional." "Systems explanations" is a currently popular euphemism for some accounts that accomplish the role of functional explanation. The new term sounds up-to-date and scientific, and it avoids many of the old unpleasant associations with functionalism. Nevertheless, these "systems" explanations have all the essential features of functional explanations. This point will be further elaborated in connection with the next question about functional explanations.

## The Consistency of Functional Explanations with Scientists' Understanding of Causality

Functional explanations have been denounced by some as being incompatible with normal scientific understanding of causality. There is a strong intuitive feeling that a really good explanation will refer to the cause or causes of that which is explained. The only causes mentioned in some functional explanations are those that have traditionally been called "final causes," such as purposes, ends, or goals. We sometimes explain the hard-working habits of a student by referring to the fellowship that the student is trying to win. The bowerbird's nest-decorating behavior is explained in terms of its goal of enticing the female to enter. Final causes have even been attributed to inanimate objects; for example, the acorn is said to develop in the way it does in order to become an oak tree.

The causal status of such purposes, ends, and goals is somewhat dubious. It is a fundamental principle of modern science that no cause can occur *after* its effect. Yet, purposes, ends, and goals—or at least the achievement of such—clearly come *after* the events that they are invoked to explain. Because of this reversed temporal order, most scientists would not regard any explanation that depended upon "final" causes as a genuine causal explanation.

Nevertheless, many explanations that refer to ends, purposes, and the like do not involve any objectionable appeals to final causes. Explanations that refer to the goals of human agents lose their questionable causal status when we realize that although the ends occurred after the actions designed to bring them about, the desires, motives, intentions, and decisions of the actors preceded their goal-directed activities. These *preceding* psychological states, not the ends achieved, are reasonable candidates for causes in explanations of purposive human behavior. Modern psychological theories have presented a strong case for the existence of unconscious desires, motives, and the like. These, as well as conscious states, may serve as legitimate candidates for causes.

There are, of course, many problems involved with uncovering and understanding the psychological states that give rise to human behavior. These difficulties should not be minimized. In the first place, there is no completely satisfactory psychological theory that analyzes what have been called "psychological states." Are these states actually internal mechanisms that are causally efficacious, or merely a convenient way of characterizing patterns of behavior, behavior whose causes lie in such factors as environmental conditioning? This is a central source of controversy between behavioral and cognitive psychologists, and it is a deep and difficult issue. Aside from that general theoretical problem, as we have seen, archaeologists must be wary of attributing their own, or contemporary,or ethnocentrically derived psychological states to the prehistoric situations they study. Fortunately, it is not necessary to have a completely satisfactory account of these states for the purpose of eliminating any dependence on "causes" which follow their effects in explaining purposive behavior. Even though our understanding of psychological states may be quite rudimentary, the mere admission of some such causes, along either behaviorist or cognitivist lines, will prevent the unacceptable employment of "final causes" in explaining human actions of a purposive sort. The causes of purposive behavior—whatever they may be—at least do not follow their effects.

Although we are willing to attribute conscious or unconscious psychological states to people, and perhaps to some animals, we hesitate to assign such complicated patterns of beliefs, desires, and motives to lower forms of animal life, plants, and nonliving things. At the same time, it is plausible to describe some behavior of these things as "goal-directed" or "purposive." Purposive behavior is commonly attributed to machines of various sorts, such as guided missiles. Such purposiveness is sometimes explained by referring to the purposes of the human designers of these machines. Only mechanistic causes are involved in the operation of these machines, and the goals achieved by them are not in any real sense *their* goals, but rather those of their designers. Though this sort of account may work for man-made machines, it will not work for plants and animals. Living things exhibit behavior, such as heliotropism, or the cowering movements of young fowl when the shadow of a predator-like figure flies over them, that is in some sense similar to human purposive behavior. But many scientists are reluctant to credit the design of these organisms to the purposive behavior of some Designer.

Modern evolutionary biology, with its principles of adaptation and natural selection, avoids this controversial issue by giving us a way of explaining such natural processes and phenomena without invoking a Designer. When we say, for example, that a plant has an exploding seed pod in order to succeed in the struggle for survival, we mean that plants with built-in scattering mechanisms have a statistically better chance of surviving and reproducing themselves. Plants without some such device would go extinct rather quickly in an environment where there were few animal seed carriers or other means of seed dispersal, for all the seeds would fall at the base of the plant and crowd one another out of existence (Wilke *et al.* 1972).

Purposive behavior of humans may change the selection patterns that occur in nature. People who want seed for planting will find it easier to hand collect from plants with less efficient scattering mechanisms, and this intervention will select plants with limp pods over those with explosive pods. So, explanation of the emergence of a particular plant may involve the expression of human purposes along with other forces of natural selection, but no appeal to "final causes."

Natural selection and human intervention are invoked by archaeologists to explain the emergence of the corn and bean diet in America. Together corn and beans provide a complete source of proteins. Those prehistoric peoples who subsisted on such a diet were more apt to survive to adulthood and to reproduce themselves than those who lacked essential proteins. Once this process had begun, because dietary patterns tend to be stable—a practice whose explanation would probably involve some references to conscious and unconscious purposes of human agents—the corn and bean diet, persisted. Notice that this account makes no assumption that the corn and bean diet was adopted because any persons were aware of its value in terms of protein adequacy.

One interesting feature of this account of the adoption of the corn and bean diet, taken from Martin and Plog (1973), is that in the entire section devoted to "Explaining Spatial and Temporal Variability in the Distribution of Domesticates," there is no use of the words "function" or "functional explanation." It may be obvious that the explanations that are offered are functional, but perhaps this is not mentioned because of archaeologists' negative associations with this term. Alternatively the authors may regard these explanations as something different, perhaps as "systems explanations." This view is supported by citations of Flannery as a major source of their account, and Flannery's insistence on the usefulness of systems theory for archaeology (Flannery 1973).

The functional explanations offered by Martin and Plog and by Flannery have been purged of any objectionable reference to purpose. They do not make use of final causes; they do not attribute purposes to inanimate objects; nor do they presuppose a purposive designer of the universe. But functional explanations that are reformed in this way nevertheless remain functional explanations, and relabeling them "systems explanations" does not remove their dependence on functional considerations.

## Some Connections between Functional Explanations and Systems

The concepts "functional explanation" and "system" are intertwined with one another in several ways. However, the connections between these two have little to do with what is ordinarily called "General Systems Theory," in spite of some archaeologists' claims to the contrary. General Systems Theory, inspired by and associated with the work of Ludwig von Bertalanffy, was officially organized as a research program in 1954 (Boulding 1972). A primary objective of the program was to provide a definition of "system" that would be broad enough to embrace the many different types of physical, biological, social, and symbolic systems. Program participants hoped to find a definition that would also be rich enough to enable them to develop a highly general, but precise body of principles that would characterize the fundamental features of systems. In spite of a great deal of effort, General Systems Theory has remained at a programmatic stage (Berlinski 1976; Salmon 1978). The real importance of the concept of *system* for functional explanations is its ability to free these explanations from objectionable appeals to purposes as final causes. This is particularly true of *feedback* systems, as seen in the history of development of the feedback concept.

Some of the first important work on the problem of legitimizing the concept of purpose in explanation was done by Rosenblueth *et al.* (1943).

In this early paper, they tried to demonstrate, by analyzing the behavior of such things as machines designed to impinge upon a moving luminous goal, that only antecedent mechanistic causes were involved in explanations of such behavior, even though these explanations mentioned or referred to purposes. The authors did not solve the problem by appealing to intentions of designers, but rather suggested that *all* purposive behavior could be described in mechanistic terms by using the concept of "negative feedback." This term, borrowed from physics and engineering, is now a part of our everyday vocabulary, and is used to describe the behavior of an object when signals from some goal are used to restrict outputs that would otherwise go beyond the goal. Rosenblueth *et al.* distinguished this from "positive feedback," which occurs when the output energy of a machine is returned as input with the same signal as the original output. In other words, negative feedback adjusts or corrects some behavior of the machine (or system), whereas positive feedback reinforces a particular sort of behavior. These feedback concepts, so prominent in Wiener's later work, entitled *Cybernetics*, have figured largely in the General Systems Theory program, and have also been used by Flannery (1968). But it is important to recognize that in this early paper (Rosenblueth *et al.*, 1943) "feedback" was introduced merely to remove some objectionable features, such as final causes, from functional explanations. The authors were not trying to construct an alternative type of explanation. In fact, one of the primary aims of their work was to try to reinterpret "purpose" so that its use in ordinary scientific explanations would not be offensive.

The role of systems in functional explanation has already been mentioned in the discussion of Radcliffe-Brown's work. Radcliffe-Brown's conception of societies, or social systems, was modeled on biological systems. Some of the most familiar and respectable functional explanations occur in biology, where the presence of some feature is explained in terms of the role or function it performs in maintaining the organism of which it is a part. For example, the presence of kidneys is explained by their role in removing impurities from the body. Such functional explanations are understood in mechanistic terms. No conscious or unconscious purposes are attributed to kidneys, nor is any designer of kidneys invoked. This consideration is useful for application of functional considerations to social systems, where one might like to claim that social practices fulfill certain functions even though the people who engage in the practice do not have that function in mind.

Of course, before the presence of something can be explained in terms of its utility for a system, the system in which the feature plays a role must be identified. In biology, many easily recognizable systems, such as human organisms, circulatory systems, and reproductive systems, are available. Outside of biology, there are other more or less clear examples of systems. Once a system has been delineated, the roles of various components in the system are examinable.

Archaeologists are keenly aware of this organizing feature of systems. What Flannery, who has already been mentioned as a major proponent of a "systems approach," has done in some of his work is to outline types of systems, such as food-procurement systems, and then to offer functional explanations to account for the presence of various features of these systems. He postulates various negative and positive feedback mechanisms that control stability and change in the systems.

Flannery's work on the development of agriculture in Mesoamerica is known to almost every student of archaeology. The material evidence on which his account is based consists of large quantities of plant and animal remains preserved in dry caves in certain areas of Mexico. Besides the food remains, there are remnants of the technology associated with food procurement and consumption—implements and facilities that are easily identified by using ethnographic analogies. These remains are datable by fairly reliable techniques, and there is evidence for a gradual change in patterns of dominant plant and animal species after a long period of stability. Before 5000 B.C., the material remains suggest a hunting–gathering economy. By 1500 B.C., the domestic species that usually are associated with agriculture dominate. Flannery sees his task as the explanation of how and why this change took place.

He believes that these changes "can best be characterized as one of gradual change in a series of procurement systems, regulated by two sorts of mechanisms, called seasonality and scheduling (1968:68)." He provides an account of how small bands of hunter–gatherers exploited, adapted to, and preserved a fragile environment with rather slim resources. Seasonality was exemplified in the Indians' use of maguey, which they harvested only after the plants had flowered, sent out pollen, and were already dying. Another example is their intensive collecting of mesquite pods during the brief season after ripening—thus preventing consumption by animals—and their drying and storing the pods for later use. Skill in scheduling was shown by employment of traps for catching rabbits. This method involved little expenditure of energy, left trappers free for other tasks, and took advantage of a fairly abundant year-round resource. Decisions about what to gather or hunt were necessary when several choices were available. Flannery's analysis suggests that these decisions were made in a way that made fullest possible use of the environment. At the same time, a balance or equilibrium that guaranteed continued availability of resources was maintained. Instances of seasonality and scheduling are characterized by Flannery as *negative feedback* mechanisms that preserved stability of the fragile ecosystem.

There were minor changes in the environment however, and Flannery suggests that they were probably the result of chance genetic changes in some plants. These changes were reinforced because they made these plants more valuable to man. Two chief examples are maize, with its increases in cob and kernel size, and beans, which became more water soluble and developed limp pods.

Flannery does not see any great invention or discovery of planting, and believes that seed scattering by gatherers had been practiced from the beginning. The evidence for this is the general sophistication of hunter–gatherers in dealing with their environment. Such sensitivity makes it most unlikely that the group in Mexico did not know the relation between seeds and plants. Flannery believes that the accidental changes in corn and beans merely made their cultivation more worthwhile, and that people simply exercised their customary opportunism and took advantage of this new resource. The deliberate cultivation of corn and beans, selective breeding of superior strains, the greater reproductive success of those who adopted the corn and bean diet—all these factors were part of a positive feedback cycle that enabled these cultigens to dominate the food procurement system.

Leaving aside all considerations of the persuasiveness of Flannery's arguments, it does seem clear that *systems* are important in his discussion because of the framework they provide for functional explanations. This point deserves emphasis because of suggestions in the literature that Flannery offers a model of explanation that is an alternative to Hempel's models of explanation, and better suited to archaeologists' needs. LeBlanc (1973), for example, has attributed to Flannery the use of a systems model of explanation developed by Meehan (1968).

## Models of the Phenomena and Models, or Patterns, of Explanation

To say that Flannery adopts a systems model of explanation is misleading, though there is a sense in which this claim is true. Flannery does provide a systems model of the *development of agriculture*, which he then uses for providing functional explanations of various aspects of food procurement systems. His model of the development of agriculture is offered as an alternative to a model of the phenomena that would postulate the beginnings of agriculture at a particular time and place (its invention or discovery), and then its spread by a process of cultural diffusion. Diffusionist models and systems models of the phenomena disagree about such facts as whether there was a discovery of agriculture. They also disagree about the types of generalizations that are relevant to explanations of the phenomena. For example, are the appropriate laws those of cultural diffusion or the laws of natural selection? They further disagree about the nature of evidence that should be sought in order to provide details within the models. There is, after all, not much point in searching for the first corn cob if a diffusionist model has been rejected (Salmon 1980).

Models or patterns of explanation, in contrast to models of the phenomena, attempt to provide a theoretical basis for distinguishing good explanations from poor ones. They present explicit criteria of adequacy for *scientific* explanation. They are concerned primarily with certain formal features of explanation, such as logical relations between the facts to be explained and the explanatory information. The usual way they do this is to provide a schematic representation to which explanations that are "scientific" must conform. Such patterns, or models, tend to be neutral with respect to matters of fact, and state only general requirements, such as "Any explanation must contain at least one universal law as part of the *explanans*.†" Construction of these models has occupied a number of philosophers of science, notably Hempel (1965), and at least one social scientist, Meehan (1968). However, Flannery's model of the phenomena is neither an example that follows Meehan's model of explanation nor an alternative to the models of explanation offered by Hempel and others. Models of the phenomena, in spite of their explanatory features, should not be confused with models of explanation.

Perhaps another example will make the distinction clearer. In the early part of this century, two different models of the structure of the atom were proposed. Thomson suggested a "plum pudding" model in which the positive charge permeated the whole atom, and the negative particles were embedded throughout, like the raisins in a plum pudding. Rutherford suggested a "planetary" model in which the positively charged nucleus formed the center of the atom with negatively charged atoms in orbit around it. These alternative models of the phenomena provided different frameworks for the explanation of the behavior of subatomic particles. Rutherford's model was retained, and the other was rejected, because testing confirmed that alpha particles behaved during scattering experiments in ways that were understandable on the planetary model, but not on the other.

In commenting on one such experiment, which resulted in alpha

---

†Explanations have two parts: that which does the explaining, the *explanans;* and that which is explained, the *explanandum.*

particles being scattered backwards, when they were fired at an atom, Rutherford said, "It was almost as incredible as if you fired a 15-inch shell at a piece of tissue paper and it came back and hit you (Holton 1973:459)." Such backwards scattering, or bouncing back, could be understood only if the alpha particles had hit some concentrated mass, not if they had hit a diffused (though positively charged) medium.

Situations in which scientists can perform "crucial experiments," such as the scattering experiment just described, to select between two competing substantive models are unfortunately rare. It would be a mistake to expect to find a single experiment or observation that could decide between a diffusionist account of the development of agriculture and a systems account. Yet, choosing between these two models of the phenomena is an empirical matter. The factual question of how agriculture developed will be answered—if it ever is answered—by examining evidence. Although no one expects to construct a crucial experiment or make a key find that would silence all opposition, workers do hope to find enough data to make their models more than merely plausible accounts.

In the absence of crucial experiments, one model may be adopted not because there is a great deal of *direct* supporting evidence but rather from indirect support which argues for its compliance ("fit") with other theories that are themselves well supported by empirical data. One model may also be selected over another because of its ability to generate an interesting research program. Many archaeologists have abandoned diffusionist models for reasons such as these. Evolutionary systems models, of the type proposed by Flannery, have suggested new approaches to problems where diffusionist research seemed to lead only to dead ends. Furthermore, many archaeologists perceive systems models as more apt to be successful because of their similarity to successful explanatory models in other areas of science.

Once a researcher does make a commitment—even though it is only tentative—to one of these models, the chances for finding a crucial experiment wherein the two can be directly compared is lessened considerably. Investigations conducted within a given framework will be aimed primarily at working out the details of that approach, rather than comparing it to some rival approach. A researcher who goes into the field looking for such features as feedback loops, mechanisms that promote equilibrium in the face of pressures for change, multiple interacting causes which emphasize development of a system in terms of internal factors, and other such "systemic" features will certainly view archaeological remains differently from the diffusionist. The latter will seek the origins of various items of material culture by looking for similarities to items belonging to other groups, and will attempt to establish that these groups were in contact with one another. The success of one model or another will be judged by the usual criteria applied to theories (see Chapter Seven of this volume).

Regardless of disagreement about which model of the phenomena is correct, workers may be in complete accord with respect to such formal principles of explanation as the necessity for laws and the linking of the laws to the events to be explained by the means of statements of initial conditions. There is no indication at all that Rutherford and Thomson, for example, were adopting different criteria for scientific explanation, though they certainly differed in their explanations (or "explanatory models") of the phenomena.

In contrast to work that attempts to establish a model of the development of agriculture that can fit the facts into an intelligible pattern, questions about the correctness of various models of explanation are not similarly empirical. The superiority of a particular set of critieria for adequate explanation is a philosophical question, one settled by conceptual considerations, argument and counterexample, and matching preanalytic conceptions of "good" explanations with various candidates for a model of explanation. Perhaps this point can be made more convincing by considering some questions that arise in trying to determine a satisfactory model: Are explanations implicit arguments? If they are arguments, must they be deductively valid? Can statistical laws play a role in explanations? Is it possible to have adequate explanation without invoking any laws? It is certainly difficult to imagine the factual information that could settle questions such as these.

This is not to say that philosophers work on these problems in complete isolation from all real scientific work. Explanations that are regarded by most scientists in some advanced scientific discipline as "good" are often used as a starting point for developing a theory of scientific explanation. From these explanations, philosophers try to abstract the beneficial features in order to build their models. If they are confronted with actual explanations in science that are widely regarded as satisfactory, but do not fit their models, the models may be revised. This is a very different enterprise from that involved in choosing between two different models of the phenomena.

It is unfortunate that the expression "systems explanation" has a number of distinct referents: functional explanations, substantive models of archaeological phenomena, and philosophical criteria for adequate scientific explanation. I am not proposing any terminological reform here, but I wish to point out that a criticism of a set of philosophical criteria (such as those presented in Meehan, 1968) should not be taken as a condemnation either of functional explanations or of viewing archaeological phenomena in the context of some system.

## Difficulties in Fitting Functional Explanations with Some Standard Models of Scientific Explanation

What has been said so far may suggest that because construction of models of the phenomena and models of explanation (in the philosophic sense) occur at distinct levels of inquiry, adoption of a particular model of the phenomena neither forces nor precludes any views about the correctness of philosophical models. Although this is partly true, it needs qualification. Functional explanations, even those that contain no objectionable references to purposes, do not fit comfortably with some standard philosophical models. If, for example, a systems model of the development of agriculture is adopted by an archaeologist, then functional explanations will be prominently featured in elaborating the details of the model. After all, a primary motive for systematizing such features as food procurement is to provide a framework for functional explanations. But if functional explanations are important to the account of the phenomena adopted, then the (philosophical) model of explanation that is accepted must be one that can accommodate functional explanations.

Functional explanations seem not to conform to some standard models of explanation because, when an attempt is made to fit the logical structure of functional explanations to the prescribed pattern, the explanations seem to account only for the presence of some set of "functional equivalents," any of which could serve the same purpose or play the same role as the item to be explained. These explanations do not give any account of the reason for occurrence of a particular item from the set.

Returning to the previous example of Radcliffe-Brown's functional explanation of joking relationships, it is clear that although such relationships are quite pervasive, their existence in face of a threat of conflict between a man and his wife's kin cannot be deduced, or even held to be highly probable. That the joking relationship avoids conflict may be well established, but we cannot show that such a relationship must exist if the function of social stability is to be achieved. There may be other means of achieving the same end. In fact, as Radcliffe-Brown shows (1952:Chapter 5) in other situations that are similar in most relevant respects, an avoidance relation is functionally equivalent to the joking relation.

In Malinowski's version of functionalism, the same problem with functional equivalents arises. Malinowski attempts to explain social facts in terms of the functions they serve in fulfilling basic human needs, such as the need for food or shelter. But the presence of a *particular* way of fulfilling a need seems to be unexplained in this view, because there are so many alternative arrangements that adequately fulfill human needs for food, shelter, and companionship (Malinowski, 1948).

Because of problems with functional equivalents, Hempel (1965) and others have said that functional "explanations" are not really explanations at all. At best they are heuristic devices or partial explanations that require the inclusion of other considerations in order to become genuine explanations. This view of the matter is closely linked to acceptance of a particular model of explanation which has been developed and discussed by Hempel (1942, 1965), Nagel (1961), Braithwaite (1953), and Popper (1959). It has been so widely accepted that, in spite of some dissent (Scriven 1962; Dray 1957; W. Salmon *et al.*, 1971), it has been characterized as *the* model of scientific explanation.

The model's elegance allows for brief characterization: an explanation is an argument whose premises are statements of laws and of particular facts (initial conditions), and whose conclusion is a description of the phenomenon to be explained. This explanatory argument is designed to show that the phenomenon was to be expected in light of the explanatory facts cited in the premises. In the exemplary cases, the relationship between explanatory premises and event to be explained is one of deductive entailment: hence, the name of the model—Deductive–Nomological, or D–N. For example:

> Whenever droughts of a prolonged and severe type occur over a period of several years, people whose subsistence base is agriculture either leave the area or die (*law*).
>
> Droughts of a prolonged and severe type occurred over a period of years in eastern-central Arizona during the fourteenth century (*initial conditions*).
>
> Therefore, the people dependent upon agriculture for subsistence either left the area or died (*phenomenon to be explained*).

Now consider what happens when we try to put a functional explanation of why some plants have a certain kind of seed pod into this form:

> Plants of type *X* thrive only if their seeds are scattered (law). Plants of type *X*, in circumstances *Y*, are able to scatter their seeds if they have pods which are easily shattered by winds (law).
>
> Plants of type *X* are thriving in circumstances *Y* (initial condition).
>
> Therefore, plants of type *X* have seedpods that are easily shattered by winds (phenomenon to be explained).

The conclusion of this explanatory argument does not follow from the premises as it should in a D–N explanation. Some scattering device is necessary for this type of plant to survive, but nothing in the explanation tells us why we should expect plants of type $X$ to have pods that are shattered by winds rather than, for example, spontaneously exploding pods. The desired conclusion would follow deductively if the occurrence of "if" in the second law statement were replaced by "only if." But unfortunately, this alteration would simply rule out the actual functional equivalents for seed scattering, and would spoil the explanation by robbing the altered premise of its truth.

If the conclusion were weakened to read, "Plants of type $X$ have seed pods which are easily shattered by winds, or some other scattering device," then both truth and the proper logical relationship would be preserved. But then only the existence of some functional equivalent to wind–shattered pods is explained, not that particular scattering device.

Functional explanations such as this fare no better under the model, also offered by Hempel, that allows explanations whose laws are statistical generalizations instead of the universal laws required by the D–N model. In this Inductive–Statistical (I–S) model, the explanatory premises are supposed to render the explanadum phenomenon highly probable. But in functional explanations that use statistical laws, what can be shown with some degree of probability is just some member of a set of functional equivalents, not a particular member.

Many archaeologists as well as philosophers have accepted these models of explanation and thus regard functional explanations as defective D–N or I–S explanations. At best, functional explanations provide necessary, but not sufficient conditions for the occurrence of the event to be explained.

Meehan's (1968) systems model of explanation has been mentioned several times. In view of the connections between systems explanations and functional explanations, it is appropriate to discuss Meehan's model at this point, even though Meehan himself does *not* mention difficulties with functional explanation as one of his reasons for rejecting Hempel's models. The standard models are inadequate because, Meehan believes, Hempel confuses logical with empirical factors, neglects the predictive function of science, and fails to provide for mutliple causal factors and feedback processes.

In order to examine the virtues of Meehan's model vis-à-vis Hempel's, it is necessary to see just what Meehan has in mind when he talks about explanations that conform to a systems paradigm. He presents the following fairly concise statement of criteria of adequacy for systems explanations:

First, the phenomenon to be explained must be embedded in an empirical description that is dynamic and not static, that stipulates change as well as differences. The phenomena will be defined in terms of such changes. Second, a system, a formal calculus, is used to generate entailments or expectations with reference to a set of symbols. Third, the symbols or variables in the calculus are "loaded," given empirical referents so that the entailments of the formal system have empirical meaning defined in terms of the concepts used to load the basic symbols. If the loaded system is isomorphic to the situation in which the phenomena occurs, the system provides an explanation for the event (Meehan 1968:56–57).

Meehan uses the term "system" to refer to a set of symbols along with rules for manipulating them, whereas we have been using the term primarily to refer to complex empirical phenomena, such as the food-procurement system that concerns Flannery. Both uses of the term are legitimate, but to avoid confusion I will distinguish between *formal* systems (per Meehan) and *empirical* systems in the ensuing discussion. Meehan's goal is to explain empirical phenomena by first embedding them in empirical systems and then by finding or devising formal systems that fit dynamic descriptions of the empirical systems well enough to predict behavior of the phenomena. In his view, a formal system (which is, apparently, just a mathematical model) that has the appropriate fit and predictive power simply *is* an explanation of the type of phenomenon whose behavior it predicts.

Before considering the relative merits of Meehan's and Hempel's analysis, I want to consider three rather general questions regarding this approach to explanation: (a) Is this model especially suited to the social sciences? (b) Is this model able to handle functional explanations? (c) Does the model capture our intuitive standards for satisfactory explanation?

The answer to the first question seems to be negative. Oddly enough, Meehan gives not a single example of an explanation in social science that conforms to his model. However, formal systems, of the type to which he refers, abound in the physical sciences. Typically, they take the form of a set of differential equations used to predict dynamic behavior in physical phenomena, such as the equation characterizing induced electromotive force in a circuit as proportional to the rate of change of magnetic flux through the circuit. Complex sets of equations, such as Maxwell's equations, involving many variables and characterizing feedback processes, are commonplace. Some attempts have been made to characterize social phenomena using sets of differential equations (Hamblin and Pitcher 1980), but these are exceptions rather than the rule. In general, the social sciences have not been able to construct mathematical models that approach the success of those in the physical sciences. So, it would seem that a model of explanation that demands such precise formalization is ill suited to explanation in the social sciences.

In looking at the second question, regarding the feasibility of Meehan's model for functional explanations, it is important to distinguish several meanings of the term "function." Thus far we have sometimes talked about ascribing a function to an item, as in "The large open space at this site functioned as a ball court." This involves merely saying how something was normally used. Other times, "function" has referred to the role of some component of a *system* in maintaining that system, as in "Seasonality and scheduling functioned to stabilize the prehistoric food-procurement system in the Valley of Mexico."

A different, though very common, use of "function" is "to signify relations of dependence or interdependence between two or more variable factors, whether or not these factors are measureable (Nagel 1961:523)." As Nagel points out in the passage from which this quote was taken, this last sense of the term is one commonly employed in mathematics when we wish to express that the value of one variable is uniquely determined by ("is a function of") some other variable or variables. This use of "function" is common in physics as well, as when we say that except at extreme values of pressure and temperature, the pressure of a gas in a closed container is a function of its volume and temperature. It is this sense of "function," rather than those previously mentioned, that is captured in Meehan's model. However, this type of functional analysis is by no means unique to the social sciences. The ideal gas law is a formal system in Meehan's sense, and one that can be fitted with empirical phenomena in the way his model demands. Moreover, explanations of phenomena such as the behavior of gases are typically used to exemplify the Deductive–Nomological model of explanation, and Meehan has done nothing to show that these D–N explanations are defective.

If we leave aside certain problems with precise calculations, or if we regard such precision as a goal that may be reasonable but not yet attained by the social sciences, we can find numerous examples in which the interdependent variable sense of "function" is employed. Nagel mentions sociologists' claims that "the suicide rate in a community is a function of the degree of social cohesion in that society (Nagel 1961: 523)."

Sometimes the interdependence of variables in a system is such that the value of one of the variables in the system is kept within a certain range by appropriate adjustments in the other variables. Such systems are, of course, those in which feedback mechanisms are operating, and they are the ones for which many reserve the special label "functional system." Examples of such feedback systems can be found in physical, biological, and social sciences. Of special interest to archaeologists are ecological studies concerning relations between social groups and their environments.

In a volume entitled *Man, Culture, and Animals* (Leeds and Vayda 1965), several studies of functional systems are presented. These are directed mainly at identifying and describing the various components of functional systems and their effects upon one another, rather than asking why some particular mechanism instead of some functional equivalent is present in a system. Leeds, for example, in his study of the Chukchi tries to demonstrate the functional relationship between a crucial variable, reindeer herd size, and a number of other cultural and environmental variables, such as marriage practices, patterns of sacrifice, social customs that provide training in herd management, climatic variations, and insect plagues. Using a historical source (Bogoras 1904–1909), he identifies the family as the basic social unit of the Chukchi. Because reindeer meat was the indispensible food resource in their harsh territories, and because reindeer herds were controlled by families, the maintenance of a family's herd at a size that permitted an adequate and continuing source of food was essential to survival of the basic social unit. To use a biological analogy, maintenance of herd size within certain limits is necessary for family survival just as the maintenance of body temperature within certain limits is necessary for survival of that basic biological unit, the human body.

Because empirical evidence strongly supports the dependence of families upon their herds, it is reasonable to seek the mechanisms controlling herd size, in other words, to identify and elaborate the functional system that has reindeer herd size as its crucial variable. Leeds, as we have said, identifies many environmental and cultural components of this system. His functional analysis describes in detail how the various components of the system operated to keep reindeer herd size within an appropriate range of values.

Now suppose, in accordance with Meehan's model, we could devise a formal system of differential equations that modeled all the empirical phenomena in the Chukchi system in such a way that one could accurately predict adjustments in one part of the system when changes occurred in another part. Such an account would not be an explanation of why some particular trait, rather than a functionally equivalent trait, was present in the system, or even why some member of a set of traits was present. That is, it would not be a functional explanation in Radcliffe-Brown's sense, though it would be an expression of some functional relationship between variables. The kind of question this model is designed to answer is how changes in some variable in a system affect the values of other variables in the system. But this type of question is neither unique to social sciences nor problematic for traditional models of explanation in the same way as explanations of the presence of some functional trait. The feedback processes that can be accommodated in Meehan's model pose no special problems for ordinary Deductive–Nomological explanation, as explanations of the operation of thermostats and homing devices in Rosenblueth *et al.* (1943) clearly show. In view of this, I think we must conclude that Meehan's model does nothing to solve the problem of functional explanation that has been a matter of special concern for social scientists.

Turning now to the third question, concerning the proximity of the model to intuitive explanation, one can detect failure in this respect as well. Basically, what the model says is that a phenomenon has been explained when a mathematical model that is predictively successful has been produced. The mathematical model is the explanation. But this is counterintuitive, for one could, on the basis of empirical observations of repeated connections between phenomena, construct a formal system that "fit," the phenomena, but could not explain them in any ordinary sense of "explain." In Salmon and Salmon (1979), a hypothetical example was given of a formal system that expressed a regular connection between the ratio of large to small pots and duration of occupation of some types of archaeological sites. Such a formula might have been based upon empirical studies of sherds at sites whose dates were known. This formal system could be used to "predict" (or better, to *retrodict*) the duration of occupation of sites without established dates, but it certainly would not explain their duration of occupation. The formula may be a useful predictive device, but it no more explains the phenomena it "fits" than obituary notices in newspapers explain the occurrence of funerals. In fact, a formal system of this nature is something which itself cries out for explanation and encourages us to look for causal factors that could account for such an interesting connection.

Before closing the discussion of Meehan's proposed model of explanation, I want to suggest why his criticisms of Hempel's models fail. In the early (1948) paper with Oppenheim, Hempel spells out in detail the difference between logical and empirical criteria of adequacy for scientific explanation (1965:247–251). A reading of this should lay to rest Meehan's charge that Hempel confounds empirical and logical aspects of explanation. Hempel's concern with prediction as a feature of scientific understanding is evident in his meticulous presentation and defense of the thesis that scientific explanation and rational prediction are symmetric to one another (1965:367–376). Furthermore, as LeBlanc

(1973:208) correctly remarks, Hempel's account of explanation allows for any number of laws in an *explanans* as well as any number of variables in these laws, so this criticism by Meehan also fails to be effective. The inadequacies of Meehan's model of explanation for the social sciences cannot help but increase one's respect for the power of Hempel's analysis, although recognizing the intractible difficulties in providing an account fully adequate to the social sciences.

Some philosophers of science who are deeply committed to the Deductive–Nomological model have tried to develop it in such a way that it can provide a satisfactory account of functional explanation. Nagel, for example, has recognized the central role that functional explanations play in biological science, and has tried to deal with the problem of functional equivalents in his "goal-supporting" analysis of functional ascriptions (1977). Nagel maintains that so-called functional equivalents fail to count as genuine alternatives to the trait that is actually present in the system when the system and the goal which the item supports are both adequately specified. He says, for example, that—given the development of human physiology—there is no genuine natural alternative to the human heart for performing the natural function of pumping blood to various parts of the body. There is, of course, no *logical* necessity why hearts, rather than some other mechanism, should have developed, provided one ignores the constraints imposed by the actual physical situation in which this development took place. But Nagel's point is that it is not legitimate to ignore those constraints.

Although this approach to the problem of functional equivalents may be convincing when we are dealing with the development of some highly organized biological systems, it is less easy to see just what constraints operate upon the systems that concern anthropologists. One is aware of some constraints, primarily environmental, but these do not usually provide any way of ruling out various social traits that would work equally well to ensure the satisfaction of biological needs or the stability of a social structure.

In fact, training in anthropology is designed to guarantee that one who goes through it will recognize this cultural variation. One cannot become an anthropologist without becoming aware of the fascinating variety of ways human beings find to secure their physical needs and to work out satisfactory social relations. Malinowski was certainly aware of the wide variety of social arrangements that could satisfy the same biological needs, and Radcliffe-Brown was similarly aware of alternative devices for maintaining social structures.

With respect to biological examples, such as the seed-scattering devices of plants in the wild, we may lack sufficient understanding of the system in which the plant developed to allow us to see why windshattered pods rather than some other mechanism belongs to that plant, but, according to Nagel, this means only that we do not have a good grasp of certain initial conditions. In his view, this does not compromise the *logical* structure of such explanations. Nagel's primary concern in his analysis of functional explanation is to preserve the *structural* similarity between functional explanations and other scientific explanations. which he is committed to analyzing on the Deductive–Nomological or Inductive–Statistical models. With the elimination of genuine functional equivalents, he sees no impediment to saying that a functional explanation is an *argument* which concludes on the basis of laws and initial conditions that a particular item is present in a given system during a particular interval of time.

Although one logical difficulty is removed on this analysis, other difficulties remain. As Nagel admits (1977:300), explanations understood in this way cannot be regarded as *causal* explanations because the proper temporal order for causality is reversed. Applying Nagel's analysis to the seed pod example, and assuming that we had an appropriate developmental history of the plant, would involve a law-like statement of the following type: "Plants of type X in circumstances Y are able to scatter their seeds *only if* they have pods easily shattered by winds." But this statement cannot be a *causal* law, because when time period and environment are specified in this way, seed scattering is not an *antecedent* condition for the occurrence of wind-shattered seed pods. Nagel simply accepts this consequence of his analysis and says that explanations that are noncausal are appropriate in these circumstances. This strategy of giving up any attempt to understand functional explanations as causal explanations in order to preserve the "standard" logical form of explanations might be reasonable if the standard D–N and I–S models were satisfactory in all other respects, and if philosophers had no reasonable alternatives to offer. However, this is not the case.

## Some Inadequacies in the Standard Philosophical Models, or Patterns, of Scientific Explanation

In recent years, the standard D–N and I–S models of explanation have themselves been subjected to increasingly heavy attack. The criticisms were not motivated by the models' failure to accommodate functional explanations, but by other considerations, among the most important of which is the problem of *revelance*. Hempel emphasizes the importance of explanatory relevance, recognizes it as one of two systematic requirements for scientific explanation (1966:48), and understands the requirement to mean that "the explanatory information adduced affords good ground for believing that the phenomenon to be explained did, or does, indeed occur." Yet, he then goes on to claim that this requirement is met in the D–N and I–S models by insistence on deductive entailment in the one case, or high probability and "total evidence" in the other, in explanatory arguments. Two counterexamples show that explanatory relevance, in a very natural sense of the term "relevant," is not guaranteed by these logical strictures.

1. John Jones avoided becoming pregnant during the past year because he faithfully consumed his wife's birth control pills, and any man who regularly takes oral contraceptives will escape pregnancy.

This "explanation" fulfills *every requirement* imposed upon D–N explanations.

2. Susan Smith experienced only mild symptoms after her infection with valley fever (coccidioidomycosis), for she was wearing a turquoise necklace when she contracted the disease, and almost everyone who is wearing turquoise at the time of the infection has a mild case.

This "explanation" fulfills *every requirement* imposed upon the I–S explanations (Salmon and Salmon 1979:68).

It is fairly easy to see in these cases that the "explanatory" facts and laws, although true enough, are completely irrelevant. The construction of counterexamples such as these, a simple task once the basic technique is recognized, is a serious threat to D–N and I–S models. It does not matter that these "explanations" are so obviously ridiculous that no one would accept them. The point is that they conform to the models, and if the models allow such egregious accounts, then more subtly mistaken accounts, which could be seriously misleading, may be accepted. The models as they stand cannot be used as a guide or test of satisfactory scientific explanations. The models may come to be rejected—or at least revisions will be required in them—quite independently of their failure to accommodate functional explanations. Some proposed revisions of the models will be examined in the next chapter. Nevertheless, in view of difficulties with these models, there is no compelling reason to reject functional explanations as scientifically inadequate or to regard them as noncausal explanations just because they do not conform to these standard patterns.

## An Attempt to Preserve Causal Features in Functional Explanation

The failure of a philosophical model of explanation may be resolved by modification of the model, or by construction of a different model, as has already been mentioned. Alternatively, one might reject the whole concept of "model of explanation," and abandon the search for certain shared formal or logical features which model-builders attribute to all adequate scientific explanations. Such a nonformalist approach is taken by Wright (1976). Wright argues that functional explanations should not be regarded as failed or incomplete D–N or I–S explanations. He rejects all attempts to characterize explanations in terms of their structural characteristics, and prefers to focus on the *substance* of explanations. This substance he interprets as a capacity to expose causal factors. Roughly, Wright believes that we have succeeded in explaining something when we have identified its cause or causes.

Functional explanations occupy a special category in Wright's view because they refer to a special kind of cause. His analysis attempts to show just how ascription of functions fits into a causal explanation. In order to do this, he provides a way of distinguishing functional causes (or simply "functions") from other types of causes (see section entitled "An Attempt to Provide a General Method for Ascribing Functions" in Chapter Four). One feature of Wright's analysis is his insistence that merely by ascribing a function to an object we have made progress toward explaining its presence. This contrasts sharply with the view of Nagel (1977) and many others, who believe that it is important to distinguish the mere claim that something has a particular function from the process of explaining its presence in terms of that function. For these writers, ascribing functions to objects is merely a preliminary. For Wright, it is an integral part of the explanation, for he believes that to define the usefulness or importance of something is at least to begin to account for its presence. Such a view seems to accord quite closely with archaeological explanatory practice.

The substantive feature that unites all correct explanations (functional and others), is that they reveal the *causes* of the phenomena to be explained. It is tempting to ask for an analysis of "cause" itself at this point. But Wright does not accept that challenge, for he believes that there is no more fundamental concept in an analysis. He insists that "cause" must simply be accepted as a basic or fundamental notion (1976:33).

Wright's principle that distinguishes functions, or functional causes, from other causes is this: When the fact that some mechanism has a particular effect is causally relevant to the very existence of that mechanism, then that mechanism is a functional cause. Wright illustrates this principle with cases of natural functions, such as the spines of porcupines—"protection is a consequence of their being there, and this is clearly why things with spines, and hence the spines themselves have survived (1976:91)"—and with cases of conscious function, such as the design of an artifact. For example, a consequence or effect of smoke holes is the reduction of smoke in dwellings. *The fact that* smoke holes have this effect is causally relevant to the construction of smoke holes in houses (i.e., to smoke holes' "being there"). Wright takes artifact design as the clearest case of functional ascription, and his intention is to display the close parallel between conscious design and natural selection by showing the similarity between the two types of cases. Though many biologists and philosophers of biology agree with him on this point, it is a highly controversial issue, because some feel that regarding natural selection in this framework makes it seem too much like an "intelligent choosing agent" (Nagel 1977).

Whatever the overall value of Wright's account of functional explanation, and regardless of its correctness in matters of detail, Wright's insight into the causal implications of saying that something is a function is extremely valuable. Functions have always been recognized as effects or consequences, but Wright manages to distinguish these effects from other "accidental" effects by appealing to the *causal* relation between a thing's having some particular effect and that thing's existing, or being where it is. Wright's priorities in doing this offer a sharp contrast to Nagel's. Nagel views logical structure or form as the crucial element in explanation. He tries to preserve formal similarity between functional explanations and D–N explanations at the expense of causal considerations. Wright sees concern with causality as the sine qua non of explanation, and regards the shared ability to expose causes as the unifying feature of satisfactory scientific explanation, while dismissing questions about formal structure as irrelevant.

## An Attempt to Preserve Structure and Causality

Even though Wright rejects the D–N and I–S models of explanation and regards formal criteria as unimportant, his insistence on causal components of explanation does not preclude the construction of satisfactory formal models. One model which tries to capture substantive as well as formal features is the Statistical–Relevance, or S–R model, elaborated by W. C. Salmon and others in a series of papers (1971, 1975, 1979).

An important difference between the S–R model and the standard models with respect to formal requirements is that explanations need not be *arguments* to the effect that the event to be explained will, or quite probably will, occur. The demand that explanations be such arguments has been a principal barrier to fitting functional explanations within the standard models. This is because the laws and initial conditions in normal functional explanations provide necessary but not sufficient conditions for the occurrence of the item to be explained. The S–R model does not see explanations as arguments, so the criticism that a functional explanation does not provide sufficient conditions for the occurrence of some item does not apply.

Similarly, the "power to predict," which critics claim is absent in functional explanation, is not a requirement of the S–R model. The alleged symmetry between explanation and prediction is closely tied to the view that explanations are arguments. An argument is a set of statements wherein some of the statements (the premises) provide evidence for the truth of one of the statements (the conclusion). From a strictly logical point of view, all temporal relations between premises and conclusions are ignored. But if we introduce temporal considerations that place knowledge of the premises prior to the occurrence of events described in the conclusion, it is reasonable to regard such an argument as a (justified) prediction. Similarly, if the event described in the conclusion is already known to have occurred, and its determining conditions (premises) are sought, it is reasonable to regard the argument as an explanation. Hempel thus regards explanations and predictions as having the same deductive structure with only a pragmatic difference between them. Hempel offers a defense of a refined version of the symmetry between explanation and prediction, taking account of a number of critical discussions in (1965:364–376). The symmetry thesis has a strong intuitive appeal, and many archaeologists are at least implicitly committed to it, a fact which is reflected in the title of Thomas's (1974) book: *Predicting the Past: An Introduction to Anthropological Archaeology.*

The S–R model of explanation, in its crudest form, says that an event is explained when all the factors that are statistically relevant to its occurrence or nonoccurrence have been assembled, and the appropriate probability value has been determined for its occurrence in light of those factors. The model does *not* require that knowledge of the statistically relevant factors would enable one to construct an argument—either a deductively valid argument or an inductively strong argument—that has as its conclusion a description of the event to be explained. In its noninferential aspect this model of explanation has a great deal in common with the conception of explanation developed by Wright (1976) and Scriven (1975). If the view that explanations are arguments (the inferential conception of explanation) is abandoned, then it is much more difficult to make a case for the symmetry between explanation and prediction, and the criticism that functional explanations are not structurally similar to justified predictions is no longer a formidable objection to functional explanation.

To see how this view of explanation can characterize explanations in archaeology, particularly functional explanations, let us look back at the previously mentioned explanation of the prevalence of certain limp-podded plants—such as beans—in the early stages of the development of agriculture. A Statistical–Relevance explanation of this phenomenon will have two stages. First, the initial appearance of plants with limp pods will be explained as a result of genetic changes—either recombinations or mutations, according to the laws of genetic theory. Geneticists may be able to make some assessment of the probabilities involved, given knowledge of the background situation when and where plants with these characteristics first appeared. If relevant factors are unknown, then this stage of the explanation may be weak. For example, it may only be possible, against a background of genetic theory, to provide probability distributions for the occurrence of new plant forms in a very general way. In any case, this stage of the explanation does not involve any reference to function.

At the second stage, what is to be explained is the contribution of limp pods to the continued success of the plant. Here the statistically relevant factor is the probability of successful production of progeny with similar features from limp-podded plants, as opposed to the probability of reproductive success of plants with brittle, easily shattered pods. In order to assess these probabilities, it may be necessary to know something about the numbers of humans interested in plant gathering, the diets of those humans, their migratory patterns, and their methods for plant collecting. As Wilke and others (1972) have noted, different methods of seed harvesting will select for different types of plants. Hand picking favors limp pods whereas knocking seeds from plants into baskets would select for the same characteristics that ensure seed survival in the wild state. Further relevant factors would include the types of plants that were competing and aids to survival of competitors. Archaeologists would probably need to enlist the aid of geologists, geographers, and paleobotanists, and undertake extensive archaeological research in order to assign probabilities to the relative reproductive success of these plants. But if they can get enough information to do so, then they can explain, according to the S–R model, why plants with limp pods were successful.

Such an explanation would show how limp pods, in their facilitation of seed scattering and nurturing, contribute to continued existence of plants in an environment where humans hand-collect and cultivate seeds. By Wright's criterion of distinguishing functional causes, seed scattering and nurturing is the *function* of limp pods, for

1. Seed scattering and nurturing is a consequence (result) of limp pods being where they are, and

2. Limp pods are there because they result in seed scattering and nurturing (see Wright 1976:81).

The S–R model demands information about *statistically* relevant factors. Wright's account of explanation insists on exposure of *causes*. Combining Wright's insight about the causal properties of functions with the S–R model of explanation is particularly felicitous because it yields a *causal* account of functional explanation, and also preserves a certain structural similarity (though not the structure envisioned in the D–N and I–S models) between functional explanations and other scientific explanations.

The Statistical–Relevance model does try to deal with one of the most desirable features of the so-called "systems approach" to archaeology, namely, the recognition of multiple interacting explanatory factors. There are often serious problems in discerning the ways in which various statistically relevant factors operate when they are jointly present. There may also be in any given situation so many unknown or poorly understood relevant factors that it may not be possible to assign the requisite probabilities in any reasonable way. Each of these problems may arise with many of the archaeologists' functional explanations, and they perhaps are a chief source of the uneasiness regarding such explanations. But it is important to recognize that these objections are quite distinct from the difficulties of accommodating such explanations within the D–N model. If statistically relevant factors can be assessed—and this is an empirical problem—so that probabilities can be assigned with some degree of accuracy, the resulting functional explanation can be a genuine S–R explanation that has the virtue of being a causal explanation as well. No such empirical information could transform a functional explanation into a satisfactory causal D–N explanation. If a suitable analysis of functional explanation in archaeology is to be given, it is important to identify the real problems.

## Conclusion

An attempt has been made in this chapter to show that several types of functional explanation are important for archaeology. Various objections to functional explanation have been considered. In order to appreciate and answer the criticisms, it was necessary to outline several philosophical models for adequate scientific explanation. The standard (D–N and I–S) models have some trouble accommodating functional explanation. A systems model, proposed as an alternative to these models for explanation in the social sciences, was seen as no more effective than the standard models. However, the Statistical–Relevance model offers some promise, and also avoids some other problems that arise in connection with the standard models. In the next chapter, this model will be elaborated and applied to various examples, both functional and nonfunctional, of explanation in archaeology.

# CHAPTER SIX

# Structure of Archaeological Explanation

## Introduction

One searches the archaeological literature in vain for examples of explanation that conform closely to any of the models that philosophers have proposed for scientific explanation. But archaeology is not unusual in this respect. There are few explanations in any science that are delineated as precisely as may be achieved in a philosophical account. However, this is hardly surprising when one considers that although the philosophical models were drawn from actual examples in the sciences, they represented attempts to reconstruct the rationale of successful explanation. These models exhibit the implicit or hidden structure that allows an explanation to be regarded as correct.

Hempel, for example, begins his account of the Deductive–Nomological model in *Aspects of Scientific Explanation* (1965) with John Dewey's (1910) description of removing glass tumblers from a hot dishwater and placing them upside down on a plate; soap bubbles escaped from under the rims of the glasses, grew a bit, and then eventually shrank and receded into the glasses.

> "Transferring the tumblers to the plate he had trapped cool air in them; that air was gradually warmed by the glass which initially had the temperature of the hot suds. This led to an increase in the volume of the trapped air, and thus to an expansion of the soap film that had formed between the plate and the tumblers' rims. But gradually, the glass cooled off, and so did the air inside, and as a result, the soap bubbles receded (Hempel 1965:336)."

Hempel comments that Dewey's account may be regarded as an argument that the phenomenon to be explained was to be expected because of certain explanatory facts. He further claims that the explanatory facts are of two types: *particular facts*—such as the fact that those particular tumblers were transferred from hot suds to a plate—and *uniformities* expressible by means of general laws. He admits that in the given explanation, these uniformities are only referred to lightly or are not mentioned at all. For example, "this led to an increase in the volume of the trapped air," merely hints at the law connecting temperature and volume of gases. Hempel says of these suppressed statements of uniformities "they are clearly presupposed in the claim that certain stages in the process yielded others as their results (1965:336)."

This discussion is designed to raise awareness of the interpretive features of any analysis. A considerable amount of rational reconstruction is involved in his account of Dewey's explanation. His construal of this account as an *argument*, for example, may be disputed. Arguments represent attempts to support some conclusion by presenting evidence for it. The presence of an argument is often signaled in English by conclusion indicator words such as "thus" and "as a result." But these expressions, which do occur in Dewey's account, have other uses in English as well. Sometimes they simply indicate a causal connection when there is no apparent effort to marshall premises in support of some conclusion. It would be hard to believe, for example, that we are *arguing* that Nixon resigned when we say that Nixon resigned *as a result* of the investigation of the Watergate scandal and its attendant exposure of corruption in the White House. To insist that every causal claim of this sort embodies an implicit argument is to beg the question of whether or not explanations are arguments.

In a discussion of some of the difficulties in considering explanations as arguments, W. Salmon (1977) notes that explanations, but not arguments, are adversely affected by the addition of irrelevant factual information. If an argument is deductively valid—and this is the sort of argument a D–N explanation represents—then, as a matter of logic, it cannot be made invalid by inserting any amount of additional information into its premises, no matter how irrelevant such information may be. Yet, the addition of irrelevancies to a set of supposed explanatory facts would seem to weaken, and in some cases to destroy, its explanatory value. We expect explanations to cite only conditions *relevant* to the event to be explained, conditions which make a difference to its occurrence or nonoccurrence. So, in this respect at least, regarding explanations as *arguments* seems to impede rather than to promote our understanding of the nature of explanation.

Awareness of the degree of interpretive analysis that is involved in the discussion of actual scientific examples leads one to realize that there is room for alternative accounts of what is occurring in these explanations. In the following discussion several attempts at archaeological explanation will be closely examined in an attempt to expose their logical structures. The project is somewhat complicated by the fact that most nontrivial archaeological explanations are incomplete and are offered in a tentative manner. This is frequently the case because some proposed explanatory *fact* is not well enough established to command universal acceptance. When this is the case, archaeologists tend to focus on these substantive features of an explanation to the exclusion of structural issues. An effort will be made in what follows to distinguish substantive and structural questions, and to treat the two separately. It is hoped that this discussion will provide some understanding of the principles by which archaeological explanations might be judged satisfactory or deficient, and some basis for assessing philosophical models of explanation in terms of their capacity to deal with the problems that concern archaeologists.

## Explaining the Character of a Faunal Assemblage

The first example is from Binford and Bertram (1977). In this essay the authors' primary purpose is to achieve understanding of attritional processes that modify the faunal assemblages so often used by archaeologists to support inferences regarding the behavior of prehistoric peoples. These processes include weathering, deterioration due to acidic soil, and destruction by scavengers. In the course of this ethnoarchaeological study, which involved the collection and analysis of large amounts of data as well as the conducting of controlled experiments, some tentative explanations are given for the occurrence of patterns in faunal assemblages. The particular case to be examined here is the authors' explanation of the differences in the overall amounts and relative proportions of various anatomical parts of sheep on sites where free-ranging dogs are the principal agents of attrition.

One of the studied sites was a winter residence and the other the summer residence of a single Navaho family. Family members provided information concerning the number of sheep that were butchered or had died from other causes. They also provided information about the ages of the sheep at the time of their deaths, and these reports were confirmed by the examination of skeletal teeth. The informants maintained that the family's habits of consumption and practices of disposal of sheep remains did not vary significantly at the two sites. The authors collected and analyzed surviving bones from both sites. In a published article, they presented a comparative graph that exhibits the percentages of survival of various parts on the winter and summer sites. The data show (a) a greater overall amount of bone surviving on the summer site, and (b) different proportions of the various parts on the two sites. The authors offer the following account:

> The two sites are considered by both the investigators and the occupants to be essentially identical, namely, that complete skeletons were being introduced to the archaeological record. No human behavior pattern, either butchering or consumption, was contributing to the actual deletion of parts from the assemblage

that was visible archaeologically. On both sites, a constant agent of attrition was active: the same dogs who had equal and free access to all anatomical parts discarded on the site. . . . The only difference between the two samples was in the age structure of the animals exposed to attrition through dog destruction. This observation led to the surmise that differences in the age of the animals exposed to a constant agent of attrition could condition the pattern of survival noted among different anatomical parts (Binford and Bertram 1977:104–105).

In coming to their conclusion the authors had looked for differences between the two sites that could account for the different patterns of bone survival. Certain factors of known causal relevance—human practices of consumption and disposal—were not different, but the variation in survival pattern showed a (statistical) correlation not only with season of occupation but also with the mean age of death of the sheep—24 months for the winter site; 37.3 for the summer (1977:100). This difference in mean age suggested to the authors that something connected with the aging process was causally relevant to bone survival. Changes in bone structure are known to be a feature of the aging process. The authors hypothesized that, in general, bone density increases in maturing animals, and that some bones increase in density at different rates than others. They reasoned that if agents of attrition acted indifferently upon two sets of bones whose composition with respect to anatomical parts was similar, then differences in survival patterns could be attributed to difference in resistance between the two sets, and that the denser bone offered more resistance to gnawing than less dense bone.

Laboratory experiments on a relatively small number of skeletons supported the authors' views about increases in bone density with age, and also showed that this took place at varying rates for different anatomical parts. For example, experiments on several sheep showed that the pelvis and ribs of animals 19 months of age were of approximately equal density, and that although both these anatomical parts were denser in sheep 90 months of age, the pelvises at this age were half-again as dense as the ribs. Such facts about bone density were clearly relevant to both the greater overall survival of bone at the summer site, where the older animals were killed, as well as to the observed variation in proportions of the different anatomical parts on the two sites. The authors summarize the situation with respect to their progress toward an explanation:

A clear relationship between bone densities for animals of varying ages and the overall survival patterning among anatomical parts for populations of mixed age structure has yet to be demonstrated. If we can accomplish this, we will have offered an *explanation* for at least some observed and expected patterning in the survival frequencies of anatomical parts . . . (Binford and Bertram 1977:111, emphasis added).

Let us suppose, for purposes of discussion, that the clear relationship referred to above *has* been demonstrated, and then let us try to analyze the form of the resulting explanation.

## Structure of the Explanation

First, it seems clear that this is not a *functional* explanation. There is no attempt to invoke any purpose, goal, or role to account for the differences in patterning of bone survival at the two sites. Even so, it does not seem that this explanation could fit the Deductive–Nomological model. The explanatory "facts" that would support the relation between bone density and patterns of bone survival are such that Hempel would characterize them as uniformities expressible by means of general laws, but these laws would be *statistical* rather than universal. Density is seen here as increasing with age, and lawful accounts of processes associated with aging would surely have a statistical form, something like "By age $x$, $y\%$ of members of species $A$ have attained characteristic $B$." Furthermore, resistance to agents of attrition—whether this be to varying degrees of soil acidity or to variations in the strength and hunger of canine scavengers—is something whose description would surely be given in statistical rather than universally general terms. The authors are, of course, aware of the statistical nature of the phenomena they are studying, and they use standard statistical techniques to try to establish their explanatory facts. Because the putative laws in their proposed explanation are statistical, the explanation could not be an example of a D–N explanation on any reasonable reconstruction.

Hempel offers two models of explanation that employ statistical laws in an essential way. The Inductive–Statistical model, discussed briefly in Chapter Five, was designed primarily to accommodate the explanation of particular events, including particular outcomes of random sampling experiments. In this model an event is explained when it can be shown to have been highly likely on the basis of explanatory facts that include at least one statistical law. In this model, as in the D–N model, explanations are conceived as arguments, but as strong inductive (probabilistic) arguments rather than as valid deductive ones.

Because the explanatory arguments constituting I–S explanations are not deductively valid, there are important logical differences between D–N and I–S explanation. Hempel points out that when the explanatory information does not deductively imply the *explanadum*, there is room for troublesome ambiguity (1965:394). As an example of the sort of ambiguity that can arise, consider the following two explanations that are in correct I–S form, have premises that are not contradictory, but nevertheless yield contradictory *explananda*.

When pottery is manufactured by the coil-building technique, it usually retains characteristic ridges even after shaping and firing. In light of this, we might present the following I–S explanation for the occurrence of ridges on a particular finished pot *A:*

P (Ridges on pottery, given manufacture by coil-building) = nearly 1.† (law)
*A* was manufactured using the coil method (initial condition)
===== (therefore, almost certainly)
*A* has ridges.

However, because the coil-building technique does not absolutely guarantee the occurrences of ridges on the finished pot, another "explanation" is available if *A* should happen not to have ridges. Regardless of the technique of construction, special tools may be used for smoothing, and some are so effective that no ridges are likely to remain on pots that have been finished in this manner. In such a case, we might present the following I–S explanation for the absence of ridges on *A:*

P (No ridges on pottery, given use of a special smoothing tool) = nearly 1. (law)
*A* was smoothed with the special tool. (initial condition).
===== (therefore, almost certainly)
*A* has no ridges.

The particular pot *A* with which we are concerned in this example falls into two overlapping classes: (a) coil-built pots, and (b) pots smoothed with a special tool. This is shown in the following diagram, wherein the two circles represent the two classes.

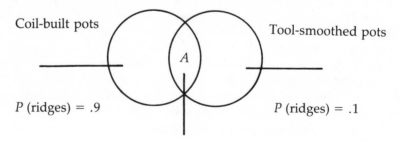

Coil-built and Tool-smoothed pots

P (ridges) = ?

† It is not required that an exact quantitative value be assigned—only that the probability be high.

The diagram illustrates how the explanatory ambiguity arises. Although the premises of each of the explanatory arguments may be true, neither of the two sets of premises embodies *all* of the evidence relevant to the occurrence of the *explanadum* event. *A* belongs to *both* reference classes, not just one, and the important probability in this case is the probability of ridges occurring on a pot that was both coil-built and smoothed.

To avoid this unhappy situation wherein different explanatory arguments, each with true premises, lead to contradictory conclusions, Hempel imposes the requirement of *maximal specificity* for Inductive–Statistical explanations (1965:399–401). This is designed to ensure that, relative to the total scientific knowledge at a given time, one takes into account *all* statistical laws and particular facts that are of potential explanatory relevance to the *explanandum* when constructing or evaluating an I–S explanation. This means, with respect to our example, that the statistical law that assigns a probability value to the appearance of ridges on a finished pot that was *both* coil-built and also smoothed by the special tool must be invoked in the explanation. It is readily apparent that in this case, as in most cases, the probability associated with the overlapping class cannot simply be calculated from knowledge of the values of each of the individual classes, but must be determined by other (empirical) means.

Introduction of the requirement of maximal specificity prevents the ambiguous situation in which one could produce an acceptable I–S explanation (i.e., one which conferred a high probability upon the *explanandum*) for either the occurrence or nonoccurrence of an event on the basis of two sets of true explanatory premises. At the same time, this requirement specifically recognizes that I–S explanation, unlike D–N explanation, is essentially relative to a given knowledge situation, for the requirement demands that we take into account the present state of scientific knowledge in choosing the appropriate reference class to which the event to be explained is assigned (Hempel 1965:402). Such dependence upon a state of knowledge at any given time naturally suggests that I–S explanations are more tentative than—and inferior to—"timeless" D–N explanations.

Although Hempel's requirement of maximal specificity rules out some of the epistemic ambiguity that may arise in connection with I–S explanation, the manner in which his requirement is formally stated (1965:394) does not rule out counterexamples of the sort presented in Chapter Five. Salmon *et al.* (1971:49–51) have suggested a reformulation and strengthening of the requirement that not only (a) the reference class must embody all relevant information—relative to our knowledge situation, but also (b) it must be the largest (maximal) class to do so. This revised requirement of *the maximal class of maximal specificity* does avoid the problems raised by such counterintuitive "explanations" as that of Mary, who is of northern European heritage, having a mild case of valley fever because she was wearing turquoise at the time of her infection. The reference class of those of northern European descent who were wearing turquoise at the time of their infection with valley fever is assigned the same probability of suffering a mild case as the still larger reference class of those of northern European descent who become infected with valley fever. Even though both of these classes embody all relevant knowledge regarding the degree of severity for cases of valley fever—and thus fulfill Hempel's requirement of maximal specificity—it is only the maximal class that avoids adding irrelevant qualifications that "spoil," at least in an intuitive sense, the explanation. Revising Hempel's requirement in favor of a maximal class of maximal specificity helps to make explicit our reasonable intuitive demand that explanations not be given in terms of irrelevant factors. These factors, such as the wearing of turquoise in our example, do nothing to show that an event is any more or less likely to occur because of their presence or absence.

Although this modification avoids some problems with Hempel's I–S model, it does not solve all of them. However, discussion of that issue will be postponed and resumed in connection with a later example.

## Deductive–Statistical Explanation— Explaining Regularities

Hempel's other model of statistical explanation, the Deductive– Statistical model, has received even less attention from archaeologists than the I–S model. This model is intended to be an account of explanation of statistical laws themselves, rather than of individual events. In explanations that conform to this model, a statement in the form of a statistical law is *deduced* (i.e., calculated with the aid of the theory of mathematical probability) from explanatory statements that essentially involve at least one law-like principle stated in statistical form (Hempel 1965:381). For example, according to this model, a statistical statement that lawfully characterizes the relative proportion of $^{14}C$ to $^{12}C$ in carbon-bearing objects that are 1000 years old can be explained by mathematically calculating the relative amount of $^{14}C$ on the basis of the statistical law that gives its half-life along with other pertinent facts regarding probabilities of contamination, corrective factors, and the like.

When Binford and Bertram state that they want to explain "at least some observed and expected patterning in the survival frequencies of anatomical parts (1977:111)," it is not entirely clear whether they want to explain a *statistical law-like statement* that gives the frequencies of survival of various anatomical parts for population with a given age structure, or whether they want to explain *particular facts,* such as the particular observed patterns of survival at various archaeological sites. They may want—and this is legitimate—to provide both sorts of explanation, but it should be noted that the explanations of these two quite distinct sets of phenomena will have different structures. What is explained (the *explanandum*) in one case will be a part of the *explanans* (the set of explanatory facts) in the other.

Let us first suppose that the *explanandum* is the statistical law. Then the explanation could conform to Hempel's Deductive–Statistical model if we interpret Binford and Bertram as indicating they would regard a statistical description of surviving anatomical parts of animals of various ages *explained* if they could calculate the appropriate frequencies of survival from statistical regularities in bone density of animals of the given age mixture, and other pertinent facts regarding attritional processes. Such a calculation, or derivation, using the laws of probability, would be analogous to the explanation of the statistical law concerning $^{14}C$ in 1000-year-old objects, and would certainly constitute a "clear relationship" between bone density and bone survival. It would be considered an explanation, according to the D–S model, of the latter in terms of the former. That is, it could be considered a deductive argument whose premises included at least one statistical lawlike statement and whose conclusion was the statistical regularity that needed explaining. (The premises of the argument may include nonstatistical laws or other information as well.)

From a philosophical viewpoint, however, there is, another way of interpreting the structure of explanations of such statistical laws. Even if there is complete agreement about what constitutes the set of explanatory facts, that is, the statistical regularities connecting age with bone density and density with resistance to agents of attrition, one could nevertheless claim that these facts have explanatory value not because they provide the premises of an argument whose conclusion is the *explanandum,* but because the explanatory facts state comprehensive physical regularities that embrace the regularity we are trying to explain as part of the larger whole (W. Salmon 1978:700). When the nature of the comprehensive regularities are perceived, and their inclusion of the *explanandum* regularity is recognized, then explanation has been achieved. In viewing the matter in this manner, we may regard a statistical regularity as *explained* when we can see how it fits into, or is subsumed under, a more general pattern of regularities. Thus, we are still operating with a "covering law" conception of explanation. But the relation between the more and less general regularities here is not *merely* a logical one between premises and conclusion of an argument, it is based in physical subsumption. If a physical relationship of this sort obtains between regularities, then it is always *possible* to construct an argument with statements of the more comprehensive regularities as premises, and to deduce, using probability theory, the limited regularity as a conclusion. But this possibility does not require us to accept the claim that the explanation *is* such an argument, or to admit that the fact that such arguments can be constructed is what makes a set of statements explanatory. These alternate ways of interpreting the nature of explanation of statistical laws make use of the same explanatory information, but they describe the relationship between explanatory facts and the *explanandum* in different ways. In looking at many actual explanations, including this one of Binford and Bertram, one might simply sidestep the philosophical question of which *model* of explanation is superior and just take comfort in reaching agreement about what constitutes an appropriate collection of explanatory facts. This is what happens, I believe, in most cases of actual explanation in scientific disciplines. This is also why it is perfectly reasonable for scientists to operate at an intuitive level with respect to standards for scientific explanation. Many explanations that are widely regarded as satisfactory would "fit" any number of models devised by philosophers. One often has to search to find the hard cases that demonstrate the inadequacy of a philosophical account of essential features of explanations. Before returning to this issue, let us take a look at what happens if we accept a rather different account of the nature of the *explanandum* in the explanation suggested by Binford and Bertram.

## Explaining the Occurrence of a Pattern

If what they want to do is explain particular events—in this case, the patterns of bone survival at various sites—then the Deductive–Statistical model is simply not applicable. In order to explain the occurrence of these patterns, Binford and Bertram might try to show that a regular relationship exists among bone age, bone density, and bone survival. However, once it was established, they would then *use* this regularity as an explanatory fact. Their demonstration of the fact might be accomplished either by empirically confirming the relationship in some appropriate manner (see Chapter Two), *or* by showing that the relationship was a deductive consequence of already established regularities. Such a derivation would have the force of demonstrating the truth of the regularity. It would not be an *explanation* of the regularity.

Binford and Bertram indicate that once a clear relationship between bone densities and survival patterns has been established, they "will have offered an explanation (1977:111)." What they may mean by this is that they will have established the right type of law-like generalization to *use* in such an explanation, not that they have actually constructed a complete explanation. Such a reading seems supported by the following:

> If we can fit an age structure to the population and thereby account for the survival population in terms of mixes of animals of different ages with their accompanying differences in bone density, these fitted mixes should correspond to the data available on both age and season of occupation for the samples. If this succeeds, we believe that a strong argument can be made that the variability has been explained, and the determinant variable is bone density, in the context of an agent of attrition, acting on population originally variable in age composition (Binford and Bertram 1977:126).

But if their sole interest is in establishing the appropriate law to use in an explanation, there is little we can say about the structure of any actual explanations that they might offer. From their claim that variability will have been explained once the statistical law that fits the data has been established, and the "determinant variable" has been identified, I believe we may infer merely that the authors see two requirements for satisfactory explanation: (a) at least one general law, that may be statistical, and (b) identification of the *cause* of the *explanandum*. Nothing at all is said about the structure of the explanation, that is, about the relation between explanatory facts and the event to be explained.

Binford and Bertram do not present examples of explanations of actually observed patterns, and one can hardly expect any, because the necessary explanatory facts are not in hand. But if the required regularities had been established, what could we say about the *form* of explanations of individual patterns? Would they fit the I–S model?

In consideration of this question, let us first present a schematic version of the type of explanatory law that Binford and his colleagues hope to establish through suitable research: "In a very large percentage of cases of exposure to a stated type of agent of attrition, a collection of faunal remains of a specified age mix at the time of death will conform within certain limits to a given pattern." With all its qualifications—"blanks" to be filled through empirical investigation to determine appropriate qualifications—this schematic version of the law-like statement is awkwardly phrased. But in its logical structure, it is similar to many familiar and simpler statistical law-like claims, such as: "In 95% of cases of series of 100 tosses of a fair coin, between 40 and 60 tosses will show heads."

Recall that, according to the I–S model, an event (and this includes an instance of a particular pattern) is explained when one can show that it was *to be expected* on the basis of explanatory information consisting of at least one statistical law and initial conditions. In I–S explanation, one need not show that the event, or pattern, *must* have occurred, given the explanatory facts, but only that its occurrence was *very likely*. This feature of the I–S model is known as the "high probability requirement." No precise figure is designated as appropriately "high." Obviously, however, "high" must be more than 50%. Various pragmatic considerations are involved in determining how high is high enough in given cases. See Hempel (1965:383f.) for further discussion of this problem.

Continuing with the coin-tossing example for the sake of simplicity, let us suppose that 100 tosses of a fair coin are made (initial condition) and that the resulting pattern consists of 55 heads and 45 tails. This pattern can be regarded as explained—in I–S fashion—by appealing to the statistical law and initial condition stated above, for on the basis of these explanatory facts, this outcome falls within the range of outcomes that are highly probable. Similarly, given a set of initial conditions that (a) stated the mix of ages at the time of death for a collection of butchered sheep, (b) information that free-ranging dogs were the only significant agent of attrition, and (c) that the dogs were operating upon complete skeletons, one who had the appropriately filled-in version of the schematic explanatory law cited above could offer I–S explanations of those patterns of sheep remains which fell within the limits specified by the law as "highly likely."

## Problems with the High Probability Requirement

The high probability requirement, which certainly has a strong intuitive appeal, is nevertheless problematic. Returning once more to a coin-tossing experiment, suppose in a series of 100 tosses, the result is 65 heads and 35 tails. This is an "unlikely" outcome, for series of 100 tosses that result in more than 60 heads (or tails) occur in only 5% of all cases. Can such an outcome be explained? Unfortunately, if one accepts the I–S model, the answer to this question must be "no." And yet it is difficult to say what more is needed for a satisfactory explanation besides the relevant statistical law and the knowledge that the coin tossing experiment was fair. Both of these bits of knowledge are in hand and we seem to understand this outcome; there is no mystery. The statistical law that gives the percentages for various kinds of patterns in a random experiment, such as the coin-tossing experiment, represents the infrequently as well as the frequently occurring patterns. Our "unlikely" result with the coins is simply a case of normal statistical variation. The only point that could possibly be added is assurance that no other factors were relevant in this case, for example, that this pattern is not a result of interference with the conditions of the experiment. But the addition of this information would not confer a high probability upon the outcome of 65 heads and 35 tails, nor would it allow the explanation to conform to the I–S model.

What we seem to have here is a conflict between two quite reasonable intuitions concerning explanations. One intuition holds that explaining an event requires showing it to be (at least) highly probable on the basis of the explanatory facts; the other intuition recognizes that improbable events do occur, and are nevertheless explainable. As frequently happens when such conflicts occur, alternative methods of resolution are available.

One alternative is to deny that science has any interest in explaining particular events, thus simply dismissing a need for any account of singular explanation. Those who take this line say that science is interested only in uniformities, whether these be universal or statistical. In the physical sciences, they point out, individual laboratory experiments are of interest because they tend to establish the existence of uniformities. Every effort is made to suppress individual circumstances that might detract from the generality of the results of such experiments. The point of explanation then is to show how uniformities are related to one another, that is, to show how some are special cases of still more wide-reaching uniformities. Particular events, according to this view, are just instances of these uniformities, and are uninteresting in themselves.

This account does not really seem to capture archaeologists' interest in explaining phenomena. Although archaeologists are concerned with explaining uniformities, they are also interested in understanding and explaining particular events: the development of agriculture in Mesoamerica, the building of Stonehenge, the abandonment of Chaco Canyon, the collapse of the Maya. There is little similarity between these individual events and the individual events that occur in a laboratory when, for example, a scientist conducts experiments to determine the melting point of copper. But this does not mean that an interest in particular events, and a desire to see them explained, is outside the scope of scientific activity. Scientists are legitimately concerned with trying to understand and explain such events as the beginning of the universe (Weinberg 1977), the low incidence of sunspots during the Maunder minimum, and the extinction of many life forms at the end of the Cenozoic. Explaining such events is a proper concern of science, and a complete account of scientific explanation must include explanation of particular events as well as uniformities (Alston 1971).

Another solution to the conflict between the intuition that wants explanations to show an event was highly probable and the intuition that admits the improbable is not thereby unexplainable is closely tied to the view, discussed in Chapter Two that statistical laws are never fundamental. These laws reflect some degree of ignorance as well as a partial understanding of how the world works. On this view, an event that is apparently improbable (such as the occurrence of 65 heads in a series of 100 tosses of a fair coin) would lose its improbable character if all the relevant facts were taken into account. In a coin-tossing experiment, these facts would include all the physical circumstances surrounding each toss in the series—the exact structure of the coin, the initial position of the coin, the details of the tossing mechanism, etc.—and all the relevant physical laws governing the behavior of such objects. This set of laws and initial conditions is enormously complex. It would be at the very least a great deal of trouble to discover and describe all the conditions, and to state the exact operations and interactions for the relevant laws for each toss. The statistical law that we use instead simply ignores all that physical complexity, but presents a good working account of a uniformity by treating coin tossing as a *random process*. This means that the outcome of each toss is considered equally likely to result in a head or a tail regardless of what has happened on previous tosses.

Processes such as fair coin tossing are sometimes called *pseudorandom*, because deterministic processes give rise to the apparently random results. Other examples of pseudorandom processes include rolling fair dice, drawing cards from a well-shuffled deck, and generating random numbers with a computer programmed for this task. In contrast to these, certain other physical processes, such as radioactive decay, are fundamentally random. In these latter cases, the best available physical theory is incompatible with an assumption of underlying deterministic processes giving rise to the observed random outcomes. When processes are perceived as random—regardless of what underlying physical mechanisms are involved—the theory of mathematical probability serves as an excellent model for the statistical aspects of the occurrence of various outcomes in long-run experiments. Thus, processes that are dissimilar in many physical respects (tossing a coin, drawing a card, radiocarbon decay) may all be regarded as exhibiting similar lawful behavior.

The statistical laws governing such processes depend upon the randomness attributed to them, not upon any specific physical laws regarding the forces applied to coins, dice, or whatever. The law "95% of a series of 100 tosses of a fair coin result in 40 to 60 heads" thus does not represent an *approximation* of those specific deterministic physical laws pertinent to the behavior of disk-like metal objects, although it gives an approximate description of the outcomes of coin-tossing experiments. The two types of laws form quite different bases for explaining the behavior of tossed coins. If one allows a statistical explanation of a random process like coin tossing, it seems incoherent to accept the use of statistical laws for the high probability cases, but to insist on shifting grounds to explain the low probability cases. If it is legitimate to use the well-established statistical law to explain the occurrence of 55 heads and 45 tails in a series of 100 tosses of a fair coin, it must be equally legitimate to invoke the same statistical law—which is the only one known to be relevant, provided that coin tossing is regarded as a random process—to explain the occurrence of 65 heads and 35 tails, even though under this law one outcome is highly probable and the other is improbable. The same law covers both sets of cases.

One might admit the point just made with respect to coin-tossing experiments, and also admit to the fundamental statistical character of radiocarbon decay, but object nevertheless that there is an important difference between the statistical laws that characterize these genuinely random and pseudorandom processes, and the statistical laws that are actually used in archaeological explanation. Although the law governing the decay of $^{14}C$ is of great importance to archaeology, it does not enter into archaeological *explanation* in such a way as to cause difficulties for the high probability requirement. The statistical law governing radiocarbon decay states that the amount of $^{14}C$ in an organism at the time of its death will be halved in 5730 years. Because of this very long half-life, the probability of a particular $^{14}C$ atom's emitting an electron and decaying during a given 24-hour period is extremely low. Yet, such events do occur, and their explanations essentially involve the statistical law of the half-life of $^{14}C$. Of course, these explanations do not confer a high probability upon the *explananda*. However, this is no real problem for *archaeological* explanation. Radiocarbon decay is a phenomenon for physics to explain. In general, the fundamentally random processes of quantum physics do not play an important role in archaeological explanation. After all, the half-life of $^{14}C$ is used to date archaeological findings, not to explain them.

Although all of the above is true, archaeological explanations do sometimes depend upon another random process, namely as genetic mutation (Flannery 1968). Scientists do not know nearly as much about genetics as they do about quantum physics. In particular, it is not known whether mutation is *fundamentally* random, or merely pseudorandom. Currently accepted genetic theory, unlike quantum physics, would not be rendered inconsistent by the addition of as yet unknown "hidden variables." Such an addition could give genetic theory a deterministic basis, making the randomness of mutations only apparent or perceived rather than fundamental. (We do believe, however, that some mutations are due to radiation, and for these at least a fundamentally random character seems likely.) Much more work in the area of molecular biology must be done before we can say whether all mutation is fundamentally random. Providing that this process is shown to have a deterministic basis, it is possible that interpretation of the laws concerning mutation will continue to be that it is a random process, ignoring underlying complex deterministic factors. In any case, insofar as archaeological explanation depends on genetic laws, it seems unwise to demand high probability of every statistical explanation.

Still, the objection might continue, genetics is another special case where archaeology is using laws developed in another discipline. Let us consider something more typical, for example, the sort of explanation Binford and his colleagues might try to give of a pattern of bone survival. The law they will use, supposing that they can establish a connection between the age-mix of animals at the time of death and the patterns of survival of bones after exposure to some agent of attrition, will not be like a law governing coin tossing (or Mendelian genetics). It will not simply ignore the operation of (known or unknown) physical forces in favor of treating various outcomes as equally likely. The law will instead recognize and take account of a factor believed to be strongly relevant (age at the time of death). Moreover, in formulating such laws, scientists typically recognize that along with factors that are mentioned in the law, there are probably other "hidden variables" operating as well. In this respect, the laws used in archaeological explanation certainly differ from the laws of fundamentally random processes, for the latter cannot countenence hidden variables without doing violence to the theory. The implicit recognition of the operation of hidden variables distinguishes these archaeological laws from the laws used in explaining pseudorandom processes such as coin tossing as well. Even though we recognize that deterministic forces govern the behavior of tossed coins, if we were to cite those physical forces, we would be shifting the grounds of the explanation; we would be refusing to consider coin tossing as a random experiment and ruling out the applicability of the statistical law.

In contrast, many of the statistical generalizations that are used in archaeological explanation can not be regarded as treating random processes, but rather as approximations to the true underlying laws, with implicit recognition that there are hidden variables unaccountable in the statistical law. These laws do reflect ignorance as well as partial knowledge of regularities. When we use one of these laws in an explanation, and an improbable event occurs, we are not satisfied to attribute it to normal statistical variation, as we would in dealing with a random process. Instead we look for the operation of some hidden variable. For example, suppose we were to find an unusually small number of pelvises surviving in a collection of bones of sheep believed to have been butchered when they were 4 to 5 years old. Such advanced age usually guarantees resistance of pelvic bones to the ravages of gnawing dogs and we would probably be reluctant to attribute the absence of pelvises to normal statistical variation. Instead we would look for some factor, such as a nutritional defect in the animals (Gifford 1981:403) or the operation of another attritional agent, that would make the observed pattern highly probable once its effect was taken into account. A reluctance to accept an explanation that confers a low probability seems reasonable here. In fact, it seems fair to say that we would simply not regard the low incidence of survival of particular kind of bone as being *explained* by citing the statistical law that says in most cases under such circumstances there will be a high incidence of survival.

When archaeologists are dealing with such nonrandom statistical laws (those which implicitly recognize the possibility of hidden variables) is the high probability requirement a reasonable one for explanation? The answer to this question is a highly qualified "yes." The qualifications are important because acceptance of a high probability requirement can easily mislead us into making unsuitable demands for satisfactory explanation. Low probabilities, *against a background assumption of the operation of deterministic causes,* signal the omission of some *relevant explanatory fact.* What we really want of explanation, whether in archaeology, physics, or whatever, is the inclusion of all relevant explanatory factors and the exclusion of irrelevant ones. We are satisfied with the physicist's explanation of the decay of a single atom of $^{14}C$, even though its decay was not shown to be probable, because we are assured that the explanation includes all that is relevant. Against the background knowledge of quantum physics, when we know its half-life we have the whole story about $^{14}C$ decay.

In contrast, we are dissatisfied with an "explanation" of a case of low incidence of survival of some anatomical part when that explanation merely invokes a law saying there is usually a high incidence. But this is not just because the explanation fails to confer a high probability upon that event. Rather, it is because we are convinced, given our background knowledge of causes operating in this type of situation, that some other relevant variable or variables have been omitted from the explanation. One might even say that there is a pragmatic rule for dealing with this nonrandom sort of statistical law. The rule requires us to look for additional relevant factors when the improbable occurs. Even though the statistical law we are using to try to explain a pattern of bone survival does not mention such variables as disease at the animal's time of death or amounts of food available to the scavengers that attacked the bones, we know such factors can affect a pattern of survival. The law tells us what happens—when all such other factors are more or less inoperative. But when an unlikely pattern occurs we look for something unusual in those factors to explain the outcome. High probability sometimes, but not always, follows from meeting the relevance requirement in explanations. The examples of explaining $^{14}C$ decay and of explanations that depend on current genetic theory show high probability and relevance do not always go together. Relevance, not high probability, is the crucial requirement for explanation.

We have seen that statistical laws used in explanations are not all alike, and that different pragmatic considerations govern their use. If a statistical law characterizes a fundamentally random process, it is unreasonable to demand a high probability for every *explanandum* covered by that law. If a statistical law characterizes a pseudorandom process, the pragmatic rule tells us to ignore the underlying deterministic laws, and to accept low probabilities occasionally as a cost of adopting a particular statistical model. However, if a statistical law represents an attempt to capture a deterministic principle, a step toward the true—but as yet unknown—deterministic law, then events that are improbable relative to such a law are not held to be explained by that law. These "improbable" events indicate some inadequacy or incompleteness in the proposed explanation, and are a signal to look for further refinements in the laws used, or for additional explanatory information of another type.

Although nonrandom statistical laws are featured in many archaeological explanations, other types occur as well. Wimsatt (1980) has argued for the importance of pseudorandomness in formulating realistic principles, particularly in ecology and biology. He, along with other scientists and philosophers who share this view, insist that the immense complexity of underlying deterministic structures frequently precludes any reasonable set of deterministic laws. Archaeology's close ties to ecology and biology make it plausible to suppose that perceived randomness is important there also, even though fundamental randomness may turn out to be unimportant in archaeology.

Because both random and nonrandom statistical laws are used in archaeological explanation, it is important to be as clear as possible about the different pragmatic considerations surrounding the uses of both types of laws. Imposing a high probability requirement upon all statistical explanations is clearly unrealistic. The high probability requirement is a feature of the I–S model of explanation, and this seriously undermines its suitability as a model for explanation in archaeology.

## Causal Relevance and Statistical Relevance

In this chapter, as in Chapter Five, there has been a continuing insistence that *relevance* relations rather than the logical relations that characterize sound deductive inference provide the basis for scientific explanations. So far the only characterization of relevance has been in statistical terms: The occurrence of *A* is relevant to the occurrence of *B* whenever the probability of *B* is not the same in *A*'s presence as in *A*'s absence. An explanation of an event, according to the Statistical–Relevance (S–R) model discussed in Chapter Five, is an assemblage of all factors statistically relevant to its occurrence, along with an assignment of the probability of the event's occurrence in the light of those factors (W. Salmon 1971:71). The model says nothing about *causes* or the necessity for a scientific explanation to be a causal explanation. Several years after the publication of this account of explanation, W. Salmon (1975, 1978) explicitly acknowledged its incompleteness and tried to supplement it with causal features. Along with the complete set of statistically relevant factors for an event's occurrence and the proper probability assignment, he now says that there must also be a *causal* account of any statistical regularity that is used in the explanation.

This modified account of S–R explanation brings it into much closer agreement with actual scientific practice, including the practice of archaeologists. This can be shown by examining two more archaeological explanations, which, although one is tentative and incomplete, do seem to fit quite nicely the S–R model when it is supplemented by causal features.

In *Before Civilization*, Renfrew proposes explaining many prehistoric culture changes in terms of population growth (Renfrew 1971:115). Renfrew notes that in recent years archaeologists have been able to estimate prehistoric population size with greatly increased accuracy, thus providing a firmer basis for establishing (statistical) correlations between increasing population size and certain other archaeologically recognizable features, such as intensification of agriculture, development of economic exchange systems, craft specialization, and changes from egalitarian to more structured social organization.

Renfrew cites, for example, Forge's claim that "the upper size limit for a neolithic egalitarian society may generally be of the order of 400–500 persons (Renfrew 1973:115)." That this is a statistical claim is indicated by the expression "may generally be of the order of," and it is reasonable, I believe, to translate this claim into the following statistical law-like statement: "The probability is very low that a neolithic society has an egalitarian social structure if its population is in excess of 500 persons.

For many societies, such as the Hohokam of southern Arizona, we have archaeological evidence both for population increases of the appropriate order and for the development of certain nonegalitarian features of social organization (Schiffer 1980). With this information, the above generalization might be used to construct an (unmodified) S–R explanation of the Hohokam's greater complexity during the Colonial Period (800–1000 A.D.) over that evidenced for the Pioneer Period (500–800 A.D.).

However, such an explanation would be weak at best. Even putting aside the legitimate worry that other factors besides population growth might have been statistically relevant to the development of more complex social structures, the explanation as it stands is not a satisfying one, for the statistical relationship that is the basis for the explanation does not tell us anything about *causes*. Statistical relevance relations, even in the limiting cases where the statistics are 100% or 0%, are *correlations* that lack the characteristic asymmetry of causal links. Because correlations are symmetric, this "explanation" cannot tell us if population growth is responsible for nonegalitarian features, if a more complicated social structure induces population increase (perhaps though a complicated feedback mechanism), or if these two features are not directly causally related, but are merely two symptoms of some common underlying causal process.

What is needed to complete the proposed explanation is something Forge provides, though in a rudimentary fashion—a *causal* account of the regularity connecting population size and nonegalitarian social structures. Forge says that "*Homo sapiens* can handle only a certain maximum number of intense face-to-face relationships, successfully distinguishing between each (quoted in Renfrew 1973:115)." According to his view, when populations grow beyond a certain size, compensatory measures, such as introducing structure or fragmentation into smaller groups, need to be taken to ensure continued communication and social integration. Although this causal account of the statistical relationship is rough and incomplete (Renfrew refers to it as a "first insight"), it does at least recognize that there must be some attempt to provide a causal basis for the Statistical–Relevance relationship if it is to have any explanatory power. The next example provides a much more detailed development of the causal relations that explain an observed relationship of statistical relevance.

In *Living Archaeology*, Gould devotes a chapter to explaining the differences between archaeologically recognizable features of "post-Pleistocene human societies in the Western and Central deserts of Australia" (Gould 1980:186–203). Especially in their faunal remains, the difference between these peoples, who left residues of roughly the same range of human activities (Gould 1980:195), is evident. Gould describes one particularly notable contrast:

> The bones at Puntutjarpa (Western desert) were broken into exceedingly small bits, rarely exceeding two centimeters in diameter or legnth. Macropod teeth there were usually split open, as were the epipheses of longbones. By contrast, the macropod remains at James Range East (Central desert) occurred in consistently larger pieces, although still much broken up when compared with the faunal remains from sites in many other parts of the world (Gould 1980:187).

What Gould has noted here is, of course, the *statistical relevance* of geographic location to the sizes of buchered bones. Appropriately, he sees this as an opportunity for *causal* explanation, and seeks possible causal processes and interactions that could connect geographic features with the sizes of archaeologically discovered bones. Several possible causes are dismissed as unlikely, for example, rock fall damage, the activities of scavenging dogs, and damage to the macropods during the act of hunting. Rock fall is a feature of both sites, but its occurrence at Puntutjarpa is too intermittent to account for the pervasiveness of the smaller bones found there. Even if the activities of gnawing dogs or the injuries inflicted during the hunting process could account for the smallness of the bones at Puntutjarpa (a doubtful case), there is no reason to believe that the two sites differed in these respects.

Gould argues that the smaller bones at Western desert sites are due to humans having broken and pounded the roasted animals in order to extract all edible portions. But this intense treatment of captured game is not attributed in an ad hoc manner to cultural preference; its explanation involves a series of *causal* processes and interactions arising from the geographic features that affect availability of water and game. Gould identifies these in some detail. Studies of kangaroo populations have shown that the availability of short green herbage and suitable cover controls the numbers of macropods in an area. Shortages in either cover or herbage, or both, cause starvation in young animals and suspension of reproduction. Absence of water catchments at close intervals is a causal barrier to human hunting activity. The combination of these factors causes reductions in the amount of game captured. The Western desert is appreciably poorer than the Central in availability of both game and water. Scarcity of a commodity is causally relevant to its conservation, and some kinds of conservation activities, such as breaking and pounding roasted game, are causal processes that result in exceedingly small bone sizes for faunal remains. Significant support for the part of Gould's causal hypothesis dealing with the treatment of roasted game is provided by ethnographic observation of contemporary Western desert Aboriginals, who routinely engage in this practice.

Besides differences in faunal remains, sites in the Western and Central deserts exhibit differences in rock art and stone tools, the Central desert being relatively richer in both these respects. However, Gould, showing his sensitivity to the need for a causal *account*, denies that the relatively richer ecological setting of the Central desert *explains* these features. The statistical relevance relation is present, just as it is in the case of faunal remains, but without a causal understanding of that relationship, there is no explanation.

## Probabilistic Causes

One could get the impression from reading the preceding example that statistical relevance relations fail to be explanatory because they are *statistical*, and that provision of a causal account of these regularities will remove that feature from an explanation. However, nothing could be further from the truth. Although not every statistical relation is a causal one, many causal relations are—to the best of our knowledge—statistical. No one denies that paresis is caused by a prior case of untreated secondary syphilis, yet only about a quarter of such cases result in paresis. Only a few still are willing to deny that heavy smoking is the major cause of lung cancer, though everyone knows that the relationship is a statistical one, and not every heavy smoker contracts lung cancer. Many persons believe, with good evidence, that Vietnam veterans' exposure to Agent Orange causes birth defects in their children who were conceived after such exposure, though this (fortunately) has not occurred in every, or even in most, cases.

The first philosophical efforts to come to terms with probabilistic causality are rather recent (Good 1961–62; Mellor 1982; Reichenbach 1956; W. Salmon 1980; Sayre 1977; Suppes 1970), but such an account is crucial for the (causally supplemented) S–R model of explanation. One persistent feature of that model is its refusal to presuppose that the world is governed entirely by deterministic laws. If the model is to insist upon *causal* explanations, then the notion of causality must somehow be separated from the notion of determinism. That is, there must be a nondeterministic, or probabilistic, account of causality.

In keeping with a probabilistic account of causality, certain familiar philosophical views of the nature of the causal relationship are abandoned. Most importantly, one gives up a view of causation which takes as its model a relation between two *events,* one of which is supposed to be temporally prior to and also a *sufficient condition* for the occurrence of the other. Although this "simplistic" view of causality has been attacked by archaeologists frequently in recent years, particularly in connection with their defense of the importance of feedback mechanims, the notion of sufficient condition as a crucial feature of the causal relationship is still predominant. This can be seen in many criticisms of functional explanation, where the complaint is that these supply necessary, but not sufficient, conditions for the occurrence of the event they are supposed to explain, as well as in other contexts (e.g. Gifford 1981:390).

Instead of taking *events* as the primitive relata in causal contexts, probabilistic versions of causality (e.g., W. Salmon 1978) take causal *processes* as fundamental. Events may be thought of as *interactions* between the processes. Causal processes are extended in space and time, and their characteristic feature is the ability to transmit causal influence or "marks" (W. Salmon 1978:690). This discussion of processes and interactions sounds rather abstract, and detailed analysis of these concepts poses challenging philosophical problems, However, the concepts of causal process and interaction are already quite familiar and easy to grasp through mundane examples. For example, weathering and trampling behaviors of animals are both examples of causal processes; the causal influence or "marks" these processes transmit when they interact with a bone lying upon the surface of the earth (another causal process) are objects of great interest to archaeologists (Gifford 1981:414–418).

Gould's explanation of the extremely small sizes of faunal remains at Puntutjarpa appeals to some widely known and well understood processes, such as droughts, and also some less well known processes, such as the reproductive processes of macropods. He gives an account, supported by empirical studies, of how such processes are affected ("marked") when they interact with one another. Again, some of these interactions are quite familiar, such as the effects of drought upon the growth of green herbage, but others are much less well known, such as the suspension of reproductive processes in kangaroos when confronted with disappearance of green herbage.

If we were to scrutinize Gould's causal account in terms of his having provided sets of *sufficient* conditions for the occurrence of the events he

describes, we would encounter problems. Droughts, amounts of herbage and cover for macropods, reproductive activity, success in hunting,
and so on, are all matters of degree. The links that bind them are probabilistic, not deterministic. And yet there is no doubt that Gould's causal
account of these processes is an excellent one. In providing his explanation, Gould has not shown that when all the missing links of the causal
chain are uncovered, the harsher environment of the Western desert is
*sufficient* to produce exceedingly small faunal remains. Instead, he has
described the chain of causally relevant processes and interactions
which explain the *statistical* connection between geographic conditions
and the character of those faunal remains. That is exactly what is required in this case for adequate explanation.

## Common Causes

In Gould's example, a long chain of causal processes and interactions
leads *directly* (though probabilistically) from geographic conditions to
sizes of faunal remains. However, there are cases wherein statistical
regularities occur without direct causal chains of any length connecting
them. In these cases the connection is *indirect*, through a *common cause.*
For example, recent excavations near Veracruz, Mexico of round to oval
mounds (1–3 m elevation and 10–50 m diameter, or slightly larger)
yielded pottery fragments, grinding stone fragments, food remains, and
fragments of wattle and daub construction (Stark and Young 1981:290).
In general, the occurrence of pottery fragments is strongly statistically
relevant to the occurrence of grinding stone fragments in mounds of this
type. Yet no archaeologists would consider this statistical relevance relation explanatory as it stands. The regular connection between pottery
fragments and grinding stone fragments needs to be causally explained,
not by showing how one of these is directly causally responsible for the
other, but by appealing to a *common cause,* in this case human habitation,
which is responsible for both types of items.

Appeals to common causes to explain statistical regularities are widespread in archaeology, and in other sciences as well. Tree ring dating
depends on this principle, for statistical regularities in ring patterns in
widely scattered trees are accountable because of shared climatic conditions, a common cause that produces the similarity in ring structure.
New techniques of lead isotope analysis, devised to trace the mine
sources of ancient silver, also depend upon this principle. Statistical
regularities in the proportion of various lead isotopes occurring in silver
artifacts is attributed to the geologic age of the source of the silver ore as
well as to the relative amounts of uranium and thorium present in the

ore-forming fields (Gale and Stos-Gale 1981:183). Because ancient methods of refining silver by cupellation left traces of lead, and because the proportions of the various lead isotopes are not altered either by refining or subsequent corrosion, these lead isotopes provide a way of "fingerprinting" ancient silver artifacts (Gale and Stos-Gale 1981:183). Gould (1980:253) and other ethnoarchaeologists would use the term "archaeological signature" rather than "fingerprints" to refer to such a distinctive mark in archaeological material, one that can inform us about the behavioral adaptation responsible for the mark. No matter what vocabulary is used, the appeal to a common cause to account for an observed regularity in these cases is obvious.

Certain features of causal processes, such as their spatiotemporal continuity, embodied in the slogan "no action at a distance," and their temporal asymmetry, which guarantees that marks transmitted in an interaction do not modify causal processes *before* that interaction occurs, place some important restrictions upon our search for the causes that explain statistical regularities. A striking case wherein temporal asymmetry forced reassessment of causal claims occurred with the "radiocarbon revolution," which showed that major megalithic structures in Britain and northern Europe antedated the civilizations that were supposed to have influenced their construction (Renfrew 1973). Evidence that both diffusionists and their critics take the "no action at a distance" principle very seriously is provided by the diffusionists' vast expenditure of effort to establish the existence of *contact* between groups who developed similar cultural features. When actual contact cannot be supported by evidence, they mount expeditions such as the Kon-Tiki to prove that contact was at least possible. Although these features of causal connections are of some help in uncovering the causal regularities that explain statistical regularities, they do not tell archaeologists all they need to know in order to discover causes.

In some cases, it is not even clear whether a statistical regularity is to be explained by appeal to a common cause or by appeal to some direct causal relation. Disagreement about this matter characteristically separates diffusionists from those who argue for "independent" development of similar cultural features in response to some common (usually environmental) stimulus.

In other cases, we may be quite sure that no direct causal processes or interactions could account for a statistical regularity, but the nature of this common cause may be partially or totally obscure. For example, archaeologists generally attribute regular patterns observed in finished artifacts to two different groups of common causes: functional causes, where the feature is controlled by the task for which the artifact was intended; and stylistic causes, dependent upon choices of the manufacturer which are not constrained by the intended task (Jelinek 1976:19–33). There are many cases wherein one is confronted with a regularity and where there is no hint about which of the two types of common cause is operative. When it is unknown what practical task, if any, an artifact was designed to perform, it may be impossible to determine whether a feature of that artifact has a functional cause or a stylistic cause.

Numerous heuristic devices to facilitate the search for causes are presented in chapters on methodology in scientific texts in most fields. Mill's Methods (Mill 1874) are examples of these, and Mill's Method of Difference, which attempts to single out causes by "comparing instances in which the phenomenon does occur, with instances in other respects similar in which it does not (Mill 1874:278)" played an important role in the examples of Binford and of Gould discussed in this chapter. Unfortunately there are no certain methods for discovering causes. Sometimes hard work discloses nature's secrets, sometimes genius is required. Luck surely plays a role, and probably, in some cases we will never find the answers we seek. But regardless of any barriers to the discovery of causes, no satisfactory theory of scientific explanation can dispense with its causal features.

# Conclusion

In this chapter, several examples of archaeological explanation, varied in their completeness as well as form and subject matter, were presented against the background of various philosophical accounts of standards for scientific explanation. With respect to explanation of particular events it was argued that, statements to the contrary notwithstanding, such explanations are scientifically important. The Statistical–Relevance model, supplemented by causal features, was demonstrated to capture more fully than other available models the beneficiating aspects of such explanations in archaeology. Furthermore, this model, in addition to its ability to "fit" explanations implicity recognized as correct by archaeologists, avoids certain problems that cannot be excised from the Inductive–Statistical model.

With respect to the explanation of regularities, a sound archaeological example that fits the Deductive–Statistical model was presented. However, it was noted that the fact that a good explanation fits a particular model does not guarantee correctness of that model, for the explanation may (and usually will) fit other models as well. Models must be tested also by seeing whether or not any obviously *bad* explanations fit them.

One defect noted in all the standard models—Deductive– Nomological, Deductive–Statistic and Inductive–Statistical—is that they depend upon *logical* relations rather than causal relations to provide relevant connections between *explanans* and *explananda*. Numerous arguments and examples were presented to try to convince the reader that *causal* relationships are necessary to provide the basis for satisfactory explanation. Viewing explanations as arguments, although natural in some contexts because of certain superficial similarities, has blinded us to some deep differences between the two. The causally enhanced Statistical–Relevance model attempts to restore an emphasis on causal relations by demanding a causal account of any noncausal regularity employed in an explanation. This insistence upon the importance of displaying causal connections is in accord with sound archaeological practice, a point demonstrated in Gould's explanation of the small sizes of faunal remains found at Puntutjarpa.

The Statistical–Relevance model is not the first philosophical account of explanation to feature causal connections as the sine qua non for correct scientific explanation. The earlier accounts of Scriven and Wright, mentioned in Chapter Five, are somewhat unsatisfactory, however, because they do not provide an analysis of the nature of causal relationships. In contrast, proponents of the Statistical–Relevance model regard a clear account of the nature of causal connections, including an account of probabilistic causality, as essential to the model's success.

The structural aspects of individual explanations by no means exhaust the archaeologists' interest in the topic. A much broader view of the problem of explanation raises questions about the nature of explanatory theories and how to devise such theories. These questions will be addressed in the next chapter.

# CHAPTER SEVEN

# Theory Building in Archaeology

## Introduction

Widespread agreement exists that archaeology lacks well developed theories that command acceptance. However, agreement halts at this point. The nature of theories, the best way to begin to build a theory, whether or not archaeological theory should be a part of a general theory of social science—all of these are matters of dispute. The term "theory" is itself used in many different ways. Unless otherwise noted, it will be used here to refer to a set of interrelated, rather high-level principles or laws that can provide an explanatory framework to accommodate a broad range of phenomena. Phenomena of interest to archaeologists include, but are not confined to, patterns of connection between human behavior and material remains, relations among the remains themselves, relations between material remains and the physical settings wherein they are found, as well as aspects of social, political, and economic organization of prehistoric societies.

It is obvious that our understanding of empirical phenomena is enhanced when we are able to see connections among things that at first seemed utterly disjoint. Theories fulfill this function, and provide a broad perspective for ordering and arranging not only isolated facts, but also various regularities that the facts exemplify. Ideally a theory, or a comprehensive system of theories, would be broad enough to account for all the observed regularities recognized by archaeology and also be detailed enough to account for any specific archaeological phenomenon. Comprehensive and detailed theories of this sort are extremely rare, even in the most advanced sciences. The construction of such a theory of archaeology would seem to be merely an ideal, not a realistic goal.

A few scientific theories, such as Newton's theory of the motion of particles, have been strikingly successful at doing the things theories are designed to do. It is only natural then that various aspects of such theories are taken as patterns or guides for theory building in other areas. One feature of such theories is the apparent emphasis on careful definition of their crucial terms. Accordingly, in archaeology, as in other social sciences, one approach to theory building has been to start by providing a set of definitions (Dunnell 1971).

Another aspect of some highly successful scientific theories is their deductive structure. At least since the time of Descartes, there has been a strong commitment to the view that success in science can be achieved by constructing theories on the model of Euclidean geometry. A relatively small number of propositions are stated as axioms, and all the other statements (the theorems) of the system are then deduced from these initial propositions. Because adherence to the principles of deductive logic can never take one from true premises to false conclusions, the dangers of error are thus confined to errors admitted in the axioms. No new error can creep into a deductive system—unless of course one errs in a deduction along the way. This formal approach to theory building was used as early as the seventeenth century in a discipline that is not part of the natural sciences (Spinoza, *Ethics*). The technique has recently been advocated by some archaeologists (Read and LeBlanc 1978).

Each of the above approaches to theory building borrows from successful theories, but what is borrowed is a method rather than anything substantive. A substantive sort of borrowing also sometimes occurs. In such cases, the theory-builder may either try to fit archaeology with some existing theory (General Systems Theory has been suggested as a candidate), or take over—perhaps with modification—substantive principles from another discipline such as ecology or ethnography (see Schiffer 1980). Archaeologists recognized in the early nineteenth century, for example, that newly developed geological principles of stratification affected interpretation of artifacts (Daniel 1967).

The final approach to be considered here is one that believes the way to build a high-level theory is by considering large amounts of archaeological data, subjecting the materials to detailed study and thoughtful consideration, developing a set of empirical generalizations, and then trying to construct laws and higher principles to accommodate these. Much of Binford's recent work falls into this class (1972, 1977, 1978, 1980).

These different strategies form neither an exhaustive nor an exclusive set of ways to deal with the challenge of theory building. But they do provide a useful framework for a discussion of problems involved with various attempts. It should be understood that attributions of one position or another to a given author should be interpreted as indicating an emphasis on one approach rather than a total rejection or neglect of the others. Most archaeologists would probably approve a broad range of attacks on the difficult problems of theory construction.

## The Definitional Approach

In advanced sciences, such as physics, there seems to be certain "crispness" of vocabulary that is absent in the social sciences. Physicists may disagree sharply about theoretical matters, but generally the parties of such disputes do not doubt that they are using terms in a uniform manner, even highly theoretic terms that do not refer to observable entities (such as "electron"). Terminology in the social sciences, by way of contrast, ranges from common-sense expressions to esoteric jargon, with disagreements about meanings at every level. Among archaeologists, for example, it is common to find disputes about terms as basic to the discipline as "artifact," "site," and "type."

Earlier archaeologists expressed little concern for how such terms were used, and went about their work without attempting to provide any explicit definitions. They apparently assumed that a shared background and context would guarantee agreement sufficient for understanding. Contemporary archaeologists cannot even find consistency in the terminology of their predecessors, much less conformity with their own usage.

These archaeologists are often struck by curious lacunae in nineteenth-century site reports, even those prepared by competent and fastidious observers. Crania, for example, are often described in elaborate detail, whereas other human bones are barely mentioned. Some lithics are given extensive treatment, but debris and microliths—so important to modern archaeologists—are completely ignored. It is clear that many of these omissions, which are so sorely felt today, are the result of a different understanding of what constitute the data of archaeology. This problem is related to definition also, for an alternative way of characterizing this situation is to say that earlier archaeologists accepted different implicit definitions of such terms as "artifact" and "site."

Dunnell suggests that before archaeologists became interested in *testing* their claims, terminological confusions were not very important. He says that imprecision was no barrier when "archaeology could be acquired as an art—by intuitive assimilation." But he insists that things are different now: "Today the discipline must be treated as a body of knowledge which can be learned. Yet the terminological morass presents serious barriers to such acquisition (1971:185)."

Surely if it prevents successful communication, terminological confusion is a serious problem even when no testing is involved. However, it seems that a *particular kind* of attention to definition, found too often in current literature of the social sciences, is more correctly viewed as contributing to a terminological morass than alleviating it. The problem, briefly stated, is this: Terminological clarity is perceived by many social scientists as a *prerequisite* to conceptual clarity and theory construction, rather than part and parcel of these latter. In an attempt to achieve terminological clarity, certain techniques of defintion are employed. But there is an inadequate understanding of the limitations of these techniques. The consequences of failing to recognize the limitations range from the introduction of useless jargon to the production of serious misunderstandings. Some examples of the definitional approach will make these difficulties apparent.

## Operational Definition

Since Bridgman's (1927) introduction of the technique of operational definition, scientists in many fields have been attracted by the hope this method offers for firmly anchoring the claims of science in a set of publicly repeatable physical operations. Depending on the outcome of such operations, a term is correctly applicable or it is not. Terms thus tied to reality, it seemed, would be prevented from taking on new sets of meanings that could allow a wide variety of interpretations, depending on the user's or listener's past experiences. Operationally defined terms were thought to provide the satisfactory basis for a truly objective account of science.

Working out the details of this exciting proposal turned out to be extraordinarily difficult, however, and careful critical analysis shows that any broad branch of science contains terms that do not yield to operational definition. For example, even fairly simple *dispositional* terms, such as "soluble," resist complete operational definition. We usually attribute dispositional properties to things just in case they *would* react in certain ways *if* they were put to certain tests. It seems too strict to withhold the label "soluble" from a bit of salt which has not been tested, though this is what strict operationalist criteria require. There have been attempts to solve such problems by providing partial *reductions* of sentences containing dispositional terms to sentences containing only terms amenable to operational definition. This has not been entirely successful, though most scientists would count simple dispositional terms like "soluble" as satisfactorily defined when operations that *could* be performed are so clearly specified. But even such weakening of the operationalist program has not allowed it to provide definitions for highly theoretic terms (such as "electron") of advanced sciences. See (Hempel 1965:123–133) for a careful critical appraisal of the program's successes and weaknesses.

In spite of its demonstrated inadequacies, the program of operational definition has some merit, and moreover, it is not without champions, particularly among social scientists. Archaeologists should understand what can and cannot be done with this technique so that they will be able to use and evaluate operational definitions correctly.

Among those who regard operational definitions as crucial for generating the *data* of anthropology, including archaeological data, are Thomas (1976) and Plog (1974). Thomas says that "data are counts, measurements, and observations *made on* people, objects and things (1976:7)." He insists that "the most important criterion for adequate operational definition requires one to specify the procedures or processes through which data have been generated (1976:14)." Thomas does not give an extended discussion of the technique of operational definition, but he does cite with approval some examples of operational definition from the works of others. He uses these examples to point out the feasibility of constructing satisfactory definitions in anthropology and archaeology. His discussion will be closely examined because it embodies some pervasive misunderstandings of the technique.

In the first place, Thomas gives a misleading impression as to why not all terms lend themselves to operational definition. Following Harris (1964:3–6) he says, "there must always be certain 'primitive' terms which remain undefined. Physicists have difficulty in defining absolutes such as time, length, and mass. But anthropological definitions can neatly sidestep such difficulties by simply taking given primitive terms and using them as undefined physical terms to build operational criteria relevant to anthropology (1976:14)." This claim is odd for several reasons. As a practical matter, it is true that it would be foolish for anthropologists to try to provide operational definitions of each and every term they use. Physicists have provided satisfactory definitions for many physical terms used by anthropologists, and it would be pointless to duplicate their efforts. Also as a practical matter, it may be pointless for anthropologists to try to provide operational definitions of physical terms when physicists have been unable to do this.

Aside from this, however, Harris and Thomas both ignore the technical meaning of "primitive term," which depends upon a certain formal way of viewing the languages containing such terms (see the "Formal Theories" section in this chapter for further discussion of formal languages). They also fail to recognize two different genres of definitions: those that present an equivalent linguistic expression, and those that indicate extralinguistic referents of a term. Primitive terms are undefined expressions, in that they are not reducible to any more basic linguistic expressions in the specified language in which they occur. For example, one might specify a language that consisted only of certain primitive terms, such as "line," "intersects," and "between." New expressions could be added to the language by defining them in terms of the primitives: "point" is "the intersection of two lines." "Point" then is a *defined* term, relative to this language.

Such languages may be interpreted or uninterpreted. In an uninterpreted language, neither the primitive terms nor the defined terms are assigned to extralinguistic referents. One might nevertheless study certain interesting formal or structural relationships among the various linguistic elements. To interpret a language is to assign its primitives (and thus also its defined terms, because they can all be reduced to primitives) to some referent outside the language. To assign referents, is *in another sense*, to define the terms. For example, a possible interpretation of the language just discussed might assign "line" to paths of light rays, and "intersection" to the physical operation of paths crossing one another. If a language is interpreted, then all of its terms, primitive and defined, have meanings (i.e., are defined in this second sense). If the language is uninterpreted, then primitive and defined terms alike lack meaning in this sense.

The whole point of operational definition is to provide a suitable link between language and extralinguistic entities. If the program of operational definition is to be accomplished, it must provide connections for any formal languages that purport to be applicable to empirical reality. This means that the primitive terms of such languages are the expressions *most* in need of operational definition. A systematic *empirical* science cannot be built upon the basis of primitive terms of an uninterpreted formal system of language. Such a proposal is inimical to every operationalist goal.

A further oddity in the quoted passage is the citation of "time," "length," and "mass" as terms that do not have operational definitions. Thomas himself, in practice, regards providing operational criteria for artifact length, weight, and even color, as utterly unproblematic. For example, he defines length as a reading on vernier calipers (1976:16). The operationalists were not concerned originally with defining an abstract concept of "length," but rather with determining conditions under which a concrete expression, such as "This biface is 8 cm long," is correctly used. Specifying such conditions is fairly simple and in this sense "length" is an operationally defined term.

This does not mean that there are no problems with operationally defining concrete expressions that attribute a particular length to an object. Difficulties arise because we are unable to discriminate operationally between lengths that our units of measure can differentiate. Our measuring systems allow a nondenumerable infinity of real number values for length, but our discriminatory powers are considerably more restricted. As an example, a measuring instrument can only approximate the length of the diagonal of a square whose side is two feet long. Further difficulties arise because there are various operations that may be used to determine the length of an object, and we have no theory that tells us how to operationally coordinate the various results. However, such problems cannot be solved or avoided by taking "length" as a primitive.

The difficulties just mentioned are minor compared with others in the operationalist program. The deeper problems with operational definitions of anthropological terms are illustrated in Thomas's discussion of the attempt to define "acculturation" (1976:15–16). The focus of Thomas' remarks is a study by Robbins and Pollnac (1969). Because these researchers were interested in investigating relations between drinking problems and acculturation in rural Buganda, they needed some way to measure the degree of acculturation of selected households. Toward this end, a questionnaire was devised to measure what they believed to be two major aspects of acculturation: "the self-identification of informants with Western society (as seen through the use of material items) and general exposure to Western behavior and values (through formal education) (Thomas 1976:15)." The items mentioned in the questionnaire are reproduced in the following table. Thomas claims that each question can be answered "yes" or "no" on the basis of simple observation.

One of the chief advantages of operational definition is that it promotes objectivity through repeatability of results. But close examination of the items in this list leads one to suspect that this feature, regarded by Thomas as the sine qua non of operational definition, is not guaranteed. There is abundant opportunity for disagreement among observers, particularly with respect to Items 12, 16, and 21. Operational criteria for terms such as "thinks it is proper," "likes," and "prefers" are certainly matters upon which different observers might disagree. Items 18 and 19 involve *dispositional* terms that have already been mentioned as posing an impediment to complete operational definition. The activities of visiting Kampala and purchasing and reading magazines may be observed, but individuals can have certain *dispositional* characteristics, such as that of being a magazine reader, even though this may not be exhibited when the observer is present. Of course, observers can ask questions about this sort of thing, but it is common to find different answers given to different observers. It also happens that different observers interpret similar answers in different ways. Though items can be answered "yes" or "no," there is no guarantee that an informant *will* answer in just that way. If pressed, one might, but then the answer would be suspect. A different form of pressing could come up with a different answer.

Other items on the list, such as the first three, not only involve dispositional properties, but are also *vague* in the sense of being difficult to apply in borderline cases. For example, interviewers might disagree

TABLE 7.1

ACCULTURATION SCALE ITEMS FOR BUGANDAN HOUSEHOLDS [a]

1. The ability to read Luganda.
2. The ability to speak English.
3. The ability to read English.
4. Education of spouse, one or more years.
5. Education of spouse, four or more years.
6. Education of spouse, nine or more years.
7. Owns clock.
8. Owns watch.
9. Owns radio.
10. Owns iron.
11. Owns stove.
12. Respondent thinks it is proper for the husband and wife to eat at the same table.
13. Wearing Kanzu (native dress) at home with relatives and friends or when visiting relatives and friends (trad.).
14. Wearing Kanzu to work, to the local market, to towns and cities (trad.).
15. Wearing Kanzu all of the time (trad.).
16. Prefers drinking from a glass instead of gourd.
17. Has been to the bank to do business.
18. Goes to the cinema.
19. Purchase and reads magazines.
20. Visits Kampala (city).
21. Likes to straighten hair.
22. Presence of photographs on the inside walls.
23. Education of respondent one or more years.
24. Education of respondent four or more years.
25. Education of respondent nine or more years.

[a]After Robbins and Pollnac 1969.

about the level of proficiency required in order to answer "yes" to "able to read English." When there is reason to believe that different investigators using the same "instrument" will not agree in their measurements, the intersubjective agreement required for operational definition is seriously undermined. In short, because this scale contains many items that lack clear operational criteria of application, the scale cannot constitute an operational definition of "degree of acculturation among rural Buganda."

There is, moreover, an even deeper reason why this scale does not provide the desired operational definition. Acculturation is a *theoretic* term, one whose definition poses special problems for the operationalist program. Thus, it is unlikely that any such scale would accomplish the intended purpose. The basis for the distinction between theoretical terms and observational terms is the contrast between the remoteness of such abstract concepts as "electron" from any sensory experience, and the apparently close link between sense impressions and such terms as "red spot" and "shrill noise." Many writers believe that the observational–theoretical distinction is too glibly drawn and will not withstand careful scrutiny (Hesse 1974; Papineau 1979). Although I agree that a sharp distinction between observational and theoretical vocabularies is indefensible, a crude scale that admits that some terms are much more theory-laden than others seems quite plausible, and is useful for many purposes.

The observational–theoretical distinction is intimately related to the operationalist program, for expressions containing only observational terms are, presumably, those most amenable to operational definition. Originally the hope was to replace theoretic terms by equivalent complexes of observational expressions, thus securing the operational definition of theoretic terms as well. This attempt at reduction has not succeeded. Theoretic terms have resisted even the type of partial operational definition that has been somewhat helpful in dealing with dispositional terms. This failure to offer satisfactory definitions of theoretic terms has been the chief weakness of the operationalist program.

Even in a crude and desultory separation of observational and theoretic vocabulary, "acculturation" clearly falls under the heading of theoretic. It draws its meaning from a complex of concepts, including those of culture, group solidarity, self-identify, and self-esteem. Only against such a background does the concept of acculturation have any explanatory value. Only in such a context can it help to account for the drinking problems among the Buganda. The concept of acculturation is invoked by the investigators to explain certain patterns of excessive consumption of alcohol. When an explanatory concept makes an implicit appeal to a theory, as does acculturation, the concept will not yield to techniques of observational definition.

The terms related to acculturation—"culture," "self-esteem," and so forth—are no more amenable to operational definition than is the term "acculturation." This does not mean that all such terms are empirically worthless, but only that their status must be assessed in a manner different from that of observational terms. Roughly what is involved is that a whole *theory*, that is, a set of statements connecting these theoretical terms, along with detailing the connections between them and certain observational terms, must be evaluated in terms of criteria for success of theories, rather than by how well the individual items in the vocabulary meet operational standards. Anthropologists are no more obligated to provide operational definitions for their theoretic terms than are physicists. Being "scientific" does not mean providing operational definitions for each and every term used in the science.

This criticism of Thomas' account of *operational definition* should not be regarded as a complete denial of value to questionnaires such as the one he discusses. Although questionnaires cannot *define* the term in question, they can be very useful in measuring objectively the degree to which certain theoretically defined traits are present. Although discrepancies are possible in reports of observers, so also is intersubjective agreement to a large degree. However, such agreement depends on more than the nature of the questionnaire. Careful training of investigators as well as a certain shared background of information and viewpoint (a shared *theory*, however implicit, of *acculturation*) contributes immensely to such agreement.

Most anthropologists, upon reflection, would agree that the questionnaire does not really provide a *definition* of "degree of acculturation" for the following reasons. It is possible for an individual who is highly accultured to score rather low on the scale. For example, if economic considerations prevented acquisition of Western education and many material items of Western culture, acculturation could nevertheless be attributed to an individual who did everything within his power to imitate Western ways. It is likewise possible for one who scores very high on the scale not to be accultured in the relevant sense. For this person, possession of items of material culture may be only for his or her family's comfort, or for some other reason besides the individual's commitment to Western forms of luxury. Years of education may have helped this person to put Western values in proper perspective, to heighten appreciation and allow reaffirmation of the values of Bugandan culture.

What the questionnaire apparently does measure are some common *symptoms* of acculturation, and so it enables a researcher to make rough quantitative judgments that provide a basis for comparisons. With recognition of the limits of such an approach, this can be valuable. However, it is misleading to call this sort of thing "providing an operational definition of acculturation." The very construction of the questionnaire depends on a prior theoretical understanding of acculturation. The scale itself is measured against this theoretical understanding rather than vice versa.

Although acculturation is a term used more frequently by cultural anthropologists than by archaeologists, its discussion here is appropriate, because archaeologists' terminology also extends beyond that required to deal with bones, lithics, and sherds. In attempts to link material remains with past behavior, similar cultural concepts are often invoked in an explanatory situation. For example, an attempt to resist acculturation is invoked by Turnbaugh (1979) to explain archaeological remains that indicate dramatic increase in the practice of calumet ceremonialism during the eighteenth century. At that time, American Indians were undergoing sociocultural stress, allegedly induced by white contact. Turnbaugh, relying implicitly on a theoretical understanding of acculturation, argues that the increase in the use of calumet pipes was due to the participants' need to reaffirm their own cultural values in the face of pressures from an alien culture. Such uses of theoretical concepts of anthropology, acquired as part of one's training in archaeology, are very common in interpreting archaeological materials.

In this discussion of the uses of operational definition, the following points have emerged. Operational definition, that is, specification of the meanings of terms by presenting publicly observable criteria for their application, has an important role in archaeology, as in other sciences. Such definitions do provide some fundamental link between language and the world scientists are trying to describe and explain. However, it is not possible to conduct the program of operational definition with anything like the thoroughness its original proponents envisaged. It is not possible to define many archaeologically important terms in this way, nor is it possible to perform reductions of the expressions in which these terms occur to expressions that contain only terms capable of operational definition. In particular, theoretical concepts, used to *explain* what is observed, are rarely reducible in this manner. Such explanatory terms do have empirical import, but they gain this through their role in theories, and other criteria are used for judging the success of theories. For these reasons, it would be unwise to demand complete operational definition of all terms as a first step in the construction of an archaeological theory.

## Systematics

Although Dunnell (1971), like Thomas, emphasizes the importance of definition for archaeological theory, his techniques and methods are strikingly different. Instead of focusing upon the operational definition of terms, Dunnell tries to provide a basic framework for a theory of archaeology (or the branch of archaeology he calls "prehistory") by using the technique of *intensional definition* to create cultural classifications for artifacts. He regards the creation of such classifications as a primary aim of inquiry in the discipline of prehistory (1971:194), and he repeatedly emphasizes its ideational or nonempirical character.

Intensional definitions specify verbally the property or properties that an object or event must have in order to be a member of a particular class. An intensional definition of a *blob*, for example, is "a small round drop or mass of a thick, viscuous substance or liquid." Dunnell points out the a priori character of such definitions; they are not based on observations, they are *proposals* to use words in a particular way. However, determining whether an actual object or event falls into a given class, a process Dunnell calls "identification," depends on observation and experiment. Such empirical work is necessary, for he insists that classifications are useless if there is no way to connect these creations of the mind with extramental reality. Dunnell also admits that choice of a particular classificatory scheme depends on which problems the classification is designed to solve. Nevertheless, he urges adoption of a single general model of a classificatory scheme ("a unitary system of unit construction including the assumptions on which it is founded and which satisfied the requirements of science (1971:186)."

Dunnell's admission of the importance of empirical criteria in determining the utility of a classification is coupled with his own stated intent to ignore the empirical aspect of the problem while concentrating on the development of an abstract classificatory scheme. He believes that trying to tie classifications too closely to particular empirical situations has hampered the development of both a consistent terminology and archaeological theory in general (1971:5). This view of how to solve problems of definition and classification seems radically opposed to operationalism. But, from a slightly different point of view, one might say that operational definition and Dunnell's method could be regarded as complementing one another, for they try to solve the same problem by attacking it in different ways. I believe, however, that Dunnell is mistaken in thinking that theory construction can be initiated by constructing a system of definitions. Moreover, his work can be faulted on grounds he himself regards as crucial: a lack of clarity in terminology.

Although his definitions are deliberately offered as aids to increase clarity and precision, they fail to do so. The defining expressions are neither clearer nor more precise than the vague terms they are introduced to define. Although the usage of earlier archaeologists' findings may have suffered from vagueness due to their failure to specify any meanings to their terms, such specification can relieve vagueness only when the *definiens* is more precise than the *definiendum*. A few examples should be sufficient to establish this claim. Consider Dunnell's starting point, a definition of prehistory as "the science of artifacts and relations between artifacts conducted in terms of culture." This, of course, demands further definitions of "artifacts" and "culture," which he provides. "Artifact" is *"anything* which exhibits any physical attribute that can be assumed to be the result of human activity," and "culture" is "a concept relating to shared ideas used as an explanatory device." "Science" is also defined: "a systematic study deriving from a logical system which results in the ordering of phenomena to which it is applied in such a manner as to make them ahistorical and capable of explanation." Although no explicit definition for "phenomena" is forthcoming, "things" are either ideational or phenomenological, and the latter term is defined as "anything which has objective existence," and is understood to apply to those things that we can observe. The term "attribute" occurs in the definition of "artifact" and is defined as "the smallest qualitatively distinct unit discriminated for a field of phenomena in a given investigation." Dunnell does provide a list of his definitions (Dunnell 1971:199–202).

One can acquire the flavor of the enterprise from this initial foray into Dunnell's set of definitions, and I believe that it is not too difficult to support the view that this type of exercise encourages rather than resolves terminological difficulties. My objection is not that Dunnell has failed to define *all* his terms, for verbal definition must stop somewhere, either at a set of undefined ("primitive") terms or with some technique, such as operational definition or even pointing, to connect words with the extralinguistic objects that are their intended referents. But one cannot but wonder at the obscurity involved in some of Dunnell's undefined expressions. For example, allowing "artifact" to apply to attributes that *can be assumed to be the results of human activity* only slightly restricts the application of this term, because there are few restraints on what persons may *assume.*

One can sympathize with Dunnell's desire to mark the distinction between the world of ideas and more substantial aspects of reality, but his definition of the phenomenological as that which has "objective existence" merely begs the question rather than answering it. Furthermore, an attempt to explicate objective existence in terms of what can be observed is unhelpful, for it raises questions about what it means for something to be observable. Do things that need microscopes or telescopes for their detection count as observables? What about things that can be detected only by electron microscopes? What about dispositional properties? Archaeologists may be annoyed with the philosophical fussiness of these questions, and say that there is no need to answer them because all of us already have a clear enough idea of what is observable and what is not. If one agrees with this, then it seems that the original definition of "phenomenological," and perhaps even the introduction of this rather fancy adjective, were exercises in creating jargon, and do nothing to make archaeology or its theory clearer and more precise.

Further examples of unclarity are evident in the expressions "deriving from a logical system" and "to make them (phenomena) ahistorical," which occur in the definition of "science." Dunnell rightly perceives that much of the language archaeologists must use in their work suffers from vagueness. He sees this vagueness not only as masking disagreements, but also as the *cause* of disagreement about important issues. However, the nature of the reform he suggests (i.e., explicit definition of key terms) is inadequate because his definitions are couched in terms no less vague than those they are intended to clarify.

There is, of course, another difficulty: Conceptual clarity about issues as complex as those Dunnell raises is not apt to come from mere reforms in terminology. Theoretical understanding is required, not just explicit intensional definition. No doubt Dunnell would agree in part with this claim, but he would insist that such classification is the first step in theory construction.

Certainly classification has a logically prior status. It is a truism to say that without classification there is no knowledge. Knowledge of individuals involves attributing some property or properties to the individual. This means assigning the individual to some class or classes (e.g., "This object is a scraper.") General knowledge involves claims about relations of some class or classes to other classes (e.g., "Hunter–gatherers are patrilocal.") In a very obvious and straightforward way, what we know about the world depends on how we classify things in the world. Without classification there would be no explanation, no saying *why* members of one class were also members of another. Nor would there be any prediction. Both of these aspects of scientific activity logically presuppose classificatory systems.

This logical priority of classificational schemes does not, however, mean that one should try to build a theory by *first* carefully defining the classes or types of things of interest, *then* organizing the phenomena by means of this classification, and *finally* establishing connections between classes for purposes of explanation and prediction. Such an account is as much a parody of theory construction as it is of scientific investigation. Dunnell recognizes that normal scientific activity, including forming explanations, is not executed in this way. He attributes explanation and the acquisition of all new knowledge to "guessing." But he insists that the method he outlines can "demonstrate the utility of the guess and precisely convey to others the content of the guess (Dunnell 1971:42)."

In this passage, Dunnell claims to be dealing not with the order of discovery, but rather that of justification, or logical reconstruction of a science. Accounts of this type are most often presented to students and fellow scientists, because a subject matter is easier to comprehend when organized in this way. What is omitted from accounts like this are all the false starts and dashed hopes, the tentative classifications that proved fruitless, and the generalizations that failed. All the student sees is what Kuhn (1962) calls "normal science," the "truth" insofar as it is then recognized.

But Dunnell's account of his own efforts is odd in two respects. In the first place, it is just as implausible to suppose that one could take a series of "guesses," impose a classificatory system on them, and create an acceptable theory of archaeology, as it is to suppose that one could start with a classification and then fill in with appropriate empirical information to get a theory. *Concept formation*, which includes definition and the construction of schemes of classification, and *theory formation* can only proceed in a highly interactive way. Because classification is itself a theoretic activity, it cannot simply precede theory construction. But neither can it serve as a "mopping up" operation that will raise implicit theory to an explicit level.

The second reason that this account sounds so strange is that it magnifies the importance of implicit theory in current archaeology in such a way as to suggest that archaeological knowledge is highly developed in a theoretical sense, and that the "implicit theory" needs only to be explicitly stated to be available for purposes of justification and communication.

An ambiguity in the concept of implicit theory may encourage this view of the matter. Principles may be called "theoretic" when they describe relations among theoretic entities, such as "culture" or "style." In interpreting and explaining archaeological phenomena, archaeologists frequently invoke such principles without delineating a "theory of culture" or similar theory for other concepts which are used. In this sense, there is a great deal of implicit theory in archaeology.

Cognitive psychologists have developed a useful distinction between *theories*, which consist of a reasonably explicit set of statements, and *schema* (or "frames" or "scripts" or "prototypes"), which are less explicit, less detailed cognitive structures or frameworks for organizing experiences (Nisbett and Ross 1980:28). Nisbett and Ross give as examples of such cognitive structures the knowledge underlying one's awareness of what happens in a restaurant, understanding an introvert, and what to expect when a car one purchases is a "lemon." These structures are of great importance in ordering and supplementing our perceptions of events and connections between them, and this is no less true in archaeological understanding than in everyday life. Schematic, rather than genuine theoretic, structures govern our knowledge of what happens when buildings burn, when trash heaps are formed, when dwellings are abandoned. All of these schemata and many others are used in archaeological interpretation. To a large degree, nonpropositional structures such as the scenarios brought to mind in connection with these events form the "implicit theory" of archaeology.

Now these conceptual structures clearly have *something* to do with a "theory of archaeology" in the sense of "a set of interrelated principles which can provide a rather high-level framework for explaining archaeological phenomena." But the implicit theory used in archaeological interpretation and explanation cannot be transformed into a fully developed theory of archaeology by the a priori activity of formulating intensional definitions of key terms. Development of an explicit theory requires both empirical understanding and intellectual insight far beyond that required for the construction of definitions.

Perhaps the best way to understand the process of theory development and its relation to implicit theoretical knowledge is to review some historical case studies of familiar classical theories, such as Newtonian theory of motion or the theory of evolutionary biology. An interesting, nontechnical account of the development of Newton's theory is presented in Chapter 11 of Holton (1973:140–167). The author points out Newton's skill as an experimenter, his knowledge of and reliance upon data collected by others, and his inheritance of many important theoretic concepts (such as force, acceleration, and gravity) from his predecessors. He also, of course, inherited such generalizations as Kepler's laws of planetary motion and Galileo's laws of terrestrial motion. Nevertheless, Newton's formulation of the laws of motion and the law of universal gravitation required the creative activity of a genius of the highest order. It was certainly not a case of extracting, through explicit intensional definition, the implicit theory already present in the works of his predecessors.

More to the point, Newton's theory does not even presuppose precise definitions of all of the theory's key terms. Let us look, for example, at the central concept of "force." It is true that Newton begins his *Principia* with a list of definitions (Newton 1953:12–13), however, this list does not include an explicit intensional definition of "force." Instead the definitions distinguish several types of forces: innate, impressed, and centripetal. Definition V is "A centripetal force is that by which bodies are drawn or impelled, or in any way tend toward a point as to a center." Following this definition, Newton provides examples of this type of force: gravity, magnetism, and "that force, whatever it is, by which the planets are continually drawn aside from the rectilinear motions, which otherwise they would pursue, and made to revolve in curvilinear orbits (Newton 1953:13)."

Newton did not simply regard "force" as a *primitive* term, one that needed no definition. Such an attitude towards terms in purely formal theories is a modern (nineteenth century) contribution. Newton believed that the meaning of "force" was unclear, because the exact nature and cause of this power were unknown. But he defended the use of the concept in spite of its lack of clarity by appealing to its success (in the context of his laws) in providing precise quantitative descriptions of the movements of bodies. See Westfall (1971:152–158) for a clear account of Newton's work in this area. Moreover, even today, there is no satisfactory intensional definition of "force" available. Although Newton's theory of mechanical motion is widely applied, most physicists would be reluctant to try to say just exactly what is meant by "force." The fact that scientists do not argue about the meaning of the term does not mean that there are not problems with its definition, rather that the progress of science does not depend on defining all the key terms in this way.

Giere (1979:66) offers an enlightening comment upon the puzzling point that good theories do not have to present precise definitions: "Indeed, it is almost a necessary (but not sufficient) condition for a theory to be really new and important that it introduce *new* concepts, which, just because they are genuinely *new*, cannot be defined solely in terms of familiar, well-understood concepts." The fact that Newton inherited terms such as "force" and "gravity" from others does not conflict with the "newness" to which Giere refers. With Newton, "force" acquires meanings not assigned to it by any earlier "mechanical philosophers" whose work influenced his own.

It is often said that physics provides a poor model if one is trying to understand social and behavioral sciences. In many ways this is true; however, in at least one respect it is true for the wrong reasons. The usual logical reconstructions of physics present a particularly misleading picture to one who is interested in how science develops. Great care must be taken by the reader not to confuse logical priority with temporal priority. No clues are given in these accounts as to what the actual temporal order was. Historical studies of the development of theories, in contrast, can offer a great deal of insight and encouragement to a social scientist interested in theory construction. There are no recipes, of course. However, one can gain an appreciation for (a) the interplay between empirical and intellectual components, (b) the value of relatively undirected experimentation and observation, and (c) the contributions to theory made by plodders as well as geniuses. Although such studies do not convey precisely how to build a theory, they do offer some defense against mistaken advice about how it is done.

Dunnell (1971) raises important questions about organization and clarification of terminology, and the provision of a proper theoretic framework for archaeology. But his answers, deliberately divorced from substantive issues and examples, in the name of theoretical purity, tend to be oversimplified and give a misleading account of how to develop a scientific theory.

I do not wish to denigrate efforts to develop improved systems of classification. This is an important part of theory building in archaeology. But real improvements in such systems seem not to come from the abstract empirically detached approach adopted by Dunnell. What seems to work in other sciences is acceptance of an available (though admittedly crude) system, and revising it in a piecemeal manner to handle problems as they arise. Revisions of this nature may have varying results, depending on the adequacy of the original system for the subject. Either the system will absorb the revisions as refinements and improvements, or eventually it will become so encrusted with ad hoc modifications that its systematic properties will be severely diminished or lost altogether. In the latter situation, there is a pressing need to "do something," but at this point purely a priori intensional definition is insufficient. Systematization can come only with a new theory.

## Formal Theories

Formalist approaches to theory building in archaeology share the goals of Dunnell's "systematics" approach: increased clarity and precision. In an article that summarizes contributions of the "new archaeologists," and indicates new areas for exploration, Read and LeBlanc (1978) suggest the use of formal theorizing to attack the problem of theory building in archaeology. In an appendix, Read offers a tentative and incomplete formalized theory of population size and area of habitation to demonstrate the utility of such an approach.

A formalized theory presents a set of assertions (the axioms or postulates) in some specified vocabulary (the primitive and defined terms). The theory itself simply consists of these assertions and all of their deductive consequences. These consequences (the theorems) are deduced from the axioms by means of generally agreed upon (but usually unspecified) principles of logic and set theory. Plane geometry, as it is presented in the modern high school curriculum, is a familiar example of a formalized theory. Contemporary presentations of geometry differ from traditional Euclidean geometry in the attempt of the latter to define *all* of the terms of the theory. It has long been recognized that Euclid's "definitions" of some of his basic terms, such as "point," are patently circular. Modern treatments take some terms as *primitive*. Other terms are defined with respect to certain logical relations among the primitives.

Theories of this type may have many interesting properties. Logicians, for example, are often concerned to determine whether or not a particular theory is *complete*. Completeness is attributed to a theory when, for any sentence that can be expressed in the vocabulary of the theory, either that sentence or its negation is a theorem. Logical investigations may not be concerned with any particular interpretation of a theory, but only in its abstract properties.

A theory is interpreted when the items of its nonlogical vocabulary are assigned denotations or referents in such a way that the axioms of the theory could all be true statements. Euclidean geometry, for example, is given a *physical interpretation* when "line" and "point" are assigned such referents as paths of light rays and intersections of light rays. *Abstract interpretations* are also possible—"point" may have as referents ordered pairs of numbers, as in analytic geometry. In the standard language of formalized theories, interpretations are called *models*. Any theory that has a model is said to be *consistent*.

The requirements for formalized theories are minimal. There are no restrictions on the nonlogical vocabulary that may be used in such theories. All consequences of the initial set of assertions (the axioms) must also be assertions of the theory, but this does not require that any derivations of theorems actually be constructed. It should be obvious that *any* subject matter could be formalized in this way. Thus, Read's claim that "axiomatized theories can be constructed for anthropological data (1978:317)" is trivially true.†

The only interesting question is whether or not such theories are useful in archaeology. To answer the question, it is important to note the difference between the *minimal* requirements for a formalized theory and the far more significant requirements for an interesting scientific theory. A theory in the latter sense is a set of rather high-level interrelated laws that are used *to explain* some class of phenomena. Theories in the former sense, though they may be framed in any language, and may be interpreted to apply to a wide range of phenomena, need not explain *anything*.

A theory of archaeology is interesting only if it can explain archae-

---

†Strictly speaking, not every subject matter can be "axiomatized" in the sense of being expressed in a finitely axiomatizable theory. But Read and LaBlanc are using "axiomatized" simply to refer to any formal theory.

ological data. If an account merely brings together and highlights various features of the data, it can hardly be called a theory in the interesting sense of that term. Even if such accounts allow reliable predictions, they may not be explanatory theories. Explanatory theories perform syntheses, and frequently allow predictions, but they must do more than this. The *tide tables*, on which navigators depended before Newton's time, were highly accurate syntheses of data, expressed in precise mathematical terms. They also served as "theories" that are characterized as "a means by which factors affecting those patterns may be brought into focus (Read and LeBlanc 1978:317)," for they connected tidal patterns with phases of the moon. But the tide tables did not constitute a scientifically adequate theory of tidal motion. There was no adequate theory until Newton *explained* the main features of the tides through application of the law of universal gravitation (Holton 1973:154).

As noted already, formalized theories may be studied without regard to the particular content of their theorems. Logicians, for example, may try to construct proofs of completeness or consistency for formal theories without regard to intended interpretations, if any. But when a theory is constructed to formalize some empirical subject matter, such as archaeology, the situation is different.

Usually when a formal theory is constructed with an intended interpretation in mind, the assertions one expects to be forthcoming as theorems are reasonably well recognized. That is, there is usually already a well-developed stock of claims (an informal theory) that is to be subjected to formalization. Such was almost certainly the case with geometry before Euclid (Mates 1972:185), and was clearly the case with Reichenbach's *The Axiomatization of the Theory of Relativity* (1969). In devising formalizations of this type, one is interested in selecting a minimal set of assertions from which all other assertions that are already accepted can be derived. If it happens that additional "new" theorems can be generated by deriving them from the axioms, one is interested in checking them against the facts. If a theory of this type could not be used in this way, then its construction would be pointless exercise.

Of course, Read cannot be engaged in this form of enterprise, for he has not selected some informal substantive theory and tried to formalize it. Read claims to be using the axiomatic method *to construct a substantive theory*. The success of such an approach would be unprecedented. In his criticism of Read, Morgan points out that "no scientific theory has ever been constructed by first setting up an arbitrary uninterpreted calculus and then trying to find some empirical applications for it (Morgan 1978:326)."

However, on examination, Read's comments to the contrary notwithstanding, it seems that Read is not really engaged in what would normally be called the construction of an axiomatic theory. After he presents the vocabulary and the axioms, he does not follow the usual procedure of deriving some important theorems of the system. Rather, he turns to the construction of several alternative *mathematical models* and examines their "fit" with some archaeological data. The stated axioms, instead of being used as a basis for the derivation of theorems, play the role of explicit assumptions that are common to the alternative models, and the definitions are used to impose different and varying restrictions on the models that are constructed. Mathematical modeling of this type is not exactly new to archaeology. What is new is the description of it as construction of formalized axiomatic theories. I believe that this blurs some important distinctions among mathematical models, formal theories, and substantive theories of science.

## Mathematical Modeling

Mathematical models can be quite useful, but the standards for judging their success are not the same as those for judging substantive theories of empirical science (formalized or not). Mathematical models, for example, would be considered valuable if they did no more than synthesize and describe data in an elegant way. If they have predictive capabilities (as did the tide tables), so much the better. But as we have already seen in connection with the discussion of the tide tables, more— namely explanatory power—is required of *theories.*

There is a great deal of flexibility in the use of such terms as "theory" and "model." Thus, it would unreasonable to be overly critical of Read's use of terms if terminology were the only issue. However, I do not mean to criticize just Read's use of the expression "formal theory" to characterize his example. He says enough about what he is doing to lead readers to believe he is urging formal theory construction in the sense of a *formal axiomatic theory* of the type described earlier. This is also the type of theory that Morgan understood Read as presenting, and that he criticized. However, the ambiguities in "formal theory" may have misled Read and LeBlanc. Constructing mathematical models involves the use of formal methods, and it is certainly "theoretical," as opposed to empirical data-gathering work. However, this does not make every mathematical model a "formal theory" in the sense discussed.

Wartofsky (1979) developed a set of useful distinctions among theories, various models, and simple ad hoc analogies. His hierarchical arrangement is based on the strength of ontological commitment involved in the acceptance of each type. That is, rather than distinguishing analogies, models, and theories in terms of the degree of formalization involved, Wartofsky considers whether their acceptance commits one to accepting certain descriptions of the data, regularities in the data, regularities in the data as representative of law-like aspects of the world, or certain (theoretic) properties that explain these regularities. For example, some models merely summarize (some aspects) of the data, and involve no commitment beyond that to the data themselves. Yellen's map of foraging trips made by !Kung San around base camps, reproduced in Binford (1980:8), is such a model.

Most mathematical models in the social sciences—including Read's models—go beyond this simple descriptive type. They attempt to exhibit regularities or law-like properties *of the data*. These models make at least a tentative claim about the systematic nature of the data. But, as Wartofsky points out (1979:30), there is a limited commitment here, for the regularities are claimed to hold for the entities of the model itself, not for the things in the world which are "represented" in the model. Read is clearly operating under this sort of limitation when he warns that *"camp, village,* and *city* are understood to have only the meanings assigned to them (by the definitions of his "theory") and not their full range of common-usage meanings (1978:314)."

Thus, the regular connections between "area" and "population" in Read's models, hold—even tentatively—only for camps as defined in terms of non-overlapping subsets of subsets of disk-like subsets of a two-dimensional Euclidean plane. How well these entities of the model correspond with real-world camps, areas, and populations is a further question that is not answered by the model itself, but by other considerations. Archaeologists must decide if the spatial areas that are of archaeological interest are similar enough in relevant respects to the model's abstract mathematical entities for the model to be a useful representation of real camps.

Read's models, like most mathematical models, serve as computational devices. Because the entities of the model are sets and numbers, the normal operations of set theory, arithmetic, and other areas of mathematics are applicable to these entities. This means that new statements about the models may be generated merely by performing appropriate calculations, restricted only by limits imposed in the definitions and axioms. The new statements (predictions) may help in judging the adequacy of the model for representing archaeological phenomena, for if there is correspondence or "fit" between the predictions and the statements known to be true of archaeological data, there is some reason to believe that the model has captured relevant structural features of the archaeological data.

A further stage of commitment that Wartofsky describes is that of going beyond statements about entities of the model to making either tentative or absolute cognitive claims about some aspects of the real world. In these cases, there is a substantive scientific theory, put forth either formally or informally, tentatively or with confidence. Such claims fall into the category we have been describing as "theories," whereas many mathematical models do not.

The distinction at this level between two important philosophical views about theories becomes important. Realists, on the one hand, hold that theories make statements that commit those who accept them to the *existence* of certain theoretical entities (electrons, cultures, phases, etc.) and relations between these entities. Instrumentalists, on the other hand, regard even fully accepted theories, such as Newton's theory of particle motion or the atomic theory of nature of matter, as no more than elaborate means for organizing and testing our knowledge. From a strict instrumentalist viewpoint, the distinction between computational devices and genuine explanatory theories breaks down, for the best theories are just the best developed and most comprehensive computational devices. Because scientific realism is implicitly but firmly accepted by all archaeologists whose work is known to me, I shall accept the realist thesis, and will not discuss arguments for instrumentalism here.† But see van Fraassen (1980) for a sophisticated defense of the antirealist position.

The distinction between the levels of commitment (within a realist framework) to mere computational models and to broader theoretic claims can be seen clearly in a study by Hamblin and Pitcher (1980). In their defense of the view that the collapse of the Classic Maya civilization was the result of a long-term class struggle between peasants and the elite, the authors introduce and make important use of several mathematical models. However, they also present substantive theoretic claims, and moreover, they are careful to distinguish between the two types of enterprise.

Their mathematical models, in the form of differential equations,

---

†In her discussion of the debates (exemplified in the Spaulding–Ford controversy) about the basis "in reality" for typologies devised by archaeologists, Wylie (1981) characterizes the opposing views as "conventionalist" and "empiricist." But even the conventionalists, who hold that types are theoretical constructs whose utility can "only be evaluated in terms of standards of plausibility (1981:58)," because the facts are too enigmatic to support them, are *realists* in the sense that they do not deny the very existence of cultural traits. Their quarrel, it seems to me, is an *epistemological* one, based on the alleged inability of archaeologists to obtain evidence for their classifications, rather than an *ontological* one, which would question whether or not such things as cultural traits exist at all. Thus, conventionalists are not antirealists in the sense in which I have been using this term.

were tested in the course of an extensive study of contemporary and historical conflicts of a violent and protracted nature (Hamblin *et al.* 1977). The authors claim their models provide reasonably accurate descriptions of observed regularities, such as changes over time in the escalation of conflicts. But it is important to note, as do the authors, that these equations are *descriptive*. In and of themselves, they have no explanatory status, and thus cannot constitute a theory. They merely call attention to certain regularities in the observed phenomena; it is these regularities that require explanation.

The regularities described in the equations could have been characterized in ordinary, nonmathematical language. The fact that they are described mathematically imparts an attractive degree of clarity and precision to the models. This, in turn, makes questions of the applicability or "fit" of the models to other data somewhat easier to answer. Aside from elegance of expression, this is one of the chief values of mathematical models, for computation is often considered easier, more reliable, and more convincing than elaborate verbal argumentation. But it is important to remember that a description cannot be transformed into an explanation merely by translating it into the language of mathematics.

To *explain* the observed patterns that the equations describe, the authors invoke causal processes of various sorts. Their theory states that extended social conflicts, once begun, follow definite and predictable courses as a result of the operation and interaction of a number of causal processes. For example, *collective learning* in conflict situations is the causal factor used to account for the fact that, over a period of time, the relative increment of successes in trials of certain conflict strategies is a constant proportion of the relative increment of attempts. The form of equation that describes this aspect of the data is one that is characteristic for learning situations. This *learning curve*, in which the probability of success in responding to a trial of some type improves as a monotonic function of practice, was first recognized by psychologists in connection with animal learning behavior. It has since been shown to be applicable to many other learning situations, including those involving collective or social learning in humans (Pitcher and Hamblin 1980).

Collective learning is just one aspect of the theory of the progress of social conflict that the authors employ in their explanation. (The theory is designed to account only for the *progress* of conflict, not for its initiation.) Long-term conflicts, according to the theory are characterized also by escalation in aggressive behavior, and by waxing and waning movement towards a resolution. These features, each represented by a characteristic form of equation, are (like the learning curve) explained by causal processes that reinforce and interact with one another. Thus, the theory of conflict, leaving considerations of its correctness aside, fits our characterization of a set of interrelated principles that can provide an explanatory framework for a broad range of phenomena.

The causal claims that are the basis of the theory do more than provide explanations for the data under study. They also play an important role in considering how mathematical models may apply to data other than those used to generate the equations. That is, the causal factors determine those aspects of new data that are relevant candidates for testing the "fit" of the data with the models. We would be at a complete loss if given only a set of equations, then asked how well they fit with available information on the Maya. When told that an equation is characteristic of a collective learning process, we can ask what in the Mayan complex would be an archaeologically recognizable instance of collective learning in a conflict situation.

Answers to questions such as this are not trivial. Deep knowledge of the archaeological materials as well as a good deal of imagination may be involved in constructing an appropriate archaeological hypothesis and selecting data to test it. Nevertheless, the theory's causal claims guide selection of some of the data as relevant to the issue at hand, and eliminate other as irrelevant.

Hamblin and Pitcher chose to look at data concerning dated monuments at Mayan ceremonial centers in order to test the collective learning component of the hypothesis that the Mayan collapse was due to prolonged class conflict:

> The appearance of a monument complex at a ceremonial center was assumed to mark an attempt by the Classic elite to establish dynastic rule, and the production of monuments for longer than a hotun was assumed to be indicative of a success. The prediction (based on the model) was that the accumulated successes would increase approximately as a power function of the accumulated attempts (1980:258).

Some of the available archaeological data on the Maya support claims about the dates of appearance and also the dates of destruction or abandonment of these monuments. Information about the duration of monument complexes, drawn from these data, can be interpreted as indicating a process of collective learning with respect to some strategic maneuver in a class struggle: learning to establish a dynastic rule from the elite point of view, or learning to overthrow one from the other side. With this interpretation in mind, the authors examined patterns in these data to test for the presence of the collective learning curve that is characteristic of long-term conflicts. Good fit was obtained in this case, as it was for the other characteristic equations of escalation and waxing–waning progress towards resolution.

It should be clear that something deeper than the use of computational models is occurring here. The ontological commitment involved in holding that the progress of conflict is characterized by perceptual processes that give rise to escalation, collective learning, and other social processes, clearly goes beyond the acceptance of mathematical equations that allow the prediction of results in data. The use of the theory in connection with the study of Mayan society is more than an attempt to predict patterns in the archaeological data. It is an attempt to explain the presence of these patterns by showing that the collapse of the Classic society was an instance of the peasants' ultimate victory in a prolonged and bitter class struggle.

## Constructing Theories by Borrowing

The theory of the progress of social conflict, briefly and incompletely described above, was developed by sociologists. They, in applying their theory to an archaeological case, must be classified as lenders rather than borrowers. However, elements of their theory were borrowed from theories of perception and learning that originated in experimental psychology. Given the imprecise and blurred boundaries that separate the various social sciences, it would be surprising if theories which were developed in one discipline were never applicable to problems encountered in another. Borrowers—and lenders—must proceed with caution, of course. Theories of animal behavior cannot be transferred automatically to humans; theories of individual behavior may not be applicable to group behavior; theories developed to account for phenomena occurring within brief time periods may not work with long-term situations; thought processes of industrial-age *Homo sapiens* may not be taken as representative of hominids of the Paleolithic period. Such difficulties are too familiar to need rehearsal here (see Schiffer 1981).

Another problem for would-be borrowers is the widely admitted scarcity of strongly supported general theories in the social sciences (Schiffer 1975:836). The theory of conflict described above, for example, is quite new. Its support is impressive, though limited. As even its adherents admit, it is not without problems. For this reason, its acceptance and use by archaeologists must be tentative. However, it seems that any theory that is even reasonably well supported, does not seriously conflict with established archaeological principles, and addresses so directly an aspect of a problem that is of general interest to archaeologist (i.e., regularities in conflict-induced changes in societies), is worth examining for its possibilities.

Borrowing theories from another discipline does not imply passive reception of the ideas of others with no contribution of one's own. Aside from reformulating claims of the theory so that they are applicable to archaeological data, an important contribution can be made by testing such theories in new contexts. With respect to the theory mentioned, if one could look at an archaeologically attested case of a long-term conflict (i.e., one in which were present all the well-recognized qualitative indicators of such conflict) and could find the quantitative patterns predicted by the theory, this would constitute important support for the theory. Alternatively, in a case where qualitative evidence for long-term conflict was good and archaeological data were sufficiently rich to produce the quantitative patterns, absence of the patterns would undermine the theory.

## General Assumptions, Common-Sense Hypotheses, Induction, and Theories

Among contemporary American archaeologists, Binford has been outspoken in expressing his deep concern with the need for attention to problems of theory construction. His recent publications dealing with the subject are voluminous, and represent his acquisition of massive amounts of new data as well as his changing and developing views on theoretical matters (1972, 1977, 1978, 1980, 1981). His work is not easy to understand, for the issues are themselves complex, and his treatment of them does nothing to alleviate this. There has been, to the distress of his commentators, little effort on his part to go back to his earlier works and to try to integrate these with his recent pronouncements on archaeological theory building. No attempt will be made here to unravel and sort out the various strands of his thought. One rather accessible and self-contained article (1980) will be focused on and treated as an example of archaeological theorizing, rather than as an accurate summary of Binford's views. Because this piece of work embodies several important aspects of archaeological theorizing, it can be used as a convenient framework for discussing ways to deal with these problems.

In this study, Binford's overall concern is one whose importance is recognized by most archaeologists: that of understanding the behavior of people who depend upon hunting and gathering for their subsistence. Because so many prehistoric peoples, known only archaeologically, were hunter–gatherers, Binford believes that such understanding is prerequisite to interpreting many aspects of the archaeological record. His specific goal in this study is to relate different ways of constructing a hunter–gatherer subsistence strategy to variety in environmental constraints. He concludes, on the basis of this study, that the length of the growing season is the crucial factor in determining various forms of adaptation, and that this relationship has important consequences for interpreting patterns of archaeological remains. The correctness of his substantive views will not be discussed here, but rather the development of the theoretical apparatus used to present and defend them.

Some theoretically important claims that mark Binford's study are the following:

1. There are two distinct ways of working out a hunter–gatherer subsistence pattern: (a) foraging, and (b) collecting. Foraging is the pattern adopted when crucial resources are arranged at approximately equal distances from a base camp. People can then disperse frequently to retrieve them. When resources are exhausted, the entire group moves to a new base camp, and the pattern is repeated. Collecting is the strategy adopted when some crucial resources lie at a considerable distance from others. The base camp may be located near some resources, but special task forces must be sent off to collect the others. In general, the first strategy involves more frequent residential moves, whereas the second requires a different ("logistic") type of mobility to collect scattered resources and bring them back to camp.

2. These strategies may be combined in varying degrees, resulting in a range of settlement patterns.

3. The varying patterns of mobility represented by these strategies result in distinctive patterns of material remains which may be recognized archaeologically. Binford uses the term "grain" to refer to the complexity of archaeological assemblages. The finest grained are those that would normally be produced by a single activity performed over a relatively brief temporal period, such as butchering at a site occupied for two days. Coarse-grained assemblages result from a variety of activities performed over a long period.

4. "(W)e cannot hope to understand the causes of these remains through a formal comparative study of the remains themselves."

5. The best way of achieving understanding is "through direct exposure to dynamics—the ethnoarchaeological study of living systems."

6. The ultimate causes for variation in settlement subsistence strategies lie in environmental factors (Binford 1980:4–19).

Obviously some of these claims are more closely tied to empirical observations than others. The first two mentioned make classificatory claims that impose divisions upon observable phenomena. The classifications are theoretically determined, however, for one could have focused on a host of other observable differences rather than those mentioned, and devised other classificatory schemes that would have been equally well grounded empirically. The *theory* that relates settlement–subsistence patterns to environmental factors makes these particular observable differences important.

The other, latter claims are less closely tied to data. No ethnographical or archaeological observations would compel us to accept them in favor of alternative hypotheses that might also account for the data. Very roughly, one might say that the six claims listed were arranged in ascending theoretical order. I shall concentrate my discussion of the nature of the claims and their justifications on the latter, more theoretical ones.

Binford's location of ultimate causes of various subsistence– settlement patterns in environmental factors relies on the *assumption* (acknowledged as such) that the complex of activities involved in human food acquisition and forms of settlement constitute an adaptive system (1980:4). This assumption obviously has implications which go far beyond the interpretation of archaeological remains. And it should also be obvious that such an assumption could not be conclusively supported on the basis of archaeological evidence alone. This assumption, or belief, is a component of the ecological view of the world, that assumes humans in a given area belong to an interacting complex of living and nonliving things (an ecosystem), and that their behavior is best understood as a series of processes involving exchanges of matter and energy within that system. This theoretical stance thus makes some very general claims about the nature and place of human societies and the activities of members of those societies. It provides a *framework* for many lower-level accounts of patterns of human behavior, although its vagueness prevents it from having much explanatory value of its own. One cannot—at this stage at least—*derive* lower level empirical laws from the theory in the manner in which, for example, laws regarding the free fall of bodies near the earth can be derived from Newton's laws of motion and universal gravitation. Some alternative theories of ultimate causes of variation or similarity in human behavior, at roughly the same level of vagueness and generality, are normative theories of culture, which hold that cultural traits are spread by diffusion, or that the ideational entities that constitute human culture follow patterns of internal historical development.

In this particular article, Binford does not offer any argument for adopting the ecosystem theoretic framework for explanations. There is nothing wrong with this, for one would not expect a defense of the general theoretical framework in every piece of work done within that framework. Nevertheless, the question of justification is an important theoretical issue and must be challenged.

Ecosystems theory may be considered as a general principle that makes some substantive claim about the ultimate causes of human behavior. The content of this claim is falsifiable, at least in principle, for it is certainly conceivable that such variations may not be causally linked to environmental influences Because of the lack of specific content, however, there would be considerable difficulty in actually producing a falsifying instance. When confronted with a potential falsifier, one might always claim that an analysis of some other new environmental factors might yield the appropriate causal source.

The other aspect of ecosystems theory is its status as a research program. In its dual aspects, ecosystems theory resembles the theory of determinism, which makes the substantive claim that everything that happens occurs as a result of deterministic causes, and has associated with it a research strategy that advises seeking deterministic causes for every event. In our earlier discussion of methodological determinism, we saw that it is consistent to adopt this research strategy, even if the substantive claim of determinism should turn out to be false. A similar case can be made for ecosystems theory. To adopt this approach as a research strategy is to accept the view that it always makes sense to look to the environment for ultimate causes of human behavior.

There are few archaeologists' arguments that *defend* ecosystems as a correct substantive theory, although certainly many archaeologists do not doubt that it is so. Willey and Sabloff, for example, make no effort to demonstrate that environmental considerations actually overide ideational cultural influences where human behavior is concerned. Instead they argue, "By adopting the ecosystems model into his research, the American archaeologist provides a framework for his investigations with clearly defined boundaries, unifies his models with those of other scientists, and permits the quantification of his material (1980:192)." Schiffer (1981) and Hardesty (1980) are far more cautious about the benefits of "the ecosystems model." Hardesty emphasizes the variety of competing and contradictory ecological principles, and urges using archaeological data in an *interactive* way to try to develop a substantive theory. But other writers offer eliminative arguments in support of ecosystems, for example, citing the failure of diffusionist principles as explanatory devices (Harris 1968:176). Binford himself in an earlier work uses an eliminative argument as well: "The normative view (as opposed to the view that culture is adaptation to environment) leaves the archaeologist in the position of considering himself a culture historian and/or a paleopsychologist (for which most archaeologists are poorly trained) (1972:198)."

Although Binford does not here defend the ecosystems approach, he does admit that he assumes its correctness, and cites an ecosystems principle upon which his investigations depend: "(T)echnology, in both its 'tools' sense as well as the labor sense is invented and reorganized by men to solve certain problems presented by the energy–entropy (sic) structure of the environment in which they seek to gain a livelihood (1980:13)." Binford, quite reasonably, regards foraging and collecting as differing technologies, and therefore sees them as responses to different environmental challenges. He *assumes* the correctness of an approach that places ultimate causes in environmental features; he sees his job as that of determining *which* particular environmental features are causally operative in the selection of some particular variation of a foraging/collecting strategy.

Binford believes that the ecosystems approach supports a *methodological* position: to discover the particular causes of variation in human hunter–gathering behavior, investigate a variety of environments along with their accompanying settlement–subsistence strategies. If this method proves successful, thus achieving an understanding of the causes, he will have contributed to what Binford calls "general theory (1977:6–7)." The "general theory" to which he refers is devoted to explanation of causes of human behavior, with no special reference to archaeological problems concerning the relations between that behavior and its material remains. The theory that accounts for the latter, and provides the basis for archaeological interpretation, Binford calls "middle-range theory."

The term "middle-range theory" has caused some confusion, because Goodyear and others (1978) have used it in a way different from Binford (Downum 1980). These writers, following Merton (1968), use "middle-range theory" to refer to generalizations that are capable of fairly direct empirical testing. These empirical generalizations may be incorporated into a higher-level theory, one whose concepts may not have such close ties to empirically observable phenomena. Presumably, the statement "All copper conducts electricity" belongs to middle-range physical theory. This contrasts with statements of electromagnetic theory, which refer to such theoretic entities as ions and electrons, and explain the middle-range generalizations.

Ethnographic–environmental studies, so important to the development of "general theory," are also (when conducted with an eye to material remains) the best method, Binford believes, for acquiring the knowledge required to interpret the archaeological record. Just as ethnography is the road to general theory, ethnoarchaeology is the path to middle-range theory. Because the construction of both levels of theory depends on ethnographic research, it seems clear that the two can be conducted simultaneously. Certainly both aspects of theory building concern Binford in this study. He tries to establish a relation between the "grain" of archaeological assemblages and the various mobility patterns demanded by differences in subsistence technology (a middle-range problem), and he also wants to solve the general theoretic problem of which environmental factors are responsible for the various combinations of foraging–collecting strategies.

As mentioned earlier, his approach to general theory through ethnographic studies in differing environmental situations is supported by the belief that environmental constraints are the ultimate causes of human behavior. However, Binford offers a different sort of defense for the use of ethnoarchaeological methods for solving middle-range problems. He presents an argument by elimination, accepting "direct exposure to dynamics" as the best way to understand the causes of material remains, on the basis of the inadequacy of the method of formal comparative studies of those remains for this task. An eliminative argument of this sort depends on two premises. One holds that the methods mentioned exhaust the possibilities, or at least exhaust the spectrum of reasonable research alternatives at a given time. That may be the situation in this case, though no supportive evidence is presented.

The second premise involves the rejection of one of the two methods. Binford presents an analogical argument in support of this premise. He compares the study of archaeological remains with the study by medical science of the symptoms of diseases. He suggests that just as it would not be reasonable to expect medical science to determine the causes of diseases from a comparative study of their symptoms, so it is not reasonable to expect archaeologists to understand the cultural dynamics that give rise to the archaeological record from the comparative investigations of those records.

This analogical argument is not very convincing, for in many cases it seems that a great deal of our knowledge of causes depends upon comparative studies of effects. From similarities in effects, the knowledge of which is acquired through comparative studies, we may infer, with reasonable reliability in many circumstances, the operation of similar causes. This is a principle used widely in medical studies. When Semmelweis, who worked in Vienna in the mid-nineteenth century, prior to the development of the germ theory of disease, tried to find the cause of puerperal fever, he made a careful study of "dynamics." That is, he examined a wide variety of antecedent conditions to which expectant mothers were subjected in the notorious First Division of the Vienna General Hospital, where the disease was so prevalent. These investigations proved fruitless, however. Only when one of his colleagues incurred *similar symptoms* and died after receiving a scalpel wound during an autopsy did a breakthrough occur. A comparative study of the likeness of symptoms was the crucial factor in Semmelweis's coming to recognize that something in "cadaveric matter" was the cause of the disease (Burks 1977:24).

Comparative studies that demonstrate the *lack* of similarity in effects are used to infer, again with reasonable reliability, the operation of different causes. This principle is also widely employed, not only in medicine, but in many other "diagnostic" sciences. Biblical scholars, for example, use this principle when they infer on the basis of comparative studies of linguistic styles that a particular book was composed by several authors rather than just one.

These principles of inferring like or different causes from the comparative studies of effects are admittedly vague and general, and they are not adequate to pin down the precise nature of a causal process. In order to achieve this goal, these principles must be supplemented with some reliable *theory* in the area in which they are applied. Semmelweis made an inspired—and correct—guess about the relation between something in "cadaveric matter" and infection with puerperal fever. But his insight did not command the immediate acceptance of his colleagues because it did not fit well with any then-current theory of disease. He had significant success in lowering the death rate when he insisted that medical students use a chlorinated lime handwashing solution after performing autopsies and prior to the examination of obstetric patients. But these and his other experimental successes were discounted or explained away, and his ideas were ridiculed by those in power (Céline 1952).

Besides demonstrating the importance of comparative studies, the puerperal fever case can be used to support the point that without a theory, observation of dynamics is not particularly helpful. Without some glimpse of the theory, one simply does not know what aspect of the dynamics is relevant to production of the effect. Long before his grasp of the connection between the two factors, Semmelweis knew that medical students were going directly from autopsies to the examination of obstetrical patients. But he had no reason to consider this relevant until his colleague died with all the symptoms of "childbed fever." He then began to formulate the theory that something in cadavers, too small to be seen, but whose presence could be detected by smell, was carried on the hands of the medical students, and was the causal agent in the production of the disease.

The situation with puerperal fever contrasts sharply with that of "Legionnaire's disease" several years ago. Although the medical profession was at first baffled as to the exact source of the disease, it did not take long to solve the problem. The general background theory of disease available at the time enabled researchers to use the detailed formal comparative knowledge of symptoms, first to determine the type of cause, and then to isolate the guilty bacterium. In the case of "Legionnaire's disease," observation of dynamics as well as comparative studies weighed heavily, but here, because of the available theory, researchers could focus on a limited number of possible causes among the antecedent circumstances.

In view of the foregoing considerations, one must regard the rejection of formal comparative methods as not well supported by Binford's argument. His analogy with respect to medical science tends to bolster rather than to undermine the importance of comparative studies. Because there is no reason to reject comparative studies as a possible route to causal knowledge, Binford's argument by elimination in support of ethnoarchaeology fails.

Fortunately, better arguments for the importance of ethnoarchaeology are available. Ethnoarchaeological studies involve novel, interesting, and important attempts to unite causes and effects. Theories are usually developed in a very unsystematic manner. Scientists employ a variety of "methods," approaches, and techniques. Comparative studies, observations of "dynamics," extrapolation from other theories in related areas, pursuit of hunches—these and a host of other means not easily fitted within any rigorous "logic of discovery" are used. Precise methods for discovering causes are unavailable. In trying to understand the cultural and noncultural processes that produce deposits of material remains, we depend on theories propounded outside of archaeology, and upon general conceptual schemes or scenarios. Nontheoretic knowledge is exemplified in our understanding of what happens when someone loses an item that is still useful; someone else may find the item, use it for some slightly different purpose, and then lose it in a crevass where it remains undisturbed until an archaeologist uncovers it (Schiffer 1976). Gifford and Behrensmeyer (1977) employed both schematic and theoretic knowledge in their discussion of a site they had observed under occupation for four days by a hunting party. The site was abandoned, and shortly thereafter was buried in a series of floods. Finally it was excavated, with special attention paid to materials that typically interest archaeologists in cases where the processes of site formation have not been observed. Such experiments, combined with knowledge of physical theories of sedimentation, erosion, and the like, can be used to transform rather vague scenarios into genuine archaeological theory. With such work, archaeologists can support causal claims about how and why archaeologically interesting materials come to be as they are and where they are. One need not undermine the value of comparative studies to appreciate the value of ethnoarchaeology.

Additional support for the value of ethnoarchaeology comes from Binford's acceptance of the ecosystems approach to understanding human behavior. Just as ecosystems attaches special importance to ethnographic studies for the development of "general theory," so also does it support ethnoarchaeology as a method for the construction of "middle-range theory." Ethnoarchaeology can tell us something about the behaviors and other processes responsible for the production of various types of archaeological remains in a variety of environments. If the ecosystems approach is correct, then this knowledge can be combined with observation of similar site structures and similar environments to reconstruct behaviors that are unobservable. Using ethnoarchaeological evidence, similar behaviors could be inferred on the basis of observed similar causes (environments) *and* observed similar effects (patterns of archaeological remains). Ethnoarchaeological studies would thus provide the missing link—behavior—between environmental factors and archaeological residues.

As a result of his investigations, Binford claims in this article (1980) to have established several correlations in the areas of both general and middle-range theory. For example, he claims to have shown a correlation between greater seasonal variability in temperatures and heavier dependence on collecting strategies. This, in turn, is said to be correlated with the presence of greater numbers of fine-grained assemblages. He also claims support for a correlation between lower effective temperatures and increased dependence upon storage facilities. Archaeologists are better equipped than I to assess his support for these correlations. (I found, regretfully, some of his attempts at curve-fitting very unconvincing (p. 16)). In any case, Binford acknowledges the tentativeness of his conclusions and the need to look for other causally important factors.

Binford's position with respect to his adopted theoretical approach restricts the search for causal explanations to environmental factors. Binford assumes this is correct, and then tries, using empirical data, to isolate causes of the appropriate sort. Binford's approach to theory building in archaeology thus involves amalgamating archaeology with ecosystems theory. However, the degree of "borrowing" in his case is far less substantial than in the case earlier cited in which a well-defined theory of social conflict was applied to Mayan case studies. Binford borrows only the general outlook of ecosystems. Consider the specific ecosystem principles Binford claims to use:

1. "Technology . . . is invented to solve problems presented by the . . . structure of the environment (1980:14),"

2. The "law of requisite variety" that "for maximum stability, the variety of homeostatic responses required in any system is equal to the environmental challenges offered to it (1980:15).

These principles have so little empirical content that it is difficult to conceive either what evidence could falsify them or how they could guide research in any detailed way. To a large degree, the vagueness of these principles, and others proposed by ecosystems theorists, is inextricably bound up with the vagueness of such terms as "system" and "environment."

Binford would probably reject this analysis of the situation, for he does at times speak as if he is deriving substantive empirical claims from these empty principles. For example, he claims to use the "law of requisite variety" to establish that the more unstable the thermal environment, the greater the number of critical resources for human societies (1980:15). This latter claim certainly has empirical content, but it does not follow from the cited "law" alone. The law says simply, and almost tautologically, that if systems are to remain stable they require compensatory (homeostatic) devices to offset unstabilizing influences. Even if we assume that the ecosystem, whose boundaries are surely vague, in a particular area is a system that is *stable*, or is "trying" to maintain stability (and this is a large assumption), there seems to be no particular reason to assume that *the* homeostatic device that compensates for thermal instability is the number of critical resources. No evidence at all is presented to show this is the case.

The concept of "critical resource" is itself distractingly vague. Humans need food, water, and some form of shelter to survive, so we expect to find critical resources belonging to these categories. However, ethnographic studies show that collecting parties often go in search of some exotic foodstuff when nutritional demands could be met by more easily available foods. Does the exotic stuff count as a critical resource? Considerable effort is expended in many aboriginal societies in the collection of a favored lithic material, or to acquire ochre used primarily for ceremonial purposes. Do these count as critical resources? They do seem to be regarded as such by the societies that use them, at least if we are able to judge such things by the energy expended to attain them. Yet it is hard to see how the numbers of such resources can be correlated with thermal instabilities in the way that Binford's alleged derivation from the "law of requisite variety" suggests.

In an intuitive approach to the matter, it makes sense to hold that when humans live in environments with sharp seasonal changes, they will depend upon some resources at one season and others at different season, because foodstuffs are not all equally available in the various seasons, and summer's shelters may not be adequate to winter's rigors. It is also a common-sense consideration that as the number and variety of required foods and other goods increases, the less likely it will be that they will all be concentrated in a small area. It is these common-sense principles, rather than any derivation from a "law of requisite variety," that support Binford's plausible claim that "the greater the seasonal variability in temperature, the greater the expected role of logistical mobility in the settlement or positioning strategy (1980:15)."

Insofar as Binford is able to establish specific causal links between environmental factors and human behavior, he supports the ecosystems approach by supplementing its vague and loose claim about appropriate *sorts* of causes with justified claims of actual instances of environmental causality. Even if the central claim of ecosystems about the ultimate causes of human behavior should prove incorrect, these specific claims of environmental causality may still survive and be incorporated within a more adequate account of human behavior. Although Binford's studies may be guided heuristically by the ecosystems approach, their validity does not depend upon the correctness of that theory.

In this respect, work accomplished under the auspices of the ecosystems approach may resemble that done in the spirit of methodological determinism. We do not know whether determinism is true or false. But its falsity is consistent with the existence of *some* deterministic causes. Any research which has discovered and validated such causal relations will not be automatically overthrown if determinism proves false. Perhaps a better comparison is provided by examining work done under the caloric, or fluid, theory of heat. This theoretic framework is now known to be false. But many important properties of heat were discovered by scientists who worked under this approach, and their results remain valid under the best current theories of thermodynamics. The false heuristic yielded work whose truth was independent of it.

Because of considerations such as these, it seems inappropriate to characterize Binford's work as *borrowing* from ecosystems theory. A better characterization seems to be that of building theory "from the ground up." His theoretic claims are based on inductive generalizations, supported by extensive observation and reviews of ethnographic data. I am not suggesting that this is naive blind induction, for hypotheses are involved. But the hypotheses are typically common-sense notions that are used to formulate correlations. These are then subjected to checks against further data and are revised accordingly. The resulting generalizations are rather low-level, in the sense that they refer to *observable phenomena*, such as "logistic moves" (i.e., trips made by collecting parties) and numbers of residential moves, rather than to such theoretic entities as degrees of adaptation or acculturation. They all thus belong to "middle-range theory" in Merton's (1968) sense, though not in Binford's own usage of the term.

Although the generalizations are low level, they are in Binford's sense *theoretical* because they are intended to present *causal* relations rather than mere correlations between empirical phenomena. For Binford, if a claim is causal it is theoretical, and in this respect the generalizations he presents are more than "mere" empirical generalizations, even though they refer only to empirically observable phenomena.

Binford is careful to treat his results as generalizations whose applicability is limited. He does not claim that they fit all archaeologically known hunter–gatherer societies. He stresses the need to check his tentative results in settings where additional environmental constraints, such as long-term land use, are operative (1980:19). Such empirically oriented studies are a vital component in the development of archaeological theory, and they should be recognized and valued as such. There is no need to cloak them in the jargon of systems theory, or to pretend to derive them deductively from another theory to make them respectable.

Binford's actual approach to theory building—as opposed to the rhetoric in which it is usually packaged—is one which is common to many practicing archaeologists. This approach to theory building is characteristic of developing sciences, and is entirely appropriate to archaeology. Unfortunately, we cannot examine patterns of development of highly advanced sciences, to see just which types of activities resulted in significant advances and which led to dead ends. But there are no such patterns, no "recipe" for success, no way to avoid all pitfalls. Patient accumulation of details, tentative attempts to analyze and interpret, and constant search for additional data that will support or undermine results are the very substance of theory building in archaeology today.

## Conclusion

In this chapter, several issues related to the development of a theory of archaeology have been discussed. Attempts based on reforms of definitions or revisions of classificatory schemes were examined and criticized for their neglect of some complexities in the problem of formulating adequate definitions. In particular, the view that providing clear definitions is a necessary *preamble* to theory construction was rejected in light of the strong interdependence between these two activities. In theory construction, one must be especially attentive to definitions, sometimes rejecting or revising old definitions, sometimes formulating new ones. But it is not feasible to resolve definitional problems first and then persevere with theory building. The two activities must proceed simultaneously.

Another approach to theory building claims that it is both possible and advantageous to construct formal or axiomatic theories of archaeology. Any set of sentences with a specified vocabulary that meets certain formal criteria (i.e., closure under deduction) constitutes a formal theory. Although formal theories that deal with archaeological subject matter, such as the relation between habitation area and population size, are constructible, I have argued that no case has been made for their explanatory value. An ambiguity in the term "theory" has caused some confusion. In the sense in which the term is most often employed by archaeologists, "theory" refers to explanatory statements, but "formal theories" need not explain anything at all.

Formal theorizing, in still another sense, that of mathematical modeling, has some utility for theory building in archaeology. Its advantages seem largely confined, however, to clarifying and extending already formulated theories rather than to devising new theories.

Substantive borrowing of theories developed in another discipline constitutes another approach to theory building in archaeology. This technique has only limited value because of the dearth of suitable theories available for borrowing. One promising example of a theory of social conflict, borrowed from sociologists, was discussed.

The last discussed approach is, I believe, that which is most typically exemplified in developing sciences. The investigator starts with (a) a rather vague belief about the causes most likely to be operative in certain situations, (b) formulates some rough hypotheses on the basis of such considerations as familiarity with the data to be explained, general scientific background knowledge, and common sense, and (c) tries to develop and refine these tentative claims through further observation, experimentation, and reflection on the significance of the results of these activities.

There is no guarantee that such low-level empirical activity will provide the insights into appropriate theoretical concepts and relations between such concepts that are characteristic of advanced physical sciences. But such knowledge is valuable in any case, and it seems reasonable to suppose that if any remarkable theoretical insights are forthcoming they will occur to, and be appreciated by, those in possession of this knowledge.

# Concluding Remarks

Many points of contact between archaeology and philosophy have been presented in this book. The applicability of the methods of inquiry of philosophy and archaeology have emerged. By way of conclusion, it is appropriate to return briefly to the problems that gave rise to this work and to assess progress toward elucidation, if not solution. For some years now, New Archaeologists have been saying that explanations offered by many of their predecessors and colleagues were inadequate. In support of their claims, they cited works in which philosophers of science analyzed the structure of confirmation and explanation, and offered standards for scientific adequacy. However, although philosophers had established criteria according to which many archaeological explanations were judged inadequate, they had little to offer in the way of positive guidelines for constructing successful explanations in archaeology. Thus, after an initial period of hope that the philosophy of science could reform archaeological explanation, many archaeologists became disillusioned (see M. Salmon 1982).

The requirement for laws in explanations, and the apparent lack of suitable laws of archaeology has been a continuing point of contention. Some archaeologists rose to the challenge, and turned their efforts to formulating and testing possible explanatory laws. Others, pointing to a similar scarcity of laws in related disciplines such as history, raised doubts that explanation in archaeology could ever meet the standards set forth in the proposed philosophical models. Along with these advances toward and retreats from nomothetic goals, there has been a growing awareness that not all the problems lie with archaeology—that there are inadequacies in philosophical accounts of the nature of scientific explanation as well.

Interchanges between philosophers and archaeologists on these matters have stimulated research in the foundations of both disciplines: on the possibility and nature of archaeological laws and also on alternative philosophical models of explanation. One important point that emerged from the early, somewhat rancorous exchanges between archaeologists and philosophers was that the two disciplines conceived the problem of explanation in distinct ways. Archaeologists' concern was largely substantive—with the truth of broad explanatory principles and factual claims—whereas philosophers tended to ignore substance altogether in

favor of questions of logical form. Because the concerns of the two groups were so different, communication failed at crucial points.

In this book, I have tried to focus on these problematic areas because I believe that by discussing them archaeologists and philosophers can learn much from one another. Philosophers, when confronted with archaeologists' concerns about explanation, should see that their formal accounts of the structure of scientific explanation fail to capture some of its most important features. They must pay attention to some highly general but nonformal aspects of explanation (such as its causal features) if their accounts are to be adequate. They should also recognize that *functional* explanation plays a central role in archaeology, just as it does in biology. Thus, if their models are to be models of *scientific* explanation, and not just models of explanation suitable for a narrow class of explanations in the physical sciences, they must deal with functional explanation in a serious manner. Archaeologists, in coming to understand the purpose of philosophical models, should see that these cannot be expected to provide blueprints for constructing sound substantive explanations, nor to provide a basis for selecting among alternative substantive accounts. Theoretically minded archaeologists may benefit from exposure to techniques of philosophical analysis. They can, for example, easily appreciate the increases in conceptual clarity that result from isolating and separating issues in a complex problem.

Another closely related issue that motivated this study was archaeologists' discussion of whether or not archaeology is—or can be—a scientists. Much of the disagreement seems to have been based in very different, though not always explicit, understandings of what constitutes a science. Throughout the book, I have argued for a broad interpretation, one that contrasts *science*—or scientific knowledge—with *guessing*, rather than with other areas of knowledge, such as history, that do not make use of all the "scientific" techniques of laboratory sciences, such as physics and chemistry. I have also argued against a narrow view of science that would identify being *scientific* with adopting a particular *philosophical* view about correct standards of confirmation and explanation.

Under such a liberal interpretation, archaeology is quite clearly a science. The discipline already embraces a good deal of knowledge which is both well founded and systematic (i.e. *scientific*) and in all likelihood archaeology will continue to develop in this manner. Reaching a noncontroversial answer to this question is not nearly so important, though, as the method by which it is reached. By trying to develop a greater sensitivity to aspects of science that are not captured in superfi-

cial accounts of scientific method, or even in a good deal of lower-level classroom training, one can see that this broad definition of "science" is not merely an arbitrary bit of semantic juggling. Some understanding of the development of modern physics, for example, can convince us that no precise method of discovery replaces trial and error, luck, and creative genius in the enterprise of theory construction. Also, because statistical laws are fundamental in modern physics, one cannot reasonably claim that genuine science demands a full set of universal laws.

Reflection on the character of other physical sciences (such as geology, astronomy, and meteorology) enables one to see that limits on the repeatability of events one is studying, on experimentation, and on predictibility are less formidable barriers to genuine science than many archaeologists have assumed. Physical and behavioral sciences are different, of course, but many of the differences that have been claimed will not withstand careful scrutiny. The differences are more subtle than cursory studies reveal. The *impersonal* character of science, for example, refers not to a lack of interest in individual events or persons, but rather to the possibility of communication of scientific knowledge through a common language. It is important for archaeologists to have a fair understanding of the nature of science if they are not to waste their time emulating inappropriate and nonessential aspects of other sciences in their efforts to make their own discipline more scientific.

Knowledge of the methods used in science is certainly beneficial to archaeology, but what can we say about knowledge of philosophy? Knowledge of philosophy is certainly not necessary for doing either practical or theoretical archaeology. In some cases, a little philosophy has been a dangerous thing, for glib appeals to philosophical authority have occasionally interfered with archaeologists' natural good sense. But careful attention to philosophy may produce such benefits as developing some analytic skills along with a suitable vocabulary for characterizing methods of archaeology. Archaeologists may also develop critical abilities that will enable them to place less reliance on the method of citation by authorities, and equip them to assess methodological and theoretical proposals urged upon them by their colleagues. However for archaeologists who want to *know* rather than guess, Russell (1914) provides the best reasons for studying philosophy:

> But even when the desire to know exists in the requisite strength, the mental vision by which abstract truth is recognised is hard to distinguish from vivid imaginability and consonance with mental habits. It is necessary to practise methodological doubt, like Descartes, in order to loosen the hold of mental habits; and it is necessary to cultivate logical imagination, in order to have a number of

hypotheses at command, and not to be the slave of the one which common sense has rendered easy to imagine. These two processes, of doubting the familiar and imagining the unfamiliar, are correlative, and form the chief part of the mental training required for a philosopher (Russell 258).

Surely skill in doubting the familiar and imagining the unfamiliar are every bit as important to the archaeologist as to the philosopher.

# Bibliography

Alston, W. P.
    1971    The place of the explanation of particular facts in science. *Philosophy of Science* **38**:13–34

Allen, J., Golson, J., and Jones, R. (editors)
    1977    *Sunda and Sahul.* New York: Academic Press.

Ascher, R.
    1961    Analogy in archaeological interpretation. *Southwestern Journal of Anthropology* **17**:317–325.

Auden, W. H.
    1976    *Collected Poems.* New York: Random House.

Berlinski, D.
    1976    *On Systems Analysis.* Cambridge, Massachusetts: MIT Press.

Binford, L. R.
    1972    *An Archaeological Perspective.* New York: Harcourt.
    1978    *Nunamiut Ethnoarchaeology.* New York: Academic Press.
    1980    Willow smoke and dog's tails: hunter–gatherer settlement systems and archaeological site formation. *American Antiquity* **45**:4–20.
    1981    *Bones.* New York: Academic Press.

Binford, L. R. (editor)
    1977    *For Theory Building in Archaeology.* New York: Academic Press.

Binford, L. R., and Bertram, J. B.
    1977    Bone frequencies—and attritional processes. In *For Theory Building in Archaeology,* edited by L. R. Binford. New York: Academic Press. Pp. 77–153.

Bogoras, W.
    1904
    –1909    *The Chukchee,* Jesup North Pacific Expedition, Vol. 7. American Museum of Natural History, Mem. 11. Leiden: Netherlands. Brill.

Boulding, K. E.
    1972    Economics and general systems. In *The Relevance of General Systems Theory,* edited by E. Lazlo. New York: George Braziller. Pp. 77–92.

Braithwaite, R. B.
    1953    *Scientific Explanation.* New York and London: Cambridge University Press.

Bridgman, P. W.
    1927    *The Logic of Modern Physics.* New York: Macmillan.

Burks, A. W.
    1977    *Chance, Cause, Reason.* Chicago, Illinois: University of Chicago Press.

Butts, R., and Hintikka, J. (editors)
    1977    *Basic Problems in Methodology and Linguistics.* Dordrecht: Reidel.

Canfield, J. (editor)
    1966    *Purpose in Nature.* Englewood Cliffs, New Jersy: Prentice-Hall.

Carnap, R.
    1950    *The Logical Foundations of Probability.* Chicago, Illinois: University of Chicago Press.

Céline, L-F.
1952    *Semmelweis*. Paris: Gallimard.
Chagnon, N., and Hames, R.
1979    Protein deficiency and tribal warfare in Amazonia: new data. *Science*
        **203**:910–973.
Cleland, C. E. (editor)
1976    *Cultural Change and Continuity: Essays in Honor of James Bennett Griffin*. New
        York: Academic Press.
Coles, J.
1973    *Archaeology by Experiment*. New York: Charles Scribner's Sons.
Crabtree, D. E.
1966    A stoneworker's approach to analyzing and replicating the Lindenmeier
        Folsom. *Tebiwa* **9**:3–39.
Curren, C. B., Jr.
1977    Potential interpretations of "stone gorget" function. *American Antiquity*
        **42**:97–100.
Daniel, G.
1967    *The Origins and Growth of Archaeology*. New York: Galahad Books.
Davies, P. C. W.
1979    *The Forces of Nature*. London and New York: Cambridge University Press.
Deetz, J.
1965    The dynamics of stylistic change in Arikara ceramics. *Illinois Studies in
        Anthropology* **4**.
1967    *Invitation to Archaeology*. Garden City, New York: The Natural History
        Press.
Dewey, J.
1910    *How We Think*. Boston, Massachusetts: Heath.
Dickson, D. B.
1980    Ancient agriculture and population at Tikal, Guatamala: An application of
        linear programming to the simulation of an archaeological problem. *Ameri-
        can Antiquity* **45**:697–712.
Downum, C.
1980    "They may be the most comprehensive damned theory in town," an eval-
        uation of L. R. Binford's strategy for middle-range theory building. Univer-
        sity of Arizona. Unpublished.
Dray, W.
1957    *Laws and Explanation in History*. London and New York: Oxford University
        Press.
1964    *Philosophy of History*. Englewood Cliffs, New Jersey: Prentice-Hall.
Dumond, D. E.
1977    Science in archaeology: the saints go marching in. *American Antiquity*
        **42**:330–349.
1980    The archaeology of Alaska and the peopling of America. *Science*
        **209**:984–991.
Dunnell, R.
1971    *Systematics in Prehistory*. New York: The Free Press.
Ekholm, G. F., and Willey, G. R. (editors)
1976    *Archaeological Frontiers and External Connections*. Austin, Texas: University
        of Texas Press.

Feigl, H., and Maxwell, G. (editors)
1967    *Minnesota Studies in the Philosophy of Science* **3**. Minneapolis, Minnesota: University of Minnesota Press.
Feuer, L. S.
1965    Causality in the social sciences. In *Cause and Effect*, edited by D. Lerner. New York: The Free Press.
Fladmark, K. R.
1979    Routes: alternate migration corridors for early man in North America. *American Antiquity* **44**:55–69.
Flannery, K.
1968    Archaeological systems theory and early Mesoamerica. In *Anthropological Archaeology in the Americas*, edited by B. J. Meggars. Washington, D.C.: Anthropological Society of Washington. Pp. 67–87.
1973    Archaeology with a capital S. In *Research and Theory in Current Archaeology*, edited by C. L. Redman. New York: Wiley. Pp. 47–53.
Flannery, K. (editor)
1976    *The Early Mesoamerican Village*. New York: Academic Press.
Flannery, K., and Winter, M. C.
1976    Analyzing household activities. In *The Early Mesoamerican Village*, edited by K. Flannery. New York: Academic Press. Pp. 34–47.
Fritz, J.
1968    Archaeological Epistemology: Two Views. MA thesis, University of Chicago.
Gale, N. H., and Stos-Gale, Z.
1981    Lead and silver in the ancient Aegean. *Scientific American* **244**:176–192.
Geertz, C.
1975    *The Interpretation of Cultures*. London: Hutchingson.
Giere, R. N.
1979    *Understanding Scientific Reasoning*. New York: Holt.
Gifford, D. P.
1978    Ethnoarchaeological observations of natural processes affecting cultural materials. In *Explorations in Ethnoarchaeology*, edited by R. A. Gould. Albuquerque, New Mexico: University of New Mexico Press. Pp. 77–101.
1981    Taphonomy and paleoecology: A critical review of archaeology's sister disciplines. In *Advances in Archaeological Method and Theory*, edited by M. Schiffer. New York: Academic Press. Vol. 4, Pp. 365–438.
Gifford, D. P., and Behrensmeyer, A. K.
1977    Observed formation and burial of a recent human occupation site in Kenya. *Quartenary Research* **8**:245–266.
Goede, A., Murray, P., and Harmon, R.
1978    Pleistocene man and megafauna in Tasmania: Dated evidence from cave sites. *The Artefact*. Melbourne, Australia: Archaeological Society of Victoria. Vol. 3, pp. 139–150.
Good, I. J.
1961
–1962   A causal calculus I–II. *British Journal for the Philosophy of Science* **11**:305–318; **12**:43–51; **13**:88.
Goodyear, A. C., Raab, L. M., and Klinger, T. C.
1978    The status of archaeological research design in cultural resource management. *American Antiquity* **43**:159–173.

Gould, R. A. (editor)
1978    *Explorations in Ethnoarchaeology.* Albuquerque, New Mexico: University of
        New Mexico Press.
Gould, R. A.
1980    *Living Archaeology.* London and New York, Cambridge University Press.
Gould, S. J.
1965    Is uniformitarianism necessary? *American Journal of Science* **263**:223–228.
Haffer, J.
1969    Speciation in Amazonia forest birds, *Science* **165**:131–137.
1974.   *Avian Speciation in Tropical South America.* Cambridge: Publications of the
        Nuttall Ornithological Club 14.
Hamblin, R. L., Hout, M., Miller, J. L. L., Pitcher, B.
1977    Arms races: a test of two models, *American Sociological Review* **42**:338–354.
Hamblin, R. L., and Pitcher, B. L.
1980    The classic Maya collapse: testing class conflict hypotheses. *American Antiq-
        uity* **45**:246–267.
Hardesty, D. L.
1980    The use of general ecological principles in archaeology, In *Advances in
        Archaeological Method and Theory,* edited by M. B. Schiffer. New York: Aca-
        demic Press. Vol. 3, pp. 157–187.
Harris, M.
1964    *The Nature of Cultural Things.* New York: Random House.
1968    *The Rise of Anthropological Theory.* New York: Crowell.
Hassan, F. A.
1978    Demographic archaeology, In *Advances in Archaeological Method and Theory*
        edited by M. B. Schiffer. New York: Academic Press. Vol. 1, pp. 49–96.
Hawkes, J.
1968    The proper study of mankind. *Antiquity* **42**:255–262.
1971    *Nothing But or Something More.* Seattle, Washington: University of Wash-
        ington Press.
Hecht, M. K., and Stiere, W. C. (editors)
1970    *Essays in Evolution and Genetics in Honor of Theodosius Dobzhansky.* New York:
        Appleton.
Heine-Gelder, R.
1976    The problem of Transpacific influences in Mesoamerica, In *Archaeological
        Frontiers and External Connections,* edited by Ekholm and Willey. Austin,
        Texas: University of Texas Press. Pp. 277–295.
Hempel, C. G.
1942    The function of general laws in history, *Journal of Philosophy* **39**:35–48 (re-
        printed in Hempel, 1965).
1965    *Aspects of Scientific Explanation.* New York: The Free Press.
1966    *Philosophy of Natural Science.* Englewood Cliffs, New Jersey: Prentice-Hall.
Hempel, C. G., and Oppenheim, P.
1948    Studies in the logic of explanation. *Philosophy of Science* **15**:135–175 (re-
        printed in Hempel, 1965).
Hesse, M.
1974    *The Structure of Scientific Inference.* New York: Macmillan.
Hodder, I., Isaac, G., Hammond, N. (editors)
1981    *Pattern of the Past: Studies in Honour of David Clarke.* London and New York:
        Cambridge University Press.

Hole, F.
   1978    Pastoral nomadism in western Iran, In *Explorations in Ethnoarchaeology*, edited by R. A. Gould. Albuquerque, New Mexico: University of New Mexico Press. Pp. 127–167.
Holton, G.
   1973    *Introduction to Concepts and Theories in Physical Science*, 2nd ed., Revised and with new material by Stephen G. Brush. Reading, Massachusetts: Addison-Wesley.
Hooykaas, R.
   1956    The principle of uniformity in geology, biology, and theology. *Journal of Transactions of Victoria Institute* **88**:101–116.
Irving, W., and Harrington, C.
   1973    Upper pleistocene radiocarbon-dated artifacts from the northern Yukon. *Science* **179**:335–340.
Jelinek, A. J.
   1976    Form, function, and style in lithic analysis, In *Cultural Change and Continuity*, edited by C. E. Cleland. New York: Academic Press. Pp. 19–33.
Jones, R.
   1978    Why did the Tasmanians stop eating fish? In *Explorations in Ethnoarchaeology*, edited by R. A. Gould. Albuquerque, New Mexico: University of New Mexico Press. Pp. 11–48.
Kirch, P. V.
   1978    Ethnoarchaeology and the study of agricultural adaptation in the humid tropics. In *Explorations in Ethnoarchaeology* edited by R. A. Gould. Albuquerque, New Mexico: University of New Mexico Press. Pp. 103–125.
Körner, S. (editor)
   1975    *Explanation.* London and New York: Oxford University Press (Blackwell).
Kuhn, T.
   1962    *The Structure of Scientific Revolutions.* Chicago, Illinois: University of Chicago Press.
Lazlo, E. (editor)
   1972    *The Relevance of General Systems Theory.* New York: George Braziller.
LeBlanc, S.
   1973    Two points of logic, In *Research and Theory In Current Archaeology*, edited by C. L. Redman. New York: Wiley. Pp. 199–214.
Leeds, A., and Vayda, A. P. (editors)
   1965    *Man, Culture, and Animals.* Washington, D.C.: American Association for the Advancement of Science.
Lerner, D.(editor)
   1965    *Cause and Effect.* New York: The Free Press.
Levin, M.
   1973    On explanation in archaeology: a rebuttal to Fritz and Plog. *American Antiquity* **38**:387–395.
   1976    On the ascription of functions to objects, with special reference to inference in archaeology. *Philosophy of Social Science* **6**:227–234.
Longacre, W. A.
   1978    Ethnoarchaeology. *Reviews in Anthropology.* Pp. 357–363.
   1981    Kalinga pottery: an ethnoarchaeological study, In *Pattern of the Past: Studies in Honour of David Clarke*, edited by Hodder *et al.* London and New York: Cambridge University Press. Pp. 49–64.

Malinowski, B.
    1948    *Magic, Science and Religion and Other Essays.* Garden City, New York: An-
            chor Books.
Martin, P., and Plog, F.
    1973    *The Archaeology of Arizona,* Garden City, New York: Doubleday/Natural
            History Press.
Mates, B.
    1972    *Elementary Logic,* 2nd ed. London and New York: Oxford University Press.
Mayr, E.
    1978    Evolution. *Scientific American* **239:**46–55.
McBryde, I.
    1979    Ethnohistory in an Australian context: independent discipline or conve-
            nient data quarry? *Journal of Aboriginal History* **3:**128–151.
Meehan, B.
    1977    Man does not live by calories alone: the role of shellfish in a coastal cuisine,
            In *Sunda and Sahul,* edited by Allen *et al.* New York: Academic Press. Pp.
            493–532.
Meehan, E.
    1968    *Explanation in Social Science—A System Paradigm.* Homewood, Illinois: The
            Dorsey Press.
Meggers, B. J. (editor)
    1968    *Anthropological Archaeology in the Americas.* Washington, D.C.: An-
            thropological Society of Washington.
Meggers, B. J.
    1979    Climatic oscillation as a factor in the prehistory of Amazonia. *American
            Antiquity* **44:**252–266.
Mellor, D. H.
    1982    Probabilities for explanation. In *Theory and Explanation in Archaeology: The
            Southampton Conference,* edited by A. C. Renfrew. New York: Academic
            Press.
Meltzer, D. J.
    1979    Pardigms and the nature of change in American archaeology. *American
            Antiquity* **44:**644–657.
Merton, R. K.
    1968    *Social Theory and Social Structure.* New York: The Free Press.
Mill, J. S.
    1874    *A System of Logic,* 8th ed. New York: Harper.
Morgan, C.
    1973    Archaeology and explanation. *World Archaeology* **4:**259–276.
    1978    Comment on "Descriptive statements, covering laws, and theory," *Current
            Anthropology* **19:**325–326.
Mueller, J. W. (editor)
    1975    *Sampling in Archaeology.* Tucson, Arizona: The University of Arizona
            Press.
Mulvaney, D. J.
    1975    *The Prehistory of Australia.* Harmondsworth: Penguin Books.
Nagel, E.
    1961    *The Structure of Science: Problems in the Logic of Scientific Explanation.* New
            York: Harcourt.
    1977    Teleology revisited: the Dewey lectures, 1977. *The Journal of Philosophy*
            **74:**261–301.

Naroll, R.
1962    Floor area and settlement population. *American Antiquity* **27**:587–589.
Newman, J. R. (editor)
1956    *The World of Mathematics.* New York: Simon and Schuster.
Newton, I.
1953    *Newton's Philosophy of Nature: Selections from His Writings.* New York: Hafner.
Nickles, T.
1977    On the independence of singular causal explanation in the social sciences: archaeology. *Philosophy of the Social Sciences* **7**:163–187.
Nisbett, R., and Ross, L.
1980    *Human Inference: Strategies and Shortcomings of Social Judgment.* Englewood Cliffs, New Jersey: Prentice-Hall.
Papineau, D.
1979    *Theory and Meaning.* London and New York: Oxford University Press (Clarendon).
Pitcher, B. L., and Hamblin, R. L.
1980    Collective learning in ongoing political conflicts. University of Arizona. Unpublished.
Plog, F.
1974    *The Study of Prehistoric Change.* New York: Academic Press.
Popper, K.
1959    *The Logic of Scientific Discovery.* New York: Basic Books
1963    *Conjectures and Refutations.* London: Routledge and Kegan Paul.
Radcliffe-Brown, A. R.
1952    *Structure and Function in Primitive Society.* Glencoe: Free Press.
1967    *The Andaman Islanders.* New York: The Free Press.
Read, D., and LeBlanc, S.
1978    Descriptive statements, covering laws, and theories in archaeology. *Current Anthropology* **19**:307–317.
Redman, C. L. (editor)
1973    *Research and Theory in Current Archaeology.* New York: Wiley.
Redman, C. L. et al.
1978    *Social Archaeology.* New York: Academic Press.
Reichenbach, H.
1956    *The Direction of Time.* Berkeley and Los Angeles, California: University of California Press.
1969    *The Axiomatization of the Theory of Relativity.* Berkeley and Los Angeles, California: University of California Press.
1976    *Laws, Modalities and Counterfactuals.* Berkeley and Los Angeles, California: University of California Press.
Renfrew, A. C.
1969    Trade and culture process in European prehistory, *Current Anthropology* **10**:151–169.
1973    *Before Civilization.* New York: Knopf.
Renfrew, A. C. et al. (editors)
1982    *Theory and Explanation in Archaeology: The Southampton Conference.* New York: Academic Press.
Robbins, M. C., and Pollnac, R. B.
1969    Drinking Patterns and acculturation in rural Buganda. *American Anthropologist* **71**:276–284.

Rosenblueth, A., Wiener, N., and Bigelow, J.
  1966   Behavior purpose and teleology, In *Purpose in Nature*, edited by J. Confield. Englewood Cliffs, New Jersey: Prentice-Hall, Pp. 9–16. (Originally published in 1943.)
Russell, B.
  1914   *Our Knowledge of the External World*. New York: Norton.
Sabloff, J., Beale, T., and Kurland, A.
  1973   Recent developments in archaeology. *The Annals of the American Academy of Political and Social Science* **408**:103–118.
Salmon, M.
  1976   "Deductive" versus "inductive" archaeology. *American Antiquity* **41**:376–381.
  1978   What can systems theory do for archaeology? *American Antiquity* **43**:174–183.
  1980   Reply to Lowe and Barth. *American Antiquity* **45**:575–579.
  1981   Ascribing functions to archaeological objects. *Philosophy of the Social Sciences* **11**:19–26.
  1982   Models of explanation: two views, In *Theory and Explanation in Archaeology: The Southampton Conference* edited by Renfrew *et al.* New York: Academic Press. Pp. 35–44.
Salmon, M., and Salmon, W. C.
  1979   Alternative models of scientific explanation. *American Anthropologist* **81**:61–74.
Salmon, W. C.
  1967   *The Foundations of Scientific Inference*. Pittsburgh, Pennsylvania: University of Pittsburgh Press.
  1968   Inquiries into the foundations of science. In *Vistas in Science*. Albuquerque, New Mexico: University of New Mexico Press. Pp. 1–24.
  1973   *Logic*, 2nd ed. Englewood Cliffs, New Jersey: Prentice-Hall.
  1975   Theoretical explanation. In Körner, (ed.), *Explanation*, edited by S. Körner. London and New York: Oxford University Press (Blackwell). Pp. 118–145.
  1977   A third dogma of empricism. In *Basic Problems in Methodology and Linguistics*, edited by Butts and Hintikka. Dordrecht: Reidel. Pp. 149–166.
  1978   Why ask, "why?" *Proceedings and Addresses of the American Philosophical Association* **51**:683–706.
  1980   Probabilstic causality. *Pacific Philosophical Quarterly* **1**:50–74.
Salmon, W. C., Jeffrey, R., and Greeno, J.
  1971   *Statistical Explanation and Statistical Relevance*. Pittsburgh, Pennsylvania: University of Pittsburgh Press.
Sanders, W. T., and Price, B.
  1968   *Mesoamerica: The Evolution of a Civilization*. New York: Random House.
Sayre, K.
  1977   Statistical models of causal relations. *Philosophy of Science* **44**:203–214.
Schiffer, M. B. (editor)
  1978
  –1981   *Advances in Archaeological Method and Theory*. New York: Academic Press. Vols. 1–4.
Schiffer, M. B.
  1975   Archaeology as a behavioral science. *American Anthropologist* **77**:836–848.

1976    *Behavioral Archeology.* New York: Academic Press.
1978    Taking the pulse of method and theory in American archaeology. *American Antiquity* **43**:153–158.
1980    Explaining the development of complex societies: the Hohokam puzzle. University of Arizona. Unpublished.
1981    Some issues in the philosophy of science and archaeology. *American Antiquity* **46**:899–908.

Schwartz, D. W.
1978    Foreword, In *Explorations in Ethnoarchaeology,* edited by R. A. Gould. Albuquerque, New Mexico: University of New Mexico Press. Pp. vii–viii.

Scriven, M.
1962    Explanations, predictions, and laws, In *Minnesota Studies in the Philosophy of Science,* edited by H. Feigl and G. Maxwell. Minneapolis, Minnesota: University of Minnesota Press. Vol. 3, pp. 170–230.
1975    Causation as explanation. *Nous* **9**:3–16.

Simpson, G. G.
1970    Uniformitarianism, an inquiry into principle, theory, and method in geohistory and biohistory, In *Essays in Evolution and Genetics in Honor of Theodosius Dobzhansky,* edited by M. K. Hecht and W. C. Stiere. New York: Appleton. Pp. 43–96.

Smart, J. J. C.
1963    *Philosophy and Scientific Realism.* London: Routledge and Kegan Paul.

Stark, B., and Young, D.
1981    Linear nearest neighbor analysis—spatial patterns and regional growth among Classic Maya cities. *American Antiquity* **46**:284–300.

Starna, W. A.
1979    A comment on Curren's "Potential interpretation of 'stone gorget' function." *American Antiquity* **44**:337–341.

Stewart, T. D.
1931    Dental caries in Peruvian skulls. *American Journal of Anthropology* **15**:315–326.

Suppes, P.
1970    *A Probabilistic Theory of Causality.* Amsterdam: North-Holland Publ.

Thomas, D. H.
1974    *Predicting the Past: An Introduction to Anthropological Archaeology.* New York: Holt.
1976.   *Figuring Anthropology.* New York: Holt.

Trigger, B.
1978    *Time and Traditions.* New York: Columbia University Press.

Tringham, R.
1978    Experimentation, ethnoarchaeology, and the leapfrogs in archaeological methodology. In *Explorations in Ethnoarchaeology,* edited by R. A. Gould. Albuquerque, New Mexico: University of New Mexico Press. Pp. 169–199.

Tuggle, D., Townsend, A. H., and Riley, T.
1972    Laws, systems and research designs. *American Antiquity* **37**:3–12.

Turnbaugh, W. A.
1979    Calumet ceremonialism as a nativistic response. *American Antiquity* **44**:685–691.

Turnbull, H. W.
  1956    The great mathematicians. Reprinted in *The World of Mathematics*, edited by
          J. R. Newman. New York: Simon and Schuster. Pp. 75–168.
Turner, C. G. II
  1978    Dental caries and early Ecuadorian agriculture. *American Antiquity*
          **43**:694–696.
Tyler, S. A. (editor)
  1969    *Cognitive Anthropology*. New York: Holt.
van Fraassen, B. C.
  1980    *The Scientific Image*. London and New York: Oxford University Press
          (Clarendon).
Vanderwal, R. L.
  1978    Adaptive technology in southwest Tasmania. *Australian Archaeology*,
          107–127.
Wartofsky, M.
  1979    *Models*. Dordrecht: Reidel.
Watson, P. J., LeBlanc, S., and Redman, C.
  1971    *Explanation in Archaeology: An Explicitly Scientific Approach*. New York: Co-
          lumbia University Press.
  1974    The covering law model in archaeology: practical uses and formal in-
          terpretation. *World Archaeology* **5**:125–131.
Weinberg, S.
  1977    *The First Three Minutes*. New York: Basic Books.
Westfall, R. S.
  1971    *The Construction of Modern Science: Mechanisms and Mechanics*. New York:
          Wiley.
White, L., Jr.
  1962    *Medieval Technology and Social Change*. London and New York: Oxford Uni-
          versity Press.
Whitten, R. G.
  1979    Comments on the theory of Holocene refugia in the culture history of
          Amazonia. *American Antiquity* **44**:238–251.
Wilke, P. J., Bettinger, R., King, T., and O'Connell, J.
  1972    Harvest selection and domestication in seed plants. *Antiquity* **46**:203–209.
Willey, G. R., and Phillips, P.
  1958    *Method and Theory in American Archaeology*. Chicago, Illinois: University of
          Chicago Press.
Willey, G. R., and Sabloff, J.
  1980    *A History of American Archaeology*, 2nd ed. San Francisco, California:
          Freeman.
Wimsatt, W.
  1980    Randomness and perceived-randomness in evolutionary biology. *Synthese*
          **43**:287–329.
Wright, L.
  1973    Function, *Philosophical Review* **82**:139–168.
  1976    *Teleological Explanations*. Berkeley and Los Angeles, California: University
          of California Press.
Wright, R. V. S.
  1971    *Archaeology of the Gallus Site, Koonalda Cave*. Canberra: Australian Institute
          of Aboriginal Studies.

Wylie, M. A.
    1981    *Positivism and the New Archaeology*, Ph.D. Dissertation, State Univesrity of
            New York at Binghampton.
Zavallos M., C. *et al.*
    1977    The San Pablo corn kernel and its friends. *Science* **196**:385–389.

# Author Index

## A

Alston, W., 126
Ascher, R. 79
Auden, W. 1

## B

Behrensmeyer, A., 173
Berlinski, D., 90
Bertram, J., 115–116, 120–121
Binford, L., 2, 40, 45, 63, 65, 77–78,
    115–116, 121–123, 138, 141, 166–171,
    173–177
Boulding, K., 90
Braithwaite, R., 98
Bridgman, P., 143
Brodbeck, M., 2
Burks, A.W., 172

## C

Carnap, R., 9
Céline, L-F., 172
Chagnon, N., 35, 42
Childe, V., 46
Coles, J., 32, 61–62
Crabtree, D., 77
Curren, C., 60, 63, 68, 72
Cushing, F., 49

## D

Daniel, G., 141
Davies, P., 87
Deetz, J., 14, 54, 61, 65
Descartes, R., 141, 181
Dewey, J., 113–114
Dickson, D., 77
Downum, C., 170
Dray, W., 98
Dumond, D., 41, 48, 54
Dunnell, R., 7, 140–141, 150–154, 157

## E

Einstein, A., 47
Euclid, 158–159

## F

Fladmark, K., 37
Flannery, K., 58, 60, 62, 64–65, 79, 90–95,
    127
Forge, A., 132
Fritz, J., 9

## G

Gale, N., 137
Galileo, 155
Geertz, C., 21–23
Giere, R., 156
Gifford, D., 60, 135, 173
Goede, A., 39
Good, I., 134
Goodyear, A., 170
Gould, R., 75–79, 133–139
Gould, S., 79–80

## H

Haffer, J., 45
Hamblin, R., 100, 162–164
Hames, R., 35, 42
Harrington, C., 41, 48
Harris, M., 85, 144, 169
Hassan, F., 37
Haury, E., 49
Hawkes, J., 3, 21, 23
Heine-Gelder, R., 74
Hempel, C., 2–4, 23, 32, 36, 93–94, 98,
    100, 103–104, 109, 113, 117, 119,
    121–122, 124, 143
Hesse, M., 148
Hole, F., 32
Holton, G., 95, 155, 159
Hooykaas, R., 79

**I**

Irving, W., 41, 48

**J**

Jones, R., 37, 46, 48

**K**

Kepler, J., 155
Kirch, P., 32
Kuhn, T., 154

**L**

LeBlanc, S., 7, 38, 93, 103, 141, 157,
　159–160
Leeds, A., 102
Levin, M., 2, 65–68, 70–74
Longacre, W., 71, 75

**M**

Malinowski, B., 85, 98, 104
Martin, P., 49, 89–90
Mates, B., 159
Mayr, E., 86
McBryde, I., 65
Meehan, B., 37
Meehan, E., 3, 4, 94, 96, 99–100, 102–104
Meggars, B., 47
Mellor, D., 134
Meltzer, D., 4
Merton, R., 170, 177
Mill, J., 138
Morgan, C., 2–3, 159–160
Mueller, J., 50
Mulvaney, D., 86
Munsen, P., 78

**N**

Nagel, E., 2, 23, 30, 98, 101, 104–105,
　107–108
Naroll, R., 37–38, 81
Newton, I., 12, 15–16, 47, 140, 155, 156,
　159, 168
Nisbett, R., 154

**P**

Papineau, D., 148

Pitcher, B., 100, 162–164
Plog, F., 49, 89–90, 144
Pollnac, R., 146–147
Popper, K., 2, 35, 54, 98
Price, B., 9

**R**

Radcliffe-Brown, A., 85–87, 91, 96, 104
Read, D., 7, 141, 157–161
Reichenbach, H., 30, 134, 159
Renfrew, A. C., 12, 131–132, 137
Robbins, M., 146–147
Rosenblueth, A., 90–91, 103
Ross, L., 154
Russell, B., 181–182
Rutherford, E., 94–95

**S**

Sabloff, J., 3, 169
Sahlins, M., 10
Salmon, M., 49, 67, 90, 94, 103, 106, 179
Salmon, W., 23, 30, 33, 42, 45, 49, 54–55,
　98, 103, 106, 108, 114, 119, 121, 131,
　134–135
Sanders, W., 9
Sayre, K., 134
Schiffer, M., 4, 13, 23–29, 32, 60, 132,
　141, 164, 169, 173
Schwartz, D., 74–75
Scriven, M., 98, 109
Semmelweis, I., 171
Service, E., 10
Simpson, G., 79–81
Smart, J., 18–19, 79
Spinoza, B., 141
Stark, B., 136
Starna, W., 60
Stewart, J., 52
Stos-Gale, Z., 137
Suppes, P., 134

**T**

Thomas, D., 40, 50, 109, 144, 146
Thomson, J., 94
Trigger, B., 4, 20–21, 23, 47
Tringham, R., 35, 41
Tuggle, D., 3–4
Turnbaugh, W., 150
Turnbull, H., 74

Turner, C., 52, 54

**V**

van Daniken, E., 48
Vanderwal, R., 46
Vayda, A., 102
von Bertalanffy, L., 90

**W**

Wartofsky, M., 160–162
Watson, P. J., 2–3
Weber, M., 21
Weinberg, S., 125
Westfall, R., 156
White, Leslie 2

White, Lynn, 74
Whitten, R., 45–46
Wiener, N., 91
Wilke, P., 89, 110
Willey, G., 169
Winter, M., 62, 79
Wright, L., 66, 107–110
Wright, R., 69, 70
Wylie, M., 162

**Y**

Yellen, J., 161
Young, D., 136

**Z**

Zavallos M, C., 52

# Subject Index

## A

Abandonment, 34 36–37, 56, 98
Acculturation, 146–150, 177
Agriculture
  corn and bean diet, 89, 93
  development of, 92–97
  diffusion model, 93
  systems model, 93
  Valdivian Phase, 52–54
Alertness principle, 72–74
Analogy
  argument for dynamics, 171
  ascribing functions, 57–65, 79
  determining prior probabilities, 45–46, 78, 82
  in ethnoarchaeology, 58
  evaluating arguments from, 61–65
  form of argument from, 61–62
  historical, 65–66
  limitations of, 31, 65
  as model, 160–161
  number of, 63, 78
  suggesting hypotheses, 45, 78, 82
Archaeological law
  importance of, 20–29
  shared, 20
Attrition, 115–116, 123, 128–129

## B

Bayes' method, 51–55, 79
Bayes' theorem, *see* Bayes' method
Behavioral science law, 18, 21
Beringia, 50–51
Bias, 37, 71
Biological law, 18–19
Biological system, 91, 104
Bone
  dating, 41, 50–51
  density, 116, 121–123
  small size of, 133–135

survival, 115–117, 121–123, 128–130
Buganda, 146–149

## C

Calumet ceremony, 150
Causal explanation, 106–111, 123, 131–139, 163–164, 174
Cause
  common, 56, 132, 136–138
  deterministic, 128–130, 169, *see also* Determinism; Deterministic law
  environmental, 137, 167–171, 174–177
  fallacy, 55–56
  final, 87–91, *see also* Purposes
  functional, 107, 137
  hidden causal factors, 15–17, 128–129
  mechanistic, 89, 91
  probabilistic, 134–136, 139
  stylistic, 138
Chalcedony tools, 27–29
Chukchi, 102
Classification, 2, 151, 153–154, 157, 167, 177
Coccidioidomycosis, *see* Valley fever
Collecting, 167, 170
Collective learning, 163–164
Comparative studies, 171–174
Concept formation, 154, 156, *see also* Definition
Confirmation, *see also* Bayes' method; Hypothetico-Deductive method
  absolute, 36, 51
  logic of, 31–34
  relative, 36, 51
Conflict theory, 162–165, 174, 178
Context
  of association, 59–61, 63
  systemic, 60–61
Contraceptive, 106
Convenience, 66–68, 71
Corroboration, 35, 54

Covering law, 3, 27–28, 122
Critical resource, 175
Crucial experiment, 95

**D**

Deductive argument, 33
Deductive–Nomological model, 2, *see also*
    Chapters 5 and 6
    characterization, 98
    in "hard" science, 21
Deductive–Statistical model, 120–122, 138
    characterization, 120
Definition
    of abstract term, 145
    approach to theory building, 140–143,
        177–178
    of concrete term, 145
    intensional, 150–151, 153, 155
    operational, 143–150, 152
Determinism, 14, 16, 135, 169, *see also*
    Methodological determinism
Deterministic law, 128, 130, 134, *see also*
    Universal law
Designer, 89, 91
Diet
    corn and bean, 89, 93
    hunter–gatherer, 37, 42–43, 166
Diffusion, 9, 14, 47, 71, 94, 137, 168–169
Dimensional analysis, 24–26
Disconfirmation, 34–37
Dispositional term, 143, 146–148
Domain of applicability, 38
Dynamics, 171–173

**E**

Ecology
    ecological determinism, 47
    extreme ecological change, 46
    pseudorandomness, 130
    theory, 168–170, 174–176
Economy, 76–78
Ecosystems, 93, 102, *see also* Ecology,
    theory
Efficiency, 77
Empirical law, 11, 24–29
Equilibrium, 92, 95, 175
Ethnoarchaeology, 5, 58, 74–82, 167–177
Ethnocentrism, 71
Evolution

cultural, 10
evolutionary biology, 13, 19, 86–87,
    89, 155
theory, 47
Experimental archaeology, 41, 67–68, 82
Explanation, *see* specific types
Extinction of megafauna, 39

**F**

Fallibilism, 12
Falsification, 35–36, 54
Feedback
    negative, 91–93
    positive, 91–93
    systems, 90–93, 99, 103, 135
Folsom points, 77
Food-procurement system, 92–93, 97
Foraging, 167, 170
Force, 155–156
Function
    ascription of, 5, 57, 63, 101, 104, 107
    conscious, 107
    definition, 66
    different uses of term, 84, 101
    experimental assignment, 63, 82
    general method for assigning, 65–67
    goal-supporting analysis, 104
    natural, 107
Functional equivalent, 97–99, 102, 104
Functional explanation
    compatibility with change, 86
    noncausal, 105, 107
    partial, 98–99
    structural similarity to D–N, 105
Functional system, 101–102, *see also*
    Feedback system
Functionalism, 84–86

**G**

General systems theory, 7, 90–91, 141
Generalization
    empirical, 19
    existential, 11, 32
    falsification of, 13
    probabilistic, *see* Generalization,
        statistical
    scope of, 13–14
    statistical, 5, 9–10, 14, 32
    universal, 9–11, 14, 32

Genetic theory, 13, 110, 130
Grain of archaeological assemblage, 167, 171, 174

## H

High probability requirement, 124–131
Homeostatic device, 175, *see also* Equilibrium
Hypothesis
 alternative, 35, 41, 49, 52–56
 auxiliary, 36, 39–41, 52, 54
 characterization, 32
 inductive relations among, 43–46
 source as criterion for priors, 48–49
Hypothetico–Deductive method, 2, 34–36, 78–79
 for testing statistical hypotheses, 39–40

## I

Ideal gas law, 9, 24, 101
Indeterminism, 14
Inductive argument, 33–34
Inductive–Statistical model
 characterization, 99
 epistemic ambiguity, 117–120
 high probability, 125
Instrumentalism, 162

## J

Joint site, 26
Joking relationship, 85, 97–98

## K

Kalinga, 71
Koonalda Cave, 69–70

## L

Language
 interpreted, 145
 uninterpreted, 145
Law, *see also* specific types
 features of, 9–14
 generality, 9–11, 19
 role in explanation, 8, 24, 179, *see also* Chapter 6
 shared, 20

 truth requirements, 11–12
Law-like statement, 12–13
Law of motion, 12, 140, 155–156, 168
Law of requisite variety, 175–176
Lead isotope, 136–137
Legionnaire's disease, 172–173
Likelihood, 54–55
Logical consequence, 32–33
Logical structure
 of analogical arguments, 61–62
 of explanation, 108, 179–180, *see also* Model, of explanation
 of generalization, 10
Logistic mobility, 167, 177

## M

Mark, 135, 137
Mathematical law, 11, *see also* Dimensional analysis
Mathematical model, 100–103, 160–165, 178
Maximal specificity, 119–120
Maxwell's equations, 100
Maya collapse, 162–165, 174
Methodological determinism, 16, 17, 169
Mill's Methods, 138
Model
 computational, 161–165
 descriptive, 163
 of explanation, 93–97, *see also* specific types
 of phenomena, 93–97
Muon, 87
Mutation, 13, 14, 93, 110, 127–128

## N

Natural selection, 13, 89, 94, 108
New archaeology, 2, 34, 40, 41, 157
Normal science, 154

## O

Observational term, 147–148

## P

Paresis, 15, 134
Particular fact
 explanation of, 125–126, 138
 role in explanation, 113, 121

Physical science law, 9, 15, 18–19, 79–80
Planetary model of atom, 94
Plausibility, *see* Prior probability
Plum pudding model of atom, 94
Population size, 7, 37, 81–82, 131–132, 157, 161
Posterior probability, 51, 53–54
Prediction
    in confirmation, 34, 39–40, 49–50
    deterministic, 17–18
    versus explanation, 99, 103, 109
    theoretical, 153, 159, 161
Primitive term, 144, 156–158
Prior probability
    formal criteria, 42–43, 48
    material criteria, 43–45, 48
    pragmatic criteria, 47
    role in confirmation, 5, 49–55
Priors, *see* Prior probability
Pseudorandomness, 127–130
Psychological states, 88
Puerperal fever, 171–172
Puntutjarpa site, 133–135
Purposes, 85–91

Q

Quantitative transform, 24–29

R

Radiocarbon dating, 12, 19, 41, 50, 80, 127, 137
Random process, 124–130
Realism, 162
Reference class, 119
Regularity, *see* Law
Reindeer herd size, 102
Relevance
    in arguments from analogy, 46, 59, 62–63
    causal, 46, 116, 131–134
    definition, 62
    of environment to behavior, 79, *see also* Ecology, theory
    explanatory, 105–106, 114, 119, 129–134
    of form to function, 59, 79
    of residues to behavior, 76, 81, *see also* Ethnoarchaeology
    similarity, 64, 78

in variety of samples, 38
Research program, 90, 95
Residue, 75, 174

S

Scheduling, 92
Schema, 154–155, 173
Seasonality, 92
Seed dispersal, 89, 98–99, 104–105, 110–111
Selection, *see* Natural selection
Seriation dating, 14
Significant evidence, 39, 79
Simplicity, 47, 76
Smoke hole, 58, 108
Smudge pits, 63, 65, 67, 78
Social science laws, 18–19, 21–22
Social stability, 85, 97
Social structure, *see* Social system
Social system, 85–86, 90–91, 97, 104, 125, 132
Statistical deduction, 40, *see also* Deductive–Statistical model
Statistical law
    explanation of, 120–122, 131–134, 136–138
    medical, 15
    quantum physics, 16, 18, 127, 129
    random process, 124–131
    role in explanation, 96–121
    social science, 18–19, 21–22
Statistical–Relevance model
    causes in, 108–111, 131, 139
    characterization, 109
    modified account, 131
Statistical relevance relation, 131
Statistical syllogism, 45
Stern–Gerlach experiment, 16
Stone gorget, 60, 63
Superposition, 20
Syphilis, 15, 134
Systematics, 150–157
Systems explanations, 6, 87, 90, 96, 111, *see also* Systems model, of explanation
System, formal, *see* Mathematical model
Systems model
    characterization of Meehan's, 100
    of explanation, 3, 93–97
    of phenomena, 93–97

**T**

Term of description, 70
Term of interpretation, 70
Theoretic term, 147–150
Theory
  abstract interpretation, 158
  axiomatized, *see* Theory, formal
  borrowing, 140, 165–166, 174, 177–178
  characterization, 140
  ecosystems, *see* Ecosystems; Ecology,
    theory
  explanatory, 158–159
  formal, 7, 157–160, 178
  general, 170–171, 174, 177
  implicit, 7, 154–155
  informal, 159
  intended interpretation, 159
  middle-range, 170–171, 174, 177
  model of, 158
  physical interpretation, 158
Thick description, 21

Tide table, 159–160
Total probability, 53

**U**

Uniformitarianism, 79–82
  actualism 79
  methodological, 79
  substantive, 80–81
Universal law, 3–4, 14–18, 128, 130, 134

**V**

Vagueness, 146, 181
Validity, 33
Valley fever, 14, 106, 120
Variety in sample, 37

**Y**

Yanomamö, 35

# STUDIES IN ARCHAEOLOGY

## Consulting Editor: Stuart Struever

Department of Anthropology
Northwestern University
Evanston, Illinois

*Charles R. McGimsey III.* Public Archeology

*Lewis R. Binford.* An Archaeological Perspective

*Muriel Porter Weaver.* The Aztecs, Maya, and Their Predecessors:
Archaeology of Mesoamerica

*Joseph W. Michels.* Dating Methods in Archaeology

*C. Garth Sampson.* The Stone Age Archaeology of Southern Africa

*Fred T. Plog.* The Study of Prehistoric Change

*Patty Jo Watson (Ed.).* Archeology of the Mammoth Cave Area

*George C. Frison (Ed.).* The Casper Site: A Hell Gap Bison Kill on the High Plains

*W. Raymond Wood and R. Bruce McMillan (Eds.).* Prehistoric Man and His
Environments: A Case Study in the Ozark Highland

*Kent V. Flannery (Ed.).* The Early Mesoamerican Village

*Charles E. Cleland (Ed.).* Cultural Change and Continuity: Essays in Honor of
James Bennett Griffin

*Michael B. Schiffer.* Behavioral Archeology

*Fred Wendorf and Romuald Schild.* Prehistory of the Nile Valley

*Michael A. Jochim.* Hunter-Gatherer Subsistence and Settlement: A
Predictive Model

*Stanley South.* Method and Theory in Historical Archeology

*Timothy K. Earle and Jonathon E. Ericson (Eds.).* Exchange Systems in
Prehistory

*Stanley South (Ed.).* Research Strategies in Historical Archeology

*John E. Yellen.* Archaeological Approaches to the Present: Models for
Reconstructing the Past

*Lewis R. Binford (Ed.).* For Theory Building in Archaeology: Essays on Faunal
Remains, Aquatic Resources, Spatial Analysis, and Systemic Modeling

*James N. Hill and Joel Gunn (Eds.).* The Individual in Prehistory: Studies of
Variability in Style in Prehistoric Technologies

*Michael B. Schiffer and George J. Gumerman (Eds.).* Conservation Archaeology:
A Guide for Cultural Resource Management Studies

*Thomas F. King, Patricia Parker Hickman, and Gary Berg.* **Anthropology in Historic Preservation: Caring for Culture's Clutter**

*Richard E. Blanton.* **Monte Albán: Settlement Patterns at the Ancient Zapotec Capital**

*R. E. Taylor and Clement W. Meighan.* **Chronologies in New World Archaeology**

*Bruce D. Smith.* **Prehistoric Patterns of Human Behavior: A Case Study in the Mississippi Valley**

*Barbara L. Stark and Barbara Voorhies (Eds.).* **Prehistoric Coastal Adaptations: The Economy and Ecology of Maritime Middle America**

*Charles L. Redman, Mary Jane Berman, Edward V. Curtin, William T. Langhorne, Nina M. Versaggi, and Jeffery C. Wanser (Eds.).* **Social Archeology: Beyond Subsistence and Dating**

*Bruce D. Smith (Ed.).* **Mississippian Settlement Patterns**

*Lewis R. Binford.* **Nunamiut Ethnoarchaeology**

*J. Barto Arnold III and Robert Weddle.* **The Nautical Archeology of Padre Island: The Spanish Shipwrecks of 1554**

*Sarunas Milisauskas.* **European Prehistory**

*Brian Hayden (Ed.).* **Lithic Use-Wear Analysis**

*William T. Sanders, Jeffrey R. Parsons, and Robert S. Santley.* **The Basin of Mexico: Ecological Processes in the Evolution of a Civilization**

*David L. Clarke.* **Analytical Archaeologist: Collected Papers of David L. Clarke. Edited and Introduced by His Colleagues**

*Arthur E. Spiess.* **Reindeer and Caribou Hunters: An Archaeological Study**

*Elizabeth S. Wing and Antoinette B. Brown.* **Paleonutrition: Method and Theory in Prehistoric Foodways.**

*John W. Rick.* **Prehistoric Hunters of the High Andes**

*Timothy K. Earle and Andrew L. Christenson (Eds.).* **Modeling Change in Prehistoric Economics**

*Thomas F. Lynch (Ed.).* **Guitarrero Cave: Early Man in the Andes**

*Fred Wendorf and Romuald Schild.* **Prehistory of the Eastern Sahara**

*Henri Laville, Jean-Philippe Rigaud, and James Sackett.* **Rock Shelters of the Perigord: Stratigraphy and Archaeological Succession**

*Duane C. Anderson and Holmes A. Semken, Jr. (Eds.).* **The Cherokee Excavations: Holocene Ecology and Human Adaptations in Northwestern Iowa**

*Anna Curtenius Roosevelt.* **Parmana: Prehistoric Maize and Manioc Subsistence along the Amazon and Orinoco**

*Fekri A. Hassan.* **Demographic Archaeology**

*G. Barker.* **Landscape and Society: Prehistoric Central Italy**

*Lewis R. Binford.* **Bones: Ancient Men and Modern Myths**

*Richard A. Gould and Michael B. Schiffer (Eds.).* **Modern Material Culture: The Archaeology of Us**

*Muriel Porter Weaver.* **The Aztecs, Maya, and Their Predecessors: Archaeology of Mesoamerica, 2nd edition**

*Arthur S. Keene.* **Prehistoric Foraging in a Temperate Forest: A Linear Programming Model**

*Ross H. Cordy.* **A Study of Prehistoric Social Change: The Development of Complex Societies in the Hawaiian Islands**

*C. Melvin Aikens and Takayasu Higuchi.* **Prehistory of Japan**

*Kent V. Flannery (Ed.).* **Maya Subsistence: Studies in Memory of Dennis E. Puleston**

*Dean R. Snow (Ed.).* **Foundations of Northeast Archaeology**

*Charles S. Spencer.* **The Cuicatlán Cañada and Monte Albán: A Study of Primary State Formation**

*Steadman Upham.* **Polities and Power: An Economic and Political History of the Western Pueblo**

*Carol Kramer.* **Village Ethnoarchaeology: Rural Iran in Archaeological Perspective**

*Michael J. O'Brien, Robert E. Warren, and Dennis E. Lewarch (Eds.).* **The Cannon Reservoir Human Ecology Project: An Archaeological Study of Cultural Adaptations in the Southern Prairie Peninsula**

*Jonathon E. Ericson and Timothy K. Earle (Eds.).* **Contexts for Prehistoric Exchange**

*Merrilee H. Salmon.* **Philosophy and Archaeology**

*in preparation*

*Vincas P. Steponaitis.* **Ceramics, Chronology, and Community Patterns: An Archaeological Study at Moundville**

*William J. Folan, Ellen R. Kintz, and Laraine A. Fletcher.* **Coba: A Classic Maya Metropolis**

*James A. Moore and Arthur S. Keene (Eds.).* **Archaeological Hammers and Theories**

*George C. Frison and Dennis J. Stanford.* **The Agate Basin Site: A Record of the Paleoindian Occupation of the Northwestern High Plains**

*Lewis R. Binford (Ed.).* **Working At Archaeology**